INTERNET MARKETPLACES
THE LAW OF AUCTIONS AND EXCHANGES ONLINE

INTERNET MARKETPLACES
THE LAW OF AUCTIONS AND EXCHANGES ONLINE

CHRISTINA RAMBERG

Consultant Editor
CHRISTOPHER KUNER
Hunton & Williams

OXFORD
UNIVERSITY PRESS

OXFORD

UNIVERSITY PRESS

Great Clarendon Street, Oxford OX2 6DP

Oxford University Press is a department of the University of Oxford.
It furthers the University's objective of excellence in research, scholarship,
and education by publishing worldwide in

Oxford New York

Auckland Bangkok Buenos Aires Cape Town Chennai
Dar es Salaam Delhi Hong Kong Istanbul Karachi Kolkata
Kuala Lumpur Madrid Melbourne Mexico City Mumbai Nairobi
São Paulo Shanghai Singapore Taipei Tokyo Toronto

Oxford is a registered trade mark of Oxford University Press
in the UK and in certain other countries

Published in the United States
by Oxford University Press Inc., New York

British Library Cataloguing in Publication Data

Data available

Library of Congress Cataloging in Publication Data

Data available

ISBN 0–19–925429–X

1 3 5 7 9 10 8 6 4 2

Typeset in Times by
Cambrian Typesetters, Frimley, Surrey
Printed in Great Britain
on acid-free paper by
Biddles Ltd., Guildford and King's Lynn

PREFACE

I was inspired to write this book by Arthur Sculley and William Woods. In late 1999 they wrote the book *B2B Exchanges—The killer application*. They described in enthusiastic terms how business would change as a result of the new technological means of assembling the worldwide supply and demand for certain products and services in closed communities on the Internet. They also pointed out the challenges and problems involved in adapting business to these major changes. My aim has been to supplement their book with a study of the legal dimension. I wanted to ascertain whether the expected changes in business models would also mean changes for the law. Furthermore, I wanted to investigate how the legal infrastructure of closed Internet marketplaces could be most efficiently designed.

Now, that the IT hype has cooled down considerably it may be questioned whether business-to-business exchanges really will become 'the killer application'. There is no certain answer. Personally, I am convinced that we will see an increasing number of transactions concluded in Internet marketplaces. I also believe that this will lead to changes in business models and in the law. However, I am not sure how fast the transformation will be. For some areas of trade the change has already happened, for some it will come eventually, and for others still it may never happen. In many cases the transformation is likely to start by way of electronic procurement initiated by single buyers and then expand to take the form of collaborations between many buyers as reversed auctions. Some marketplaces will eventually evolve to become exchanges. In this book I aim to cover the design of the legal infrastructure for all these different types of transactions.

I hope that this book will be of interest to lawyers generally interested in how the changes in business models affect the law and that it will be of assistance to lawyers seeking practical advice on how to draft contracts between parties acting in Internet marketplaces.

I thank many of my friends and colleagues for their inspiration and valuable advice, and would particularly like to mention Bo Dahlbom, Marcel Fontaine, John Gregory, Susanne Hansson, Douglas Hibbs, Manfred Holler, Rolf Höök, Gustaf Johnssén, Mathias Klang, Christopher Kuner, Carolina Landys, Ruben Lee, Nicklas Lundblad, Suman Naresh, Jan Ramberg, Erik Røsæg, and William Woods. For invaluable help with language editing I would like to thank Richard Dey.

Christina Ramberg
Christina.Ramberg@law.gu.se
Göteborg, Sweden
March 2002

CONTENTS

TABLE OF NATIONAL CASES

TABLE OF EUROPEAN, INTERNATIONAL, AND NATIONAL LEGISLATION AND CONVENTIONS

INTRODUCTION

Introductory remarks

Many believe that the technical possibilities for establishing meeting places on **1.01** the Internet with the purpose of assembling the worldwide supply and demand of almost any kind of product will create a revolution for business. The fact that the Internet makes it possible easily to gather a large amount of the supply and demand and thereby establish increased liquidity in the markets, is likely to lead to a substantially increased use of electronic auctions and exchanges.[1] If this prediction comes true, business will face tremendous changes in how to buy and sell products and services. This study will analyse the new legal questions that will follow the changes in business concepts.

The Internet marketplaces described in this book are closed communities, ie a **1.02** website that can only be accessed after a subscription procedure has been completed. The marketplaces which are examined are not open to everyone, but participation is based on a contractual relationship between the participant and the operator of the marketplace. A marketplace's level of service may cover a spectrum of activities, from simple electronic noticeboards where sellers and buyers having found each other negotiate the transaction offline, to electronic procurement systems;[2] and to the most sophisticated scenarios where all services are provided, including logistics, credit referencing, payment guarantees and insurance.[3]

---

[1] R E Hall, *Digital Dealing* (2001) at <http://www.stanford.edu/~rehall/LinoleumReport.pdf> 12: 'Auctions fit so naturally on the Internet that auction volume there has reached startling levels—in 2000, Internet auctions made deals for more than a trillion dollars in goods and securities.'

[2] FreeMarkets provide such private procurement facilities, see Hall (n 1 above) 17 ff.

[3] See for a description of different services, M Bichler, *The Future of e-Markets: Multidimensional Market Mechanisms* (CUP, 2001) ch 2.

1.03   There are already many examples of Internet marketplaces which may be operated by an independent intermediary or be set up by the party taking the initiative
in the transaction. Examples of interesting exchange sites are Nasdaq, eSTEEL,
PaperExchange, CATEX (for insurance), ELRiX (for standardized risks),
PlasticsNet (for plastics), Chemconnect (for chemicals), Omnexus (for thermo-
plastics), FruitLine (for fruits and vegetables), Pefa.com (for fish) and the
National Transportation Exchange. Examples of interesting auction sites are eBay
(where consumers offer goods to consumers), Bidlet (where new manufactured
goods are offered to consumers), GoIndustry.com (for used surplus equipment),
MetalSite, Autodaq (where used cars are offered to used-car dealers (business-to-
business)). A special type of marketplace is Covisint, where the car manufacturers Daimler-Chrysler, GM, Ford, Renault and Nissan ask for competing offers
from suppliers of goods and services.[4]

1.04   Markets have three main functions: matching buyers to sellers; facilitating the
exchange of information, goods, services, and payments associated with a market
transaction; and providing an institutional infrastructure, such as the legal and
regulatory framework which enables the efficient functioning of the market.[5]
This book combines a consideration of aspects of economics and computer
science with an analysis of the relevant legal and regulatory framework. It
focuses on the design of optimal rules and norm structures for conducting business in Internet marketplaces where the transactions are carried out as auctions or
exchanges.

Aim of the study

1.05   A problem for practising lawyers is to understand the new kinds of business
transactions and how they relate to the law. This study aims to help lawyers
understand electronic auctions and exchanges and identify the relevant legal
problems and challenges. To understand the norm design of an Internet marketplace completely, it is necessary to be familiar with the business realities and the
potential practical problems arising from such activities. With this in mind this
study often refers to and explains the relevant business models of auctions and
exchanges.

1.06   A particularly important issue is how the legal infrastructure of the marketplace can
be used to establish the necessary trust and confidence between the participants.

---

[4]   See for a compilation of auction site, <www.internetauctionlist.com>. A very helpful profile of
49 selected business-to-business enterprises operating in Europe is made by Goldman Sachs Global
Equity Research, *B2B e-Commerce/Internet Europe—The Old World Meets the New Economy* (2000)
(at <https://www.gs.com>) 67 ff.
[5]   Y Bakos, 'Bundling information goods: pricing, profits and efficiency' (1991) *Management
science* 45 (12) referred to by Bichler (n 3 above) at 2.

This study therefore aims to explain the legal dimension related to building trust in electronic auctions and exchanges. Traditionally, the national legislature has been anxious to protect trust.[6] Auctions and exchanges require trust and confidence. There must be trust with respect to liquidity, accurate information, competition, equal treatment of bidders, rational behaviour by bidders and firm rules so that bidding strategies can be used efficiently. When there is no basic trust and confidence there are negative consequences for the price-setting mechanism.

If the participants cannot be sure that there are in fact objects offered and a poten-   **1.07** tially large number of bidders for those objects (liquidity in the marketplace), the price-setting mechanism will not be efficient and participants will be reluctant to be involved. If information provided in the marketplace cannot be trusted and relied upon as accurate, participants will run the risk of making wrong decisions and consequently refrain from taking part in the marketplace. If the bidders are not participating on equal terms the price-setting mechanism will be affected and participants will not dare to be involved. If participants are allowed to use bidding strategies that manipulate the price-setting mechanism, the participants will not trust the marketplace and therefore refrain from taking part. If the rules are not definite, but can be changed or used with 'flexibility', there is a risk of manipulation and, consequently, the marketplace will not be able to attract participants.

Because of the reduced influence of the state, it is vitally important that the   **1.08** Internet marketplace *itself* is focused on the design of efficient and enforceable rules for the marketplace. The operator[7] of a marketplace and the participants in a marketplace cannot rely on the state effectively to secure the participant's confidence in the marketplace, but increasingly the operator must build the foundations for such confidence by itself. This is mainly done via the membership terms, the conditions of sale and the technical structure of the Internet marketplace. This book shows how Internet marketplaces interact with national states. In this lies an important qualification: this study does not examine the Internet as a whole, but only the rules related to closed Internet marketplaces where commercial dealings are carried out.

When I refer to Internet marketplaces I have in mind closed communities, ie a   **1.09** website that can only be accessed after a subscription procedure. The marketplaces I am examining are not open to everyone, but participation is based on a contractual relationship between the participant and the marketplace operator.

---

[6] Lee says that the broad goals of regulators of financial and commodity markets typically are investor protection, economic efficiency, fairness, market integrity and the minimization of systematic risk: R Lee, *What is an Exchange? The Automation, Management and Regulation of Financial Markets* (OUP, 1988) 251. All these goals seem to involve in essence the aim of protecting trust in the marketplace.

[7] I will call the body in charge of the design and transactions carried out in a marketplace the 'operator'. Other terms have been used, Bichler, for instance, calls these bodies 'brokers' (n 3 above).

1.10 The idea specifically and determinedly to *design* rules for a marketplace is rather new. Such norms historically have developed slowly by a process involving actual behaviour, the power structure of the parties involved and the power structure of society as a whole. Consequently, the development of norms in traditional marketplaces has necessarily been slow and is often without anyone intentionally steering the content of such rules. In Internet marketplaces the marketplace operator actively conducts the norm design. It must, however, be emphasized that the operator of an Internet marketplace is restricted in the design of the rules by the participants' expectations and sense of what is fair. For the marketplace operator it is more a question of codifying the participants' expectations and existing behaviour than introducing wholly new regimes.

Scope

1.11 In this study I do not describe the governance, ie the ownership and control, of the Internet marketplace. This is an important and interesting issue but this study is based on the assumption that there is a need to create efficiency, trust and confidence no matter who operates and controls the marketplace.[8]

1.12 A fundamental and crucial problem for the emerging electronic exchanges and auctions is the role of traditional intermediaries. In markets where deals have been concluded by individual negotiations, intermediaries have played the important role of assembling information about potential buyers and sellers and this knowledge enabled the intermediary to match deals. When the information about supply and demand, buyers and sellers becomes transparent, the role of intermediaries is likely to change as buyers and sellers may easily acquire knowledge without the help of an intermediary. In this study I do not provide an analysis of the position and role of intermediaries.[9]

1.13 This study will not analyse the different methods of pricing the services provided by an Internet marketplace. The marketplace can do this by membership fees, transaction percentage (commission/brokerage), fees for accessing information, fees for advertisements (such as banners), or a combination of any of these.[10] Pricing policy is obviously an important factor in attracting participants to the marketplace. Since pricing methods are more a question of business strategy than law, I have chosen not to deal with them here.

---

[8] Lee points to three main categories of exchange: commercial mutual non-profit, consumer co-operative, and for profit forms: Lee (n 6 above) chs 2 and 3. In ch 9 Lee provides an analysis of the governance of financial marketplaces.

[9] For such an analysis, see Lee (n 6 above) chs 4 and 5.

[10] For an analysis of pricing in financial exchanges, see Lee (n 6 above) ch 6; and see also a survey by S A Gidel, 'The Business of Exchanges' *Futures Industry*, 8 September 1997 11–14.

Competition and anti-trust law aspects of electronic commerce are important. It **1.14** is difficult to say whether the marketplaces will become huge dominant giants in their respective branches of trade or decentralized into many smaller units. It is likely that different branches of trade will undergo different developments in this respect. An electronic auction or exchange needs to attract many participants in order to function efficiently. This creates a risk that the marketplace becomes too dominant. There are several marketplaces whose activities have been investigated by competition and anti-trust agencies (eg in the US and in Germany[11]). This study will not to any great extent cover the anti-trust and competition law aspects of Internet marketplaces dominating their field of trade and their relationship to other competing marketplaces within the same field.[12] The marketplace itself has an interest in ensuring participants that competition within the marketplace is efficient. This internal aspect will be dealt with in this study. Furthermore, the marketplace will be anxious not to abuse its dominant position, since such behaviour might hamper the participants' trust in the marketplace. This aspect related to competition will also be taken into account in the study.

Consumer protection in relation to e-commerce is an often-debated issue, for **1.15** instance within the OECD. This study is mainly focused on business-to-business auctions and exchanges.[13] I do not agree with the idea that there is a fundamental difference between the need to protect consumers and the need to protect businesses. Both businesses and consumers benefit from honest behaviour and general trust in marketplaces. There is a common interest in preventing fraudulent behaviour both in business-to-business and business-to-consumer transactions. Thus, many of the conclusions and recommendations given in this book for business-to-business transactions apply equally to business-to-consumer transactions. In the area of consumer law, we often find mandatory national legislation that restricts the scope for freely designing the conditions of sale and membership terms. This study does not generally take such mandatory national legislation into account but only mentions it in isolated examples.

---

[11] For a useful analysis, see R B Bell and W F Adkinson Jr, 'Antitrust Issues Raised by B2B Exchanges' (2000 Fall) *Antitrust* 18; and Linklaters & Alliance in Goldman Sachs Global Equity Research, *B2B e-Commerce/Internet Europe—The Old World Meets the New Economy* (2000) appendix B, 143 ff. There is much concern in Washington DC about the collusive potential of B2B marketplaces. In summer 2000, both the Federal Trade Commission (FTC) and the Department of Justice (DoJ) (ie both the bodies concerned with anti-trust enforcement in the US) launched investigations of such marketplaces: the FTC is investigating Covisint, formed by the car companies GM, Ford, Daimler-Chrysler, Renault and Nissan, and the DoJ is looking into the marketplace sponsored by six (unnamed) meat-packing companies. The aim of both investigations was to determine whether, in these marketplaces, information becomes more easily available to some participants than to others, and/or more easily available to participants than to non-participants so as to operate as a barrier to entry.   [12] See Hall (n 1 above) ch 7.

[13] An interesting study for consumer auctions online is P Selis, A Ramasastry and C S Wright, 'Bidder Beware: Toward a Fraud-Free Marketplace—Best Practices for the Online Auction Industry', a Report for the State of Washington Attorney-General's Office (17 April 2001) at <http://www.law.washington.edu/lct/publications.html#bidder>

1.16   The study covers norm design only of Internet marketplaces. In non-Internet marketplaces the same types of fundamental problems are present, but because of the great differences in the practical means for controlling the relevant activities, the conclusions and recommendations presented here are limited to Internet marketplaces. Despite this qualification the study may also provide a deeper understanding of non-Internet marketplaces.

1.17   The focus of this study is on auctions and exchanges. The perspective is sometimes wider and covers other types of Internet marketplaces and many of the issues examined are also of interest outside auctions and exchanges. I have, however, only had auctions and exchanges in mind when putting this study together.

1.18   Some believe that the peer-to-peer technique may be used for Internet marketplaces. By using this technique the function of the marketplace operator is largely diminished.[14] The users are thus able to communicate more directly than by the technique where everyone 'meets' at a particular web page. I am personally sceptical that the role of the marketplace operator will become superfluous. The peer-to-peer technology may be developed to serve the needs of Internet marketplaces, but I believe that the task of establishing the necessary trust and confidence cannot be handled by the technology alone. In this study I will not investigate peer-to-peer marketplaces that do not use an overall responsible marketplace operator.

1.19   Intellectual property law in relation to auctions and exchanges online is not examined in this study. In the US there are many examples of marketplaces claiming that their mode of operation is protected either by copyright or patent law. I do not cover this question because it is quite separate from the legal questions regarding the relationship between the parties acting in the marketplace, ie the participants and the operator.[15]

Method

1.20   My intended reader is a legal adviser to operators and participants in Internet marketplaces. I would like to show the many different available options in relation to designing the rules of a marketplace and point out the implications of these options.

1.21   This study takes a non-national approach, which is quite uncommon in legal literature. I provide an analysis of the functions of the auction and the exchange

---

[14] A Oram (ed), *Peer-to-Peer Harnessing the Benefits of Disruptive Technologies* (O'Reilly, 2001).

[15] See Hall (n 1 above) ch 8 for illustrations of Internet marketplaces claiming copyright or patent rights. See also the German case *OLG Köln, Urteil vom 2.11.2001—6 u 12/01—Ricardo.de/Rolex* in *K&R* 2/2002, 93.

and point out some related general legal problems. These problems are likely to appear in all jurisdictions. My aim is not to make a traditional comparative study with a detailed analysis of how one jurisdiction is different from another. The focus is not on examining the applicable law and its default rules—rather I use cases and legislation in different states to illustrate how these problems may be solved or what problems may occur. Solutions in different legal systems are examined with the sole intention of learning from good and bad experiences.

In chapters 2 and 3 I provide a platform upon which I make my detailed analysis. **1.22** Chapter 2 describes the autonomous nature of the Internet marketplace. It provides the framework for legal and technical design. Chapter 3 describes the relationships, on the one hand, between the participants, and on the other hand, between the marketplace and the participants. Understanding these relationships is essential for designing the most efficient norm structure.

By comparing Internet marketplaces with traditional marketplaces and analysing **1.23** the new technological setting, I intend to show how the norm structure can be efficiently designed in electronic auctions and exchanges. I cover the content of membership terms, the conditions of sale, and the technical design steering the way transactions are conducted.

Throughout the study I make references to procedures and rules in auctions and **1.24** exchanges operating online. These references are made with the intention of illustrating how different problems are solved in practice and sometimes to confirm assumptions about how things are carried out in practice. Making such references poses problems from a methodological point of view. First, Internet businesses have a strong tendency to change their operational modes frequently. Thus, the procedures to which I refer might have been changed. I can provide no assurance that the procedures to which I refer are still in use. Due to the fact that I have been preparing this study for some time, it is even possible that the changes may have been made a long time ago. Secondly, making the references does not purport to be of any scientific empirical value. The auctions and exchanges which I mention are not chosen by any scientific method, but are simply websites that I have happened to come across during my work and found to be particularly significant.

It is now possible in practice to implement many of the theories in economics **1.25** about efficiency in marketplaces. This implementation, however, will not be carried out mainly by the national legislator, but by the operators of different marketplaces. This is fully in accordance with mainstream economic theory generally warning about the negative effects of state regulations and advocating instead individual regulation by the parties involved. There is thus a close relationship between the legal and economic sides of the questions dealt with in this study. I do not intend to make any statements about economics but only wish to shed some light on how some of the economic theories can be carried into effect by the design of rules and norms for the Internet marketplace.

The transition towards the Internet marketplace and online auctions

1.26 In traditional markets there are barriers to attracting many participants due to *time* and *geographic location*. Participation in traditional auctions could be costly and inefficient due to bid preparations costs or exposure constraints (ie total amount of bids submitted).[16] In an Internet marketplace the bidders may submit bids 24 hours a day, 365 days a year from anywhere in the world. Internet auctions are not costly: the bid preparations are minimal and there is normally no reason to restrain the amount of bidders.

1.27 From a theoretical point of view it is thus easy to understand that there are significant factors in favour of holding auctions on the Internet. As early as 1967 it was stated that electronic auctions were not at all a new phenomenon.[17] As already mentioned, electronic auctions cover commodities, financial products, metals, agricultural products, unique items of fine art, manufactured goods, travel, insurance, surplus goods, damaged goods, space in containers, trucks, used cars and ships. There are also wholly automated processes based on auctions in the area of power distribution where there is no human interaction.

1.28 Naturally, there are also factors working against the increased use of electronic auctions. The changed roles of the intermediaries in business is one of these. The uncertainty related to anonymity is another factor hindering the development of electronic auctions. Furthermore, the increased transparency of the price-setting mechanism may lead to a lack of interest in participating in electronic marketplaces. It has been said that if markets are too perfect, there is a risk that many potential participants refrain from taking part because transparent competition results in the profit margins becoming too low.[18] Another problem related to auctions and exchanges is that it is difficult to have negotiations on terms other than the price. This latter problem, however, may be solved by advanced computer systems allowing for bundling of bids and multi-attribute auctions.[19]

---

[16] R Wilson, in P Newman, M Milgate and J Eatwell (eds), *The New Palgrave Dictionary of Money and Finance* (1992) 198.

[17] R J R Cassady, *Auctions and Auctioneering* (University of California Press, 1967) ch 14, Modern Communication Systems.

[18] See Barrie Nalebuff in <NYTimes.com>, 13 December 2000. See also Hall (n 1 above) 4.

[19] See Bichler (n 3 above) chs 5–7. The International Chamber of Commerce in Paris is developing contract formulae that will facilitate negotiations in a standardized electronic environment (see <www.iccwbo.org>).

Effects of the transition to the online auction

It used to be the case that the goods sold in the auction were only a fraction of the total supply, but that the auction price still influenced the whole market by serving as a reference price for negotiated deals.[20] When a greater part of the total amount of transactions is made in the marketplace, the prices in the market will better reflect the 'true' price. Furthermore, when an online auction is an available alternative, presumably fewer transactions will be individually negotiated as at least one of the parties normally would be able to see that it can make a better deal in the online auction as compared with the individual negotiation. **1.29**

The Internet has provided a powerful tool with which to change the price-setting mechanisms in trade. Evolution from manufacturer-controlled market value to online markets is anticipated. Some believe that fixed prices will pass into history. I, however, share the view that fixed pricing will never disappear, but that the Internet is changing the balance in favour of dynamic pricing. The case for dynamic pricing is compelling for both buyers and sellers. The OECD has predicted that: 'More and more products will be subject to differential pricing associated with customized products, fine market segmentation and auctions as it becomes easier to change prices'.[21] Stuart I Feldman at the IBM Institute for Advanced Commerce has said: 'We've suddenly made the interaction cost so cheap, there's no pragmatic reason not to have competitive bidding on everything'.[22] **1.30**

The broker, whose role it was to function as an aggregator of disparate buyers and sellers, will to a large extent be transformed into marketplaces—exchanges or auctions. The broker's former value lay in his connections and knowledge about the market. In an Internet marketplace this information is transparent and accessible to all participants. **1.31**

As a summary of the effects of the transition towards electronic auctions Bichler has stated:[23] **1.32**

Auctions have proven to be very efficient negotiation protocols that converge to an equilibrium very quickly, which is important in situations where transactions need to occur at a rapid rate. Considering political contexts, auctions are also widely perceived as fair. In fact, they reflect the general shift of power towards the consumer, as sellers who do not offer some form of negotiation may be in danger of falling behind or being considered consumer-unfriendly. Aside from theoretical arguments, auctions have a number of practical advantages for both seller and buyer:

---

[20] See Cassady (n 17 above) 42. Now this reference price is available on a global scale (if there is general access to the information in the marketplace).

[21] OECD, *The Economic and Social Impacts of Electronic Commerce* (2001) available at <www.oecd.org/subject/e_commerce/summary.html>.

[22] Cited in Bichler (n 3 above) 139.   [23] Bichler (n 3 above) 201, 202.

- An auction mechanism releases the bid taker from having to negotiate with several bidders individually, thus saving time.
- A bid taker can have several bidders compete against each other in an open-cry manner. As shown in subsection 5.4.2, this type of information revelation leads to a sense of competition among bidders, which is likely to impact on the equilibrium values in real-world auctions, although this is contrary to game-theoretical predictions.
- Finally, electronic brokerages of this type also lead to advantages for the bidders. They can participate in negotiations with buyers/sellers they would otherwise never have access to. Moreover, these electronic trading floors enable bidders to learn more easily about their buyer's needs and their competitor's strength.

In this study I will describe some of the basic features of price mechanisms based on auctions and exchanges and analyse what impact this may have on general trade law.[24]

---

[24] The efficiency of electronic markets has been analysed and questioned by economists. See Y Bakos, 'A Strategic Analysis of Electronic Marketplaces' (1999) *MIS Quarterly*, 15(3), 295–310; K Crowston, 'Price Behavior in Electronic Markets', Paper presented at the 18th International Conference on Information Systems (ICIS 1997), Atlanta; H G Lee, 'Do electronic marketplaces lower the price of goods?' *(1998)* Communications of the ACM, 41(1), 73–80; V Choudhury, K S Hartsel and B R Konsynski, 'Uses and consequences of electronic markets: an empirical investigation in the aircraft parts industry' (1998) *MIS Quarterly*, 22(4), 471–507, all referred to in Bichler (n 3 above) 7.

2

THE RELATIONSHIP BETWEEN INTERNET MARKETPLACES AND NATIONAL STATES

Introduction

An electronic marketplace can be managed from anywhere and simultaneously **2.01** from many places. This makes it possible for the marketplace operator to choose its own jurisdiction.[1] In theory, it may even choose to have no jurisdiction at all— to be wholly independent and located only in cyberspace. In practice, however, it is not likely that such autonomous 'bubbles' in cyberspace will develop in relation to electronic commerce. Anyhow, there is an enormous potential for the operators of marketplaces to design the rules and norms independently of the national state. This might be perceived as a valuable freedom. However autonomy also has its costs. An autonomous Internet marketplace can no longer rely on the help of the national state and, consequently, must solve problems that were formerly solved by the state. In this chapter I will describe the national state's powers and functions in relation to Internet marketplaces.

---

[1] The operator or 'owner' of the marketplace could be anyone: former intermediaries, participants, or wholly independent persons.

2.02 It is essential to emphasize that my study is merely aimed at commercial transactions in closed communities where access is admitted only to members of the particular marketplace. There has been an animated general debate concerning the autonomous Internet as a whole, including every legal aspect of the Internet such as child pornography, privacy and freedom of speech. My analysis is limited to transactions made in a marketplace allowing access only for participants and the substantive terms stipulated for these transactions: typically contract law, the law of sales and services and, to some extent, consumer law. In areas outside such closed communities the national legislator may fulfil wholly different functions and have different means of exercising control and making legislation efficient. The following analysis does not attempt to be anarchic and plead for a wholly unregulated Internet. I simply want to show that for commercial transactions traditional national regulation might to some extent be efficiently substituted by self-regulation and that self-regulation indeed is necessary due to the reduced power of the national state.

2.03 From a general point of view the development of norms in the Internet society is interesting. Nihoul says, with reference to the industrialist society: '. . . the legal system was regarded as a body of binding sentences expressing a project designed by a central authority. That project was supposed to become reality, ie to be implemented by the members of society under the threat of sanction.'[2] In contrast to the industrialist concept of the legal system, the information society does not build on centralization. It is rather a question of dispersion of decision-making power. The fact that public authorities do not principally create law is not inconsistent with democracy. On the contrary, it is in harmony with the basic concept of democracy since it provides an opportunity for individuals to participate in the norm-making process.[3] The norm design of Internet marketplaces is an example of decentralized law-making where territoriality matters less. There are similarities with the law-making of private law in medieval times, where the customs and usages—rather than the feudal prince or king—was the source of the rules for business transactions. It has been said: 'Maybe we are moving back to the medieval system, which was non-territorial in so far as territoriality was not the defining characteristic of organization. Political rule was not premised on territorial delimitation. Feudalism, the Church and the Holy Roman Empire represent three different organizational forms in the Middle Ages, which lacked territorial fixity and exclusiveness.'[4] It is fairly easy to see the members of the medieval Hanseatic League as centres of power equivalent to the emerging

---

[2] P Nihoul, 'Will Electronic Commerce Change the Law?' in C T Marsden (ed), *Regulating the Global Information Society* (Routledge, 2000) 79–90 at 82.   [3] ibid, 82, 83.

[4] C Jönsson, S Tägil and G Thörnqvist, *Organizing European Space* (SAGE Publications, 2000) 66. See also J P Barlow, 'Thinking Logically, Acting Globally' (1996) *Cyber-Rights Electronic List*, 15 January: '. . . the Internet is too widespread to be easily dominated by any single government. By creating a seamless global-economic zone, borderless and unregulatable, the Internet calls into question the very idea of a nation-state.'

Internet marketplaces. They lacked borders and were functionally rather than geographically integrated.

How the national state's power over the Internet is limited

It has often been pointed out that globalization limits the power of the national **2.04** state. When companies and persons are able to choose from where to conduct their transactions, the legislator's ability to regulate markets is reduced.[5] National states used to be able to steer or regulate business behaviour. Nowadays, the state instead is anxious to enact legislation that attracts business. This has been called the 'race to the bottom', meaning that states try to attract business by abolishing rules that protect weaker parties and by lowering taxes. We know of this phenomenon from earlier experience in relation to shipping and 'flags of convenience', ie ships carrying the flags of the countries providing the most favourable rules. This experience shows how difficult it is to prevent the 'race to the bottom' when states begin to compete with each other in order to attract business. It should, however, not be forgotten that there are also 'races to the top' where national states compete to attract businesses in the financial sector by imposing heavy regulation that ensures trustworthiness in a market.[6]

In the present era of globalization there are still opportunities for the national state **2.05** to reach out more or less effectively in cyberspace.[7] In order to present an accurate picture of the power of the national state the following must be acknowledged:

(a) national states may co-operate and create *international treaties* that apply worldwide;
(b) important states may *boycott* states that provide safe harbours for unwanted business behaviour;
(c) the national state may *forbid its citizens to do business* in unwanted Internet marketplaces (see, for a comparison, the US restrictions on trade with Cuba);
(d) there is also, at least in theory, a power to influence the behaviour of cyberspace activity by threatening to *shut down the IP address* of the Internet marketplace;

---

[5] See, for example, the problems in relation to the French state's attempts to forbid the part of the Yahoo!-auction website providing Nazi memorabilia from being accessible to French users: P Selis, A Ramasastry and C S Wright, 'Bidder Beware: Toward a Fraud-free Marketplace—Best Practices for the Online Auction Industry', a Report for the State of Washington Attorney-General's Office (17 April 2001) at <http://www.law.washington.edu/lct/publications.html#bidder>.

[6] A Sculley and B W Woods, *B2B Exchanges* (ISI Publications, USA, 1999) 150.

[7] The Internet is by no means impossible to regulate. See C T Marsden, 'Introduction: information and communications technologies, globalisation and regulation' in Marsden (ed) (n 2 above) 2, with references to A M Florini, 'Who does what? Collective action and the changing nature of authority' in R Higgot, G Underhill and A Bieler (eds), *Non-State Actors and Authority in the Global System* (Routledge, 2000).

(e) the national state may by co-operative means facilitate *self-regulation* and guide it in desirable directions by, for instance, developing self-regulatory agencies, codes of conduct and rating systems.[8]

These different means by which the national state can reach out in cyberspace involve major political effort and sometimes entail work over many years. It is quite likely that the state will be much less regulatory in the future due to the practical problems of effectively executing national regulation. While acknowledging that there is still some power left for the national state to enforce legislation in cyberspace, it is clear that in practice it must be much more careful before introducing new regulations, since it will involve much more effort than previously to make the regulation effective in practice. The debate concerning to what extent the power of the national state is limited will not be analysed in depth here.[9] My main concern is to show that marketplaces nowadays cannot rely as much on the help of the national state as they used to, but must to a greater extent take their own initiatives to protect their interests in establishing trustworthiness in order to attract participants.[10]

The relationship between the Internet marketplace and the national state

2.06 Studies in economics have shown that for a state to prosper it must have the power to ensure the basic rights of property and ownership. Formerly, many business transactions were dependent on the latent threat of extreme measures which (with some minor exceptions) the national state had the monopoly on exercising. In effect, these measures included execution obligations and imprisonment—and in some countries, even killing people. Naturally, there are many other and complex reasons why people comply with norms and rules. The national state's power is *ultimately* ensured by the threat that these extreme sanctions on which they have a monopoly will be exercised unless, for instance, promises are kept, debts are paid and fraudulent behaviour avoided. Luckily, these extreme measures are rarely used in practice.

2.07 It is interesting to note how little support from a national state an electronic marketplace needs. An Internet marketplace could function quite well without a structure based on a latent threat of violence or other extreme sanctions. An Internet marketplace has at its disposal a more sophisticated—but yet more

---

[8] See, for instance, M E Price and S G Verhulst, 'In search of itself' in Marsden (ed) (n 2 above) 57–78.

[9] See D R Johnson and D G Post, 'The Rise of Law in The Global Network' in B Kahin and C Nelson (eds), *Borders in Cyberspace* (MIT, 1999) 12, pointing to the likelihood that local regulatory structures will be superseded by new structures that better fit the online phenomena.

[10] See for an introduction, Marsden (ed) (n 2 above) *passim*.

powerful—sanction than violence: access denial. A participant acting against the rules set up by the marketplace can be excluded from the marketplace.[11] If the marketplace is dominant in its field the access denial makes the excluded participant 'cyberspace-handicapped'. There is a parallel in more primitive societies, where misbehaving members became outcasts, which in effect meant that they would face certain death alone in the wilderness. Before using such drastic sanctions, the Internet marketplace could demand from misbehaving participants the payment of fees to the marketplace comparable to the fines paid to a national state. It should be acknowledged that access denial is ineffective against one-off fraudulent participants whose actions will not be detected until carried out. None the less, access denial remains a powerful disincentive for repeat players because it represents a threat to their very existence in the Internet marketplace community.[12] Furthermore, access denial may not be an efficient sanction when there are substitute markets available. In chapter 16 different means of excluding certain participants are described in detail.

Also before the Internet there were examples of marketplaces that opted out of the legal system and still succeeded in preserving a high degree of trustworthiness, for instance the diamond market that has been thoroughly examined in an often-cited study by Bernstein.[13] The strong social pressure created in traditional physical marketplaces could be supplemented or substituted in Internet marketplaces by a technical structure that automatically identifies unwanted behaviour and by using a transparent exclusion procedure.   **2.08**

To say that many Internet marketplaces do not necessarily need the help of the national state is not to say that they cannot benefit from belonging to a certain jurisdiction.[14] A typical example is the extensive SEC regulation in the US. At first one might believe that a marketplace would be anxious *not* to fall under such a regulatory and bureaucratic scheme. However, since the SEC regulation has created trustworthiness, a marketplace may want to signal its own trustworthiness by showing that it belongs to the US jurisdiction.[15]   **2.09**

---

[11] See Johnson and Post, (n 9 above) 22, 31; R L Dunne, 'Deterring Unauthorized Access to Computers: Controlling Behavior in Cyberspace Through a Contract Law Paradigm' (1994) 35 *Jurimetrics J* 1, 12; Selis, Ramasastry and Wright (n 5 above) 33.

[12] Selis, Ramasastry and Wright (n 5 above) 33.

[13] L Bernstein, 'Opting Out of the Legal System: Extralegal Contractual Relations in the Diamond Industry' (1992) 21 *Journal of Legal Studies* 115, reprinted in part in R Barnett, *Contracts: Theory and Doctrine* (Little, Brown & Co, 1995).

[14] Coase argues 'economists observing the regulation of . . . exchanges often assume that they represent an attempt to exercise monopoly power and restrain competition. They ignore, or at any rate, fail to emphasize an alternative explanation for these regulations: that they exist to reduce transaction costs and therefore to increase the volume of trade.': R H Coase, *The Firm, the Market, and the Law* (University of Chicago Press, 1988) ch 9. Johnson and Post say that '. . . insofar as consensually based "law of the Net" needs to obtain respect and deference from local sovereigns, new Net-based lawmaking institutions have an incentive to avoid fostering activities that threaten the vital interest of territorial governments.' (n 9 above) 18.   [15] Sculley and Woods (n 6 above) 150.

2.10 Below I shall point to some functions of the national state traditionally associated with ensuring trust and confidence in marketplaces and explain to what extent these functions can be managed by the Internet marketplace without the help of the state.

Default rules

2.11 The national state has often performed an important service to citizens by providing default rules that stipulate what the parties should do in the absence of a particular contractual agreement. The default rules in private law were of great value since they lowered the costs of concluding agreements. The parties did not need to agree on all terms, since they were already provided by the default rules in national law.

2.12 The default rules in private law were codified in parallel with the development of the industrialist-capitalist society, starting in the mid nineteenth century and really taking off at the beginning of the twentieth century. The industrial-capitalist society was characterized by mass transactions and scale efficiency. The information age is often said not to have these characteristics. At least the new information technology makes it possible to tailor transactions and create scale efficiency at a lower level than in the industrial-capitalist society. In Internet marketplaces it is rather easy to stipulate and customize efficient rules for different types of transactions. Thus, appropriate rules can be developed by the marketplace at a relatively low cost without the help of the national state. A legislature is rarely able successfully to codify very specific default rules for different branches of business or trade without running into complicated questions of definitions and scope of application. A legislature, therefore, often has to lay down rather general rules, whereas an Internet marketplace can establish rules that are specifically aimed at and adopted for a particular type of transaction.

Mandatory rules to ensure fairness

2.13 In the late twentieth century many mandatory rules were enacted with the aim of protecting weaker parties, mainly within the area of consumer law but also for business-to-business transactions. This type of regulation ensured trust for situations where the market forces were not strong enough to create fair rules. The operator of an Internet marketplace can, as an independent third party, require that the participants include certain types of clauses in their conditions of sale. These, in a way, can be said to be norms of a mandatory nature. The reason for the marketplace to have such requirements is the same as in the national state: to ensure fairness and trust, which in turn is essential to attract liquidity. It is not likely that an Internet marketplace will have as extensive mandatory regulations as a national state. However the Internet marketplace does not *need* the *help* of the national state to ensure fairness by mandatory regulations. Another point is that the national state's ability to reach out in cyberspace with more mandatory protection than the marketplace considers necessary is limited.

Dispute resolution

Another important service of the national state is to provide a means for citizens **2.14** to resolve their disputes, normally by national courts. The courts are usually financed and administered by the state. Dispute resolution between individuals may, however, be handled with or without the help of the national state. It is quite common in business relations to provide in contracts that conflicts shall be solved privately by arbitration, without the help of national courts. It is not surprising that conflicts in Internet marketplaces—between participants in the marketplace or between the marketplace itself and the participants—are frequently solved by arbitration procedures set up according to the rules of the marketplace, eg by a permanent arbitration tribunal connected to the marketplace.[16] We see that the help of the national state is not needed for the Internet marketplace with respect to dispute resolution between participants.

Enforcement of court decisions and arbitral awards

Another traditionally important task for the national state is to execute and **2.15** enforce court decisions and arbitral awards. State authorities, such as the bailiff, can enforce court decisions that the parties do not follow voluntarily. If an arbitration award is not adhered to voluntarily, most national states have legislation acknowledging arbitral awards and making them enforceable. Internationally, many states have ratified the New York Convention 1958 on the Recognition and Enforcement of Foreign Arbitral Awards according to which international arbitral awards are enforceable.[17]

Since an Internet marketplace has no authority physically to take possession of **2.16** property in someone else's possession, one might have thought that the help of the national state would be necessary to enforce arbitral awards efficiently. An Internet marketplace can, however, rely to some extent on the threat of access denial for participants who do not adhere to arbitral awards. It is thus not always necessary to rely on the help of the national state to achieve 'voluntary' execution of an arbitral award. In some instances the threat of access denial might not be severe enough and the participant entitled to damages may need a national authority to help him enforce an arbitral award. Normally, a national state would recognize the award and enforce it when the arbitration procedure is in accordance with the requirements in the New York Convention.[18]

---

[16] See ch 18.   [17] The Convention may be found at <www.unictral.org>.
[18] Arbitration held online might give rise to complications in applying the New York Convention. This issue will be analysed in ch 18.

Prevention of transactions in stolen goods

2.17   The national state often functions as a safeguard of ownership by preventing crimes aimed at ownership by, among other things, making it difficult to trade stolen goods. There is no doubt that stolen goods will be—and already are—put into circulation in Internet marketplaces.[19] The Internet makes it possible to communicate easily with businessmen and consumers interested in certain products and services. Likewise it is easy for criminal elements to gather and find each other and form communities for criminal activities and to cheat honest people into buying stolen goods. On the Internet criminal elements are able to communicate more easily with a greater number of criminals and they also have many opportunities to hide or disguise their communication from the police. To my knowledge, the police authorities all over the world are much concerned by this problem. It must be emphasized, however, that the problem of criminals and gatherings of criminals cheating honest people is not new, but has always existed. We ought to be careful that our keenness to prevent crime does not prevent the development of efficient business procedures conducted by honest entities.

2.18   Auctions for antiques have long faced the problem of stolen goods being offered for sale. There are examples of the national state trying to prevent this from happening by licensing auctioneers and requiring them to produce catalogues of the offered goods and information about ownership.[20] In other states it has not been considered necessary to introduce such legislation, since it is often in the interests of a serious auctioneer that his auction house is well respected and not associated with crime. There are means other than criminal law available to prevent transactions in stolen goods. We see different types of blacklisting schemes administered by state authorities or private bodies seeking to prevent consumers from being defrauded.[21] A serious Internet marketplace would to a large extent be willing to co-operate with the police in order to prevent the types of crimes that may destroy the good reputation of the marketplace.[22]

---

[19] Investigations show that online auction complaints represent the largest category for Internet fraud statistics. See <www.fraud.org/internet/lt00totstats.htm>. At the same time it is argued that the amount of Internet fraud is tiny compared with the number of transactions which take place: M Bichler, *The Future of e-Markets: Multidimensional Market Mechanisms* (CUP, 2001) 131.

[20] See for instance the English legislation from the eighteenth century referred to in para 2.06 above.

[21] See for example the US Federal Trade Commission with a database helping to identify and track fraud worldwide at <www.fts.gov/bcp/reports/int-auction.htm>.

[22] Florida has introduced an online record system to allow users to enter identification numbers for everything from appliances to cars to see if they have been reported as stolen. If an item turns up in the database, users can click on it and email a tip to the police, potentially receiving a tipper's reward of up to $1,000. The website lets the public check to see if someone they know has been reported missing or is wanted by law enforcement agencies. Further information may be found at <http://www.computeruser.com/news/00/10/13/news12.html>.

The national states can by different means try to convince the Internet market-   **2.19**
places that it is of value to help the police. It is highly probable that we will find
Internet marketplaces developing a symbiotic relationship with national police
throughout the world. It is generally in the interests of Internet marketplaces to
promote an environment where participants can feel that their ownership is safe-
guarded and that their transactions are valid and not the result of criminal activity.[23] The fact that some Internet marketplaces are unwilling to provide
information to the police and that most Internet marketplaces are unwilling to
participate in police work related to crimes that do not affect the trustworthiness
of the marketplace should not be used as an argument to regulate all Internet
marketplaces.[24]

Collusion and anti-trust

A task that may sometimes be difficult for the marketplace to manage itself is   **2.20**
preventing collusion between participants who thereby destroy efficient competition, eg by forming a cartel. In the traditional setting such behaviour is controlled
by anti-trust and competition law. With the aid of administrative controlling
bodies the national state seeks out unlawful collusion and stipulates severe consequences for breach of the relevant regulations.[25]

There are three main disadvantages connected to this approach. First, it is diffi-   **2.21**
cult for the national regulations to be effective when collusion is committed from
a location abroad. When the Internet is used as a marketplace there are greater
opportunities for locating a marketplace in a state which does not have harsh anti-
trust regulations. Secondly, it is questionable whether it is appropriate to charge
all the taxpayers in a national state with the cost of the administration and control
of the anti-trust regulations. It would be preferable if the cost were borne by the
participants protected by the regulations. This is particularly so in an international
setting where taxpayers in small states would otherwise unjustifiably benefit from
the larger states' financing of administration and control. Thirdly, the anti-trust
regulations of a national state necessarily need to be general in nature. Different
types of transactions are differently exposed to the risks and types of collusion—
thus many are in favour of regulating the problem at a local level, ie by the
marketplace itself forbidding collusion in its membership terms.

---

[23] Selis, Ramasastry and Wright (n 5 above) 37.
[24] An area where it can be assumed to be particularly difficult to achieve co-operation between the
national police and Internet marketplaces is tax evasion. I will refrain from going further into the topic
of tax law and the huge challenges and changes which the new means of international electronic
communications entail for this area.
[25] For a useful analysis, see R B Bell and W F Adkinson Jr, 'Antitrust Issues Raised by B2B
Exchanges' (2000 Fall) *Antitrust*; and Linklaters & Alliance in Goldman Sachs Global Equity
Research, *B2B e-Commerce/Internet Europe—The Old World Meets the New Economy* (2000) appendix B, 143 ff.

2.22 An Internet marketplace can to a large extent deal with unwanted collusion by itself. It is often in the interests of the marketplace to have severe rules against collusion. If it becomes known among the participants that collusion occurs in the marketplace, it loses its trustworthiness and, as said earlier, it is crucial for an Internet marketplace to preserve trustworthiness and confidence. By having membership terms or conditions of sale forbidding collusion and providing for severe consequences—fees or denial of access—when such rules are broken, there is a strong incentive for participants not to collude.[26]

2.23 There are situations when an Internet marketplace by itself cannot prevent collusion. For certain types of markets, there are so few sellers or buyers that denying access to a particular participant leads to the death of the marketplace since without that important participant no one is likely to want to make transactions in that marketplace. In such situations there is no way of replacing the national state regulation preventing collusion.

2.24 National regulation on anti-trust may to some extent be ineffective in cyberspace but it is at least better than nothing. A globally enacted treaty against collusion would to a large extent enhance the efficiency of national regulation. It should, however, be emphasized that for many types of transactions the marketplace itself has enough incentive, power and influence effectively to prevent collusion.

Abuse of autonomy

2.25 The power of an autonomous marketplace in cyberspace could be abused by, for instance, denying access to certain persons or charging unreasonably high participation fees.[27] There are two schools of thought as to how abusive power should be tamed and dealt with: the market-oriented view and the regulatory view.

The market-oriented view

2.26 According to the market-oriented view, a marketplace abusing its power by wrongfully denying access to well-behaving participants or charging excessively high fees or bribes for participation would soon face competition from other marketplaces offering a platform more in harmony with what the participants perceive as fair. Market forces create an incentive for marketplaces to apply non-abusive rules for participation and to keep the costs of participation low.[28]

---

[26] See ch 15.

[27] For an analysis of abuse from a competition and anti-trust law point of view, see Bell and Adkinson (n 25 above) 18; and Linklaters & Alliance (n 25 above) 143 ff.

[28] See Johnson and Post (n 9 above) 32 referring to Tiebout's idealized model for optimal allocation for locally produced public goods provided by small jurisdictions competing for mobile residents (C Tiebout, 'A Pure Theory of Local Expenditures' (1956) 64 *J Pol Econ* 416).

Furthermore, market forces are likely to create an incentive to keep the market-place transparent, in the sense that information about how transactions are carried out may be conveyed to the participants in order for them to determine the level of ethics of participants and the marketplace operator.[29]

In traditional physical marketplaces there are substantial barriers against estab-   **2.27**
lishing a competitive marketplace. These barriers consist of geographical changes, travel expenses, costs for physically building the marketplace and costs for making the new marketplace known. An Internet marketplace wanting to compete with an existing marketplace faces barriers, but these are easier to overcome. It is relat-ively inexpensive to build the technical platform for the competing marketplace,[30] the participants need not physically travel from one geographical location to another, and information about the new marketplace can be spread quickly, effi-ciently and at low cost. It must, however, be acknowledged that there are still inconveniences in shifting from one marketplace to another. There may be prob-lems related to technical compatibility and there may also be considerable costs in teaching the users to handle a new interface. Furthermore, the cost of spreading information about the existence of a competing marketplace may also be consid-erable in times of modern communication due to the so-called network effect.[31] There are, however, technological means making it easy to search for the right auction items by various search engines and agents.[32] A particularly important barrier for competing marketplaces, whether Internet based or physical, is the start-up period before there is enough liquidity to attract more liquidity.

The ever-present latent threat of the establishment of a competing marketplace   **2.28**
has a preventive effect and in a situation where a dominating marketplace is abus-ing its power, new marketplaces will provide an alternative and a solution. The fact that switching from one marketplace to another is not easily done is efficient from an economic point of view and provides incentives for participants to express how the marketplace can be improved. This is described as the intricate relationship between exit, voice and loyalty.[33] We see that market forces are able, at least in theory, to prevent autonomous Internet marketplaces from exercising abusive power and that in practice market forces will function more efficiently in the Internet environment than in physically located marketplaces.[34]

---

[29] See for a parallel in society generally, D Brin, *The Transparent Society* (Reading, Mass, 1998).

[30] See R Lee, *What is an Exchange? The Automation, Management and Regulation of Financial Markets* (OUP, 1988) 32 and 55.

[31] See R E Hall, *Digital Dealing: How e-markets are transforming the Economy* (2001) at <http://www.stanford.edu/~rehall/LinoleumReport.pdf> 57 ff.

[32] See Bichler (n 19 above) 131 with a reference to <www.auctionwatch.com>.

[33] See A O Hirschman, *Exit, Voice and Loyalty* (Harvard UP, 1969).

[34] 'In an environment in which there is rivalry between trading systems, it is hard to conceive of any exchange or trading system, whatever its governance structure, that might not seek to attract order flow. The pursuit of this goal is likely to lead to the optimal provision of the desired regulatory object-ives. Any action by an exchange that adversely affects the quality of its market increases the poss-ibility that competing trading systems will be able to attract order flow away from the exchange. An

The regulatory view

2.29   Many would argue that it is only in theory that the competing marketplace could be established as an alternative to an abusive dominating marketplace.[35] According to this approach, there is no real incentive for the Internet marketplace to abstain from abusing its strong position. Consequently, the autonomous Internet marketplace must be controlled and regulated in order to protect the participants and 'outcasts' from being abused. As a parallel, the financial markets that emerged during the first part of the twentieth century did not manage to create enough trust by themselves and were also considered to abuse their dominating positions. Consequently they became extensively and increasingly regulated by mandatory national legislation throughout the century.

2.30   Even if there is found to be a need to regulate Internet marketplaces, regulation entails special difficulties due to their non-national nature. There are three main problems related to control of Internet marketplaces:

(a) who should exercise the control—the national state? If so, which national state? One could hope to assemble all the nations of the world and establish common regulations for control of Internet marketplaces. Even if this is possible to achieve, it will probably take a couple of decades before such global regulation is agreed upon;[36]

(b) the control against abusive behaviour needs to be of a prohibitive and mandatory nature. Such a structure might function as a hindrance to the flexibility of different marketplaces and the free development and improvement of existing marketplaces;

(c) a scheme of control is bound to create administration and bureaucracy, which is costly and time-consuming. The costs will ultimately be borne by either the taxpayers in the state exercising the control or by the participants in the marketplace.

---

exchange will therefore have an incentive to adopt whatever level of transparency best enhances market quality. This does not imply, however, that an exchange will always choose a market architecture with full transparency.': Lee (n 30 above) 260, 261.

[35] The traditional marketplace has benefits compared with newcomers. Particularly important in this respect is the 'network externality'. Furthermore, successful competition by other marketplaces requires fungibility or mutual off-set arrangements between the competing marketplaces' clearing-houses (if the objects for sale need to be registered or 'cleared') see ibid, 55. For a regulatory approach see J Goldring, 'Netting the Cybershark: Consumer Protection, Cyberspace, the Nation-State, and Democracy' in Kahin and Nelson (n 9 above) 323–54.

[36] An often-heard argument against global harmonization of law is that it will not be able to encompass different cultures. This is an important argument for many areas of law, but not so much in relation to international commercial law.

Conclusion

We see that, at least in theory, market forces are likely to prevent an autonomous **2.31**
marketplace from abusing its power.[37] We also understand that there are problems
in controlling the power of the Internet marketplace which relate to the legitimacy
of the controlling body, the costs occurring due to the control and the preservat-
ory effect of mandatory and regulatory schemes. Strange writes: '(T)he authority
of the governments of all states, large and small, strong and weak, has been weak-
ened as a result of technological and financial change and of the accelerating integration of national economies into one single global market economy.'[38] Sandel
says:[39]

The hope for self-government today lies not in relocating sovereignty but in dispersing it.
The most promising alternative to the sovereign state is not a cosmopolitan community
based on the solidarity of humankind but a multiplicity of communities and political
bodies—some more extensive than nations and some less—among which sovereignty is
diffused. Only a politics that disperses sovereignty both upward (to transnational institutions) and downward can combine the power required to rival global market forces with
the differentiation required of a public life that hopes to inspire the allegiance of its citizens.

Studies show that self-regulation may lead to cartels and monopolies since it has **2.32**
an excluding function, that is to say, the self-regulatory scheme excludes companies not participating in the scheme. In Internet marketplaces that are anxious to
attract liquidity, ie many participants and many transactions, it is not likely that
monopolies will develop even if the marketplaces are based on self-regulatory
schemes. The need to attract liquidity will probably balance and thwart the
tendency to exclude competitors. Those who do not share this prediction must at
least acknowledge that the risk of cartels and monopolies has decreased due to the
fact that the barriers against establishing competing marketplaces are lower in the
electronic setting than in the traditional physical markets.[40]

In my opinion, national states ought to rely on market forces and only intervene **2.33**
with controlling and regulatory schemes when abuse is actually taking place and
is of such importance that it threatens fundamental interests. In other words, it is
better to be proactive than reactive. I am aware that not everyone agrees with this

---

[37] For a more in-depth description of the market forces in relation to the development of competing marketplaces, see Lee (n 30 above) chs 4 and 5.
[38] Strange, *The Retreat of the State: The Diffusion of Power in the World Economy* (CUP, 1996)
14. See also R Rosecrance who in the 1980s envisioned the rise of the 'trading state': *The Rise of the
Trading State* (New York: Basic Books, 1986).
[39] M J Sandel, *Democracy's Discontent: America in Search of a Public Philosophy* (Cambridge,
Mass, 1996) 73.
[40] For a useful analysis of competition and anti-trust law issues, see Bell and Adkinson (n 25
above) and Linklaters & Alliance (n 25 above) 143 ff.

view. Again, I would like to emphasize that my opinion only refers to regulation of closed marketplaces where commercial dealings are conducted and that I do not examine other Internet phenomena.

Democracy in Internet marketplaces

2.34 Another problem with the autonomous Internet marketplace is the apparent lack of democracy. This may appear a non-controversial issue. As long as the principle of freedom of contract is acknowledged as democratic, marketplaces are allowed to contract about whatever rules they wish. It may, however, be of some interest to make a comparison between the democratic nature of the national state and the Internet marketplace, since an autonomous marketplace constitutes a community of its own that may acquire substantial power and influence.

2.35 In the democratic national state, legislation is decided by Parliament. In an Internet marketplace the operators of the marketplace set the rules. Who actually owns and governs an Internet marketplace may vary. Sometimes the participants own it; at other times an independent body owns it.[41]

2.36 The national Parliament derives its legitimacy from the constitution, which usually includes provisions on how the members of Parliament are elected and what power Parliament has. Since Parliament has high legitimacy, it may successfully enact legislation that is followed even by citizens who do not sympathize with that particular legislation.

2.37 In an Internet marketplace the designer of norms or rules (the marketplace operator) lacks legitimacy in the democratic sense. Participants adhere to the rules set by the operator of the marketplace not because the decision-maker is elected, but for pure economic reasons. By contracting to take part in the marketplace the participants accept that they are to be bound by the rules of the marketplace. If a participant does not approve of the rules, he is free not to take part (exit). A marketplace's legitimacy is based on economic attraction and not on democratic principles. It may, consequently, be questioned whether democracy is needed at all in a marketplace.[42] Post has written:[43]

There has always been a strong fictional element to using this notion of a social contract as a rationale for a sovereign's legitimacy. When exactly did you or I consent to be bound by the US Constitution? . . . But in cyberspace there is an infinite amount of space, and movement between online communities is entirely frictionless. Here, there really is the

---

[41] Sculley and Woods (n 6 above) provide examples of successful and unsuccessful ownership constellations. See also Lee (n 30 above) for an analysis of governance of exchanges.

[42] An advocate for the need for democracy in Internet business transaction is Goldring (n 35 above) 351.

[43] D G Post 'The State of Nature and the First Internet War' (1996), *Reason*, April, 33.

opportunity to a social contract; virtual communities can be established with their own particular rule-sets, power to maintain a degree of order and to banish wrongdoers can be lodged, or not, in particular individuals or groups, and those who find the rules oppressive or unfair may simply leave and join another community (or start their own).

In a democratic national state, the principle of equal treatment of citizens is of **2.38** fundamental importance. In a marketplace it is not necessary to treat everybody equally. There is always a risk that market forces are not strong enough to take care of the occasional mistreatment of small participants in a marketplace. The idea of unequal treatment depending on economic strength is offensive to many in principle. However, in comparing the equal treatment of marketplace particip- ants and citizens in a national state, we must acknowledge that the principle of equal treatment is not always upheld in practice in the state. It is a well-known fact that poor and uneducated citizens in practice face huge problems exercising their legal rights.[44] Both the national state and Internet marketplaces normally have incentives to treat all citizens/participants equally. If the national state fails to do this it can be taken to the courts of constitutional or human rights and exposed to international humiliation. In extreme cases a national state neglecting the need to treat citizens equally might face a revolution, or less seriously, the government might lose the next election. If an Internet marketplace fails in treat- ing everybody equally, it runs the risk of being exposed to negative criticism and eventually to losing its participants to competing marketplaces.

There are incentives both for national states and Internet marketplaces to treat all **2.39** citizens/participants equally. However in practice it may be that not all cit- izens/participants are strong enough to pursue their rights in this respect. All the same, I do not think that the risk of unequal treatment is necessarily greater in the Internet marketplace than in the national state. The disincentives preventing unequal treatment appear to be of equal force.

There are private institutions that lack legitimacy in the way they produce norms **2.40** and whose participants do not have an option to resort to a competitor.[45] For such institutions the problem of democracy is relevant. The marketplaces examined in this study are not monopolistic in nature, and thus market forces are often likely to manage the problem of non-democratic norm design.

Future regulation of Internet auctions and exchanges

National states have long been keen to regulate auctions and exchanges. This **2.41** chapter provides a prognosis concerning to what extent national regulation of

---

[44] A detailed examination at Columbia University of 5,760 capital cases in 1973–95 found error 'at epidemic levels': more than two out of every three capital cases reviewed by the courts were over- turned on appeal and the main victims are poor. Around 90 % of the people on death row could not afford their own lawyers. 'A Covenant with Death', *The Economist*, May 2001, 49, 50.

[45] Marsden (n 2 above) 31, gives ICANN as an example of such an institution.

auctions and exchanges will be made in the future by pointing to some issues that have been regulated historically.

2.42 In France auctions have been heavily regulated by legislation requiring the auctioneers to have licences. Until quite recently, only French citizens had the right to conduct auctions in France.[46] In the electronic environment it is difficult for a national state to impose licensing requirements since it is not always easy to determine under which jurisdiction a marketplace falls.

2.43 Licensing of auction firms started in England in 1779 mainly with the aim of helping the exchequer to collect revenues. Legislation also aimed to prevent frauds by stipulating that a catalogue approved by the sheriff must be produced to show ownership of the property being auctioned.[47] The English Auctioneers Act 1845 required the auctioneer to provide his name and place of residence in order to reduce malpractice. As described above, Internet marketplaces are likely to try to prevent fraudulent transactions without the help of the national state. The question of collecting revenues based on Internet transactions has already proved problematic in practice. It is not likely that the national state in the future will be able to implement efficient taxation of Internet marketplaces sucessfully without resorting to global multilateral treaties.

2.44 We also find many examples of national regulation of auctions in relation to default rules in contract law, eg concerning the right of withdrawal and the effect of the fall of the hammer. Such legislation also has fundamental problems in determining the applicable law and providing efficient national enforcement. It is not unlikely that such default provisions in national legislation will become less frequent in the future.

2.45 One striking and worldwide phenomenon is the national legislative regulation of stock exchanges and other exchanges for financial instruments. The relevant legislation is based on the presumption that market forces are not strong enough easily to provide competing stock exchanges where the dominating stock exchange is misbehaving. In fact, not long ago states often granted stock exchanges a monopoly. This was considered efficient since the establishment of a single exchange led to high liquidity, ie many transactions in one marketplace, which is efficient. Furthermore, the purpose of legislation on stock exchanges was to secure trust in the financial market, since lack of trust might negatively affect the whole society. Nowadays, these basic reasons for regulating stock exchanges and granting exchanges monopolies are of less importance. There is room for many

---

[46] B Learmount, *A History of the Auction* (Bernard & Learmount, 1985) 128. Also in Germany it is sometimes required that auctioneers are licensed; see T Schafft, 'Reverse Auctions im Internet' (2001) *Medienrecht 6* at 396

[47] The Spanish Ley 7/1996 de Ordenación del Comercial Minorista Art 58 also contains a provision that the objects should be properly described in order to prevent fraud; see J Ataz López, *Régimen Jurídico General del Comersio Minorista* (McGraw-Hill/Interamericana de España, 1999), 681.

stock exchanges in the world and enough liquidity in each of them due to the whole world's citizens—and not only a single nation's—being the potential participants. As described earlier, it is less difficult to establish a competing marketplace in the electronic environment. Due to the competitive structure a marketplace is forced to create trustworthiness by itself through not acting abusively. The only remaining reason for regulating stock exchanges by national legislation is to 'help' the exchange to create trustworthiness. Although the regulation is often launched as a consumer protection activity, it is in effect a question of ensuring the general trust in the marketplace which is essential to its survival. It is extremely important always to bear in mind the underlying reasons for introducing regulatory schemes. In these times of rapid change it is also necessary to re-examine old regulatory schemes to check whether they are in harmony with the new *raison d'être*.

The future ability of the national legislature to prescribe mandatory legislation **2.46** affecting the inner life of Internet marketplaces will probably be limited. This is due to the problems for the national state in monitoring activities conducted in cyberspace. An additional explanation is that a single national state can hardly claim to have any authority over an autonomous Internet marketplace. Examples of legislation not likely to prevail in the Internet environment are the French and German requirements of authorization for selling new goods in an auction and the French law that auction sales of second-hand goods may only be conducted by public officers.

History teaches us that auctions may create hostile feelings and frustration. As an **2.47** example, in the US auctions were viewed with much scepticism during the nineteenth century. Auctions were described as a monopoly and thus unjust by giving to a few what ought to be distributed among the mercantile community generally. The commission paid to the auctioneer was claimed to be unconstitutional. Many anti-auction meetings were held and an Anti-Auction Committee was established in 1826. The reason was, among others, fear of international competition and change in the distribution systems. The committee met resistance and did not succeed in prohibiting or limiting auctions.[48] This example illustrates that the public may demand that the legislator take action and introduce restrictions and prohibitions in times of change. The public's feelings may become frustrated in situations where the national legislature is not able to 'reach' the auction with its legislation. As mentioned above, the use of electronic auctions and exchanges will probably lead to quite substantial changes in how business is done in the future. In the period of transition it is likely that those who find it difficult to adapt to the changes will be very critical of the institutions of auctions and exchanges.

---

[48] Learmount (n 46 above) 84–90.

Summary and conclusion

2.48 We are likely to see Internet marketplaces develop a mixture of autonomy and dependency on national jurisdictions.[49] As Reidenberg writes: 'Rules and rule-making do exist. However, the identities of the rule makers and the instruments used to establish rules will not conform to classic patterns of regulation.'[50] What is rather new is the increased ability of an Internet marketplace to choose to what extent it allows a national jurisdiction to 'interfere' or 'help'.

2.49 The analysis shows that in some instances market forces are not enough to protect vital interests and in such situations national regulation is the only solution. This is the case in relation to some types of transactions exposed to a large risk of collusion, to enforcement of obligations against participants independent of the marketplace, to enhance the trustworthiness of marketplaces dealing with transactions that are sensitive to fraud, and to safeguard ownership by preventing thefts and dealings in stolen property.[51] Another important task for the national state is to facilitate and stimulate the establishment of competing marketplaces, thereby helping market forces instead of trying to control them.[52]

2.50 Outside this limited area, Internet marketplaces are well-suited to protect the public and internal interests by self-regulatory means.[53] Although traditionally

---

[49] L Lessig, *Code and other Laws of Cyberspace* (Basic Books, 1999) 206 (with a reference to W Wriston, *The Twilight of Sovereignty* (New York, 1992)).

[50] J R Reidenberg, 'Governing Network and Cyberspace Rule-Making' (1996) 45 *Emory Law Journal* 911 at 911, 912; id, 'Governing Networks and Rule-making in Cyberspace' in Kahin and Nelson (n 9 above) 96: 'For global networks, governance should be seen as a complex mix of state, business, technical, and citizen forces.' See also C Karnow, *Future Codes* (Artech House, Boston, 1997) 5–11, 223. As said by D Wall, 'The new electronic lawyer and legal practice in the information age' in Y Akdeniz, C Walker and D Wall (eds), *The Internet Law and Society* (Longman, 2000) 113: 'The law itself is plural, decentralised and now comes from multiple sources with more rules and standards being applied by more participants to more varied situations, which means that legal outcomes are contingent and changing. Galanter also concludes that more outcomes are being negotiated rather than being decreed. Because law is contingent (conditional), flexible and technically sophisticated, he argues that legal work has become increasingly costly, yet desired.' With a reference to M Galanter, 'Law Abounding: Legislation Around the North Atlantic' (1992) 55(1) *MLR* 900.

[51] A Sculley and W Woods (eds), *Evolving E-markets: building high value B2B exchanges with staying power* (ISI Publication Ltd, 2000) 153.

[52] Lee concludes in his extensive study on exchanges (n 30 above) 316: '. . . and finally, implementing the joint strategy of separating the regulation of market structure from the regulation of other areas of public concern, and employing competition policy to regulate market structure. This last strategy is recommended as being the best way of classifying and regulating exchange and trading systems.'

[53] 'Meanwhile, the door is open for private companies to move directly into the rule-making business. Although companies cannot write the rules of intellectual property rights, they can establish rule bound areas of the Internet virtual communities which rules are enforced. In those areas, companies can perform the functions that government are not yet capable of fulfilling. For a fee or by contract, they can protect the rights of on-line property. Just as merchants in medieval times developed the customs and practices that eventually became commercial law in Europe, so can contemporary companies and entrepreneurs create the rules of electronic commerce.' D Spar and J I Bussgang, 'Ruling the Net' (1996) 129 *Harvard Business Review* 125–33.

we have been used to national regulation, it will most probably become less important. Internet marketplaces are likely to solve the problems just as well, if not even better, by themselves. This is particularly the case for norms relating to contract law in the broader sense. Rules with their origin in the *lex mercatoria* rarely generate any political controversy. This factor, in combination with the problems for the national state in 'reaching out' in cyberspace, leads me to believe that such areas of law are best left to be self-regulated by Internet marketplaces. The development of mandatory regulation of contract law—for consumer transactions as well as business-to-business transactions—will in the future probably be limited to crucial issues. The opportunites provided by the Internet for effective development of fair rules for consumers through market forces are likely be quite satisfactory.

It is crucial to identify where national regulation is needed and for the national **2.51** state to concentrate its efforts in these areas. This study shows that it is in the interest of a marketplace itself to create rules and norms that protect confidence in the marketplace and, consequently, that the marketplace itself secures the general interest of a fair and balanced structure. Finally, the study shows the interdependency of Internet marketplaces and the national states.

3

EFFICIENT NORM DESIGN IN THE INTERNET MARKETPLACE

Introduction

The increased ability to steer and monitor transactions made in an Internet **3.01** marketplace is a major difference from what was feasible in traditional 'physical' marketplaces. This chapter will describe how the opportunities for or feasibility of surveillance are different in the Internet setting as compared with physical marketplaces. The chapter will also explain how this increased ability to steer and monitor makes it possible, and perhaps even necessary, to examine all contract law rules in a new light. This chapter is intended as a basis for the following detailed chapters and to provide an understanding of the large variety of options available to solve problems in relation to electronic auctions and exchanges. With a deeper knowledge of the relationship between the structure of norms and surveillance for conformity with those norms, there should also come a greater ability to provide potential solutions.

This chapter mainly deals with contract law. For all marketplaces, whether 'phys- **3.02** ical' or digital, it is of the utmost importance that promises are kept. Without a basic rule of binding promises there will be no trust associated with the marketplace and without trust no one will be willing to make any transactions.

Using the participants in the marketplace as monitors

Norms or rules related to private law have developed over thousands of years. **3.03** So far it has been efficient to use the individual parties in the marketplaces as monitors of each other's behaviour. When a rule stipulates that A is entitled to damages when B breaks his promise to A, there is an incentive for A to take action against B and to ask for compensation. In this scheme the individuals act as the 'police' and are the safeguards for the implementation of society's basic understanding that promises must be kept. It is not primarily a question between A and B—even though the rule at first might give this impression—but a question of the interest of society as a whole, as society benefits when promises are generally kept.[1]

Using the national state as the monitor

3.04 There are other possible ways of using the binding-promise principle beyond having the individual contracting parties as watchdogs. Rather late in the day we have seen the development of 'market law'. This is public law aimed at protecting the well-functioning market. When someone misbehaves he is harming the market as a whole. In public market law misbehaviour results in liability to pay a fee to the state as a representative of the market. Such a fee acts as a disincentive for market participants and not as economic compensation for harm suffered by any individual. Public market law deals with the individual's relationship with the market as a whole. In public market law the national state acts as a representative for the market and market law thus deals with the relationship between the individual and the state. Private law deals with the relationship between individuals. It is often difficult to understand how market law relates to and influences traditional private law.

3.05 Market law is sometimes inefficient. For some market rules huge bureaucracies have been created in order to investigate whether unlawful behaviour takes place, eg within the area of competition law. Despite such controlling bodies, many contracts still contravene the applicable regulations. Another strategy is merely to rely on reports from participants in the marketplace, eg consumer protection by market law. The main drawback of such regulations is that reports are rarely made as the individual consumer is given no benefits for making a claim. Because of the inefficiencies of systems involving controlling bodies and reports by market participants the national state is thrown back on using the participating individuals as safeguards of the binding-promise principle.

Using the marketplace operator as the monitor

3.06 Internet marketplaces can to a large extent steer the participants' behaviour by making it technically impossible for them to act against the stipulated rules. For example, when there is no 'I-withdraw' icon available, bids cannot be withdrawn because a withdrawal cannot be communicated.

---

[1] M Ridley, *The Origins of Virtue* (Penguin, 1997) *passim.*

What is new and fascinating with the Internet marketplace is that the operator of **3.07** the marketplace can monitor each transaction. Often the monitoring is done automatically and misbehaviour can be identified immediately. When a participant acts against the stipulated rules, he is immediately 'seen' by the monitor. The stipulated sanctions for such misbehaviour can be executed directly and automatically.

The means of surveillance varies depending on what system is used in the **3.08** Internet marketplace. When, for example, the marketplace provides services related to the settlement of deals, it is possible to check automatically whether promises are fulfilled. When the Internet marketplace does not provide settlement, the fulfilment of the promise cannot be monitored and controlled by the operator of the Internet marketplace.

How the new means of monitoring affect the design of norms

Because technical steering and monitoring is possible in the Internet marketplace **3.09** there is less need to use individual participants as safeguards of the general interest that promises are kept. An Internet marketplace does not always need the help of other actors to identify misbehaviour in order to ensure trust and confidence in the marketplace. This is an important difference from what we have become used to in the traditional marketplaces where it is in practice impossible for the national state to identify individuals breaching promises without the help of the other participants.

As a consequence of this fundamental difference, each rule related to the effects **3.10** or consequences of breach of contract must be analysed in a new light. To what extent has any individual participant suffered economic damage by the misbehaviour? Also to what extent is the general trustworthiness of the marketplace harmed by the misbehaviour? The sanctions and effects of each type of misbehaviour should then be properly balanced either to compensate the marketplace as such, or to compensate an individual participant, or both.

In the traditional physical marketplace it was often appropriate to overcompen- **3.11** sate an individual party in order to achieve a preventive effect or deterrent against breach of promises—this took the form of giving him an incentive to sue the party in breach. In a steerable and monitorable Internet marketplace such overcompensation is not always needed.

Stock exchanges are a special case since such marketplaces, at least in theory, can **3.12** control all the trade related to the object sold in the marketplace. This is feasible because the stocks are issued by a company that is listed on the stock exchange which is also where the settlements take place, and where the transactions in the stocks are reported and communicated to the exchange's operators. Other types of traditional marketplaces lack this ability to control, since the products do not originate from a single source, eg metals, commodities, manufactured goods and services. We also know that the 'market law' of stock exchanges—ie the participants' liability towards the stock exchange—is often much more elaborate than in other traditional marketplaces.

3.13 This study will focus further on some basic rules in auctions and exchanges online and analyse what types of norm structures are most efficient in establishing a well-functioning and trustworthy marketplace. The result may appear controversial to lawyers trained in traditional contract law. Naturally, it has to be taken into consideration what is deemed by the participants to be a fair and predictable set of norms and consequences of breach. Because of old traditions, it might not be advisable always to implement a norm structure that is the most efficient from an abstract and theoretical point of view. Each marketplace has to balance the theoretically optimal solution with the users' traditional expectations.

3.14 This study aims to show how norms may be constructed in such a way as to form a well-balanced and efficient marketplace from a theoretical point of view. I believe that this can be of practical help to the designers of norms in Internet marketplaces and enable them to see the full range of possibilities available. Our way of thinking is often unnecessarily limited and burdened by traditions. Unfortunately this is particularly true for lawyers. Although I am not a believer in sudden great changes, electronic means of communication force us to see the whole concept of doing business in a new context. It also makes necessary a more creative analysis of the law related to e-business.

3.15 It is essential to stress that this study concentrates on legal issues arising from rules agreed on between the parties in auctions and exchanges online, and is not intended to be a comparative study of national law, though examples from national law are given from time to time.[2] In physical marketplaces the problems related to market law are the same. The analysis of the Internet marketplace also makes it possible for us to gain a deeper understanding of the rules and norms of physical transactions. It is, however, not possible to transfer blindly the efficient rules of Internet marketplaces to physical marketplaces, since physical marketplaces lack the extensive opportunities for monitoring transactions and introducing technical restrictions against unwanted behaviour. For physical marketplaces it is still necessary to retain contract law under which each participant acts as the 'police' or 'monitor' for safeguarding the principle that promises must be kept.

---

[2] See above para 2.21 (scope).

4

DIFFERENT TYPES OF AUCTIONS AND THE
LEGAL DEFINITION OF AUCTION

Introduction

4.01 As has been described earlier, many Internet marketplaces conduct transactions by using methods of auctions or exchanges in order to make potential buyers and sellers meet and conclude a deal. This study mainly aims at describing how the parties by agreement can regulate the details of a contract concluded in an auction or exchange. When drafting such agreements, it is necessary to understand how the agreement relates to national legislation on auctions and exchanges. This and the following chapter explain the difficulties in ascertaining to what extent national law on auctions and exchanges is applicable to transactions made in Internet marketplaces.

4.02 In national law there are rules on auctions. Such rules are applicable to transactions defined as auctions. It is not always easy to determine whether a transaction can be defined as an 'auction' in the legal sense. In this chapter different transactions will be analysed for the purpose of gaining a deeper understanding of how to define the term.

4.03 Normally, when thinking about the term, the English auction comes to mind.[1] This is an auction initiated by a seller where higher and higher bids are made orally by bidders. When no further bids are heard the auctioneer lets the hammer fall and the highest bidder acquires the item offered. As we will see in this chapter, there are many other types of transactions that in different ways resemble the English auction and the question to be considered is which of these qualify as auctions in the legal sense.

4.04 This chapter will begin by describing different types of transactions closely related to the auction. After this, I will focus on some major characteristics. Finally, I will identify the characteristics crucial for defining the auction from a legal point of view.

4.05 The analysis will show that different types of regulations need different definitions. It is not possible, nor advisable, to give a single applicable legal definition of the term auction. My intention is merely to draw attention to how difficult it may be to provide a legal definition of the term 'auction'. I will point to some of the factors that may be relevant in making a legal definition, which may be a useful guide for a definition in an individual case under the appropriate jurisdiction.

---

[1] The English auction is clearly dominating the legal mind. This is shown in the extensive comparative examination in Schlesinger's book in 1968 where sale by auction was given a particular chapter. The English auction was the only type of auction mentioned (apart from requests for bids and tenders and a mentioning of the existence of the Dutch auction by the South-African reporter). R B Schlesinger (ed), *Formation of Contracts, A Study of the Common Core of Legal Systems* (New York, 1968) Vol 1, 391–429.

The different types of auction methods have been analysed in the literature— **4.06**
mainly within economics—in order to understand the effects on bidding strategies and what methods ensure the highest or lowest prices. This book will not
provide such analyses.[2]

A short description of some types of auctions

This chapter will describe some different types of auctions and how they are **4.07**
applied in Internet marketplaces.

The English auction

The principle of the ascending-bid selling system is simple: the auctioneer seeks **4.08**
an initial bid from one of the assembled buyers with the expectation that those
interested in the item or lot will bid against one another until all but the highest
bidder are eliminated. If there is no reserve price (by which the seller sets a minimum price) or when the last bid equals or exceeds the reserve price, the item or
lot is 'knocked down' to the one remaining bidder.[3]

The English auction is quite easily adapted for electronic systems.[4] In electronic **4.09**
versions of the English auction bids may be submitted electronically by clicking
a box on the website of the auctioneer or by the use of a joystick. Bids could also
be submitted orally via the Internet connection. The oral electronic auction
requires that the auction be carried out in real time, which has so far proven to be
somewhat problematic for technical reasons. In the international arena the time
zones may create a problem if the intention is to include the whole world in the
bidding procedure.

The Dutch auction[5]

The Dutch system, instead of starting at a relatively low price level and ascend- **4.10**
ing by steps until only one single bidder remains, follows a descending-price
pattern. The auctioneer determines the starting figure and quotes prices at
descending intervals until someone bids the item in. The prices thus nominated
are thus simply invitations to buyers to bid, and the first bidder is the one willing
to pay the most and becomes the successful bidder. In this system would-be

---

[2] For an introduction to this topic see R E Hall, *Digital Dealing: How e-markets are transforming the Economy*, 2001, at <http://www.stanford.edu/~rehall/LinoleumReport.pdf>; and M Bichler,
The Future of e-Markets, Multidimensional Market Mechanisms (CUP, 2001).

[3] R J R Cassady, *Auctions and Auctioneering* (University of California Press, 1967) 56 ff.

[4] *The eBay model*: the product is one of a kind and there are several interested buyers; the seller
wants to get one buyer to pay something close to the highest price; the seller arranges for the buyers
to bid against each other in an automated auction.   [5] Cassady (n 3 above) 60 ff.

buyers compete with one another just as they do in the English system, but the individual wanting the item most must register his bid before any other similarly motivated bidders have a chance to do so. Each bidder is competing against his own perception of the competitive structure facing him at the given moment. Usually, the first bid is the only bid, although it is conceivable, if the amount taken is optional, that the balance of a lot would be sold by continuing the price downward. In Dutch flower markets bids may be accepted for portions of a lot and are followed by bids for the remaining lot.

4.11   To illustrate how the Dutch auction works in practice, let us suppose that the lot of merchandise offered is twenty boxes of tomatoes, that the unit of sale is the kilogram, and that the estimated value of the merchandise is $1 per kilogram. It is customary for produce and related items, in contrast to works of art, to be offered on the basis of a certain price per kilogram, although the unit of sale may be a different measure. The auctioneer starts the quotations at 100 cents, say moving down rapidly at one-cent intervals—99, 98, 97, 96 . . . 88—at which point a buyer claims the merchandise by shouting 'mine'. After the auctioneer recognizes the bid, the buyer may exercise the option of taking all or only part of the lot. The balance is usually made available to other would-be buyers at the same price if there is sufficient interest. If not, the remaining lot is sold by the Dutch auction continuing downwards from 88 cents.

4.12   The Dutch auction is easily adapted to the electronic environment. It requires communication in real time. The equivalent to shouting 'mine' consists of clicking in a particular box on the auctioneer's website or by the use of a joystick. The portion of the lot is then quickly announced by pointing to an amount on the website or by using the keyboard to insert the relevant figures.

4.13   There have been discussions in economics as to which type of auction results in the highest prices. A recent study points to the Dutch auction.[6]

The combined English–Dutch auction

4.14   The combination of the English auction and the Dutch auction starts out by using the English ascending bid principle to establish a starting position for the descending process. The high bidder in the initial English phase will not be awarded the goods unless he remains the highest bidder in the second, or Dutch, phase of the auction. This combined procedure can be applied electronically by using the same means as described in the English and Dutch auctions.

---

[6] See D Lucking-Reiley, 'Using Field Experiments to Test Equivalence Between Auction Formats: Magic on the Internet' (1999) *The American Economic Review*, December, Vol 89, No 5, 1063 and P R Milgrom and R J Weber, 'A Theory of Auctions and Competitive Bidding' (1982) *Econometrica* 50, 1089–1122.

The Japanese auction or simultaneous-bidding auction

The distinct aspect of the Japanese (or simultaneous-bidding) auction is that **4.15** all bids are made by prospective buyers at the same time, or approximately the same time, using individual hand signs for each monetary unit. Theoretically, all the bids are made simultaneously, but in practice it takes several seconds for bidders to get their hands in the air and for the auctioneer to read their signals. The bidding starts as soon as the auctioneer gives the signal, and the highest bidder, as determined by the auctioneer, is awarded the lot. Although bids are registered simultaneously, some bidders might manage to raise their bids within the allotted time after seeing the signals of other bidders. As the rules do not preclude the raising of bids, the time element is crucial in determining whether the system is in fact a matter of simultaneous or ascending bidding.[7]

The Japanese simultaneous-bidding auction is well-suited to the electronic envir- **4.16** onment. In the electronic systems it is possible to create a true simultaneous-bidding system where it is not possible for the bidders to see the signals of others. Furthermore, in the electronic Japanese auction the auctioneer's determination of which bid is the highest becomes less arbitrary and more accurate. See below at 4.90 for discussion on the similarities between the electronic Japanese auction and sealed bidding.

The English clock auction (also called Japanese auction)

In an English clock-auction procedure the prices begin at some minimal value **4.17** and increase automatically, with bidders indicating at which point they choose to drop out of the auction.[8] This type of auction is also sometimes called the Japanese auction, but is different from the above-described Japanese simultaneous auction. The English clock procedure is well-suited to electronic application. It is necessary that the interested bidders for each transaction are identified in advance. The procedure can either be made in real time or by a slow procedure enabling the participating bidders to calculate at what time their maximum value is bound to be reached and thus enabling them to withdraw at a certain precise moment.

The time-interval auction (Scottish auction)

Some auctions carry a proviso that all bidding must be completed within a certain **4.18** time interval. The time-interval auction allows bidders a reasonable period in which to consider their bids, rather than forcing them to move precipitately. It

---

[7] Cassady (n 3 above) 63 ff.   [8] Bichler (n 2 above) 114.

could be used to advantage in sales of real property, where speed is not important and time for consideration may produce more and higher bids.[9]

4.19 In the electronic environment this type of auction has become popular since it does not require real-time participation. A bidder may submit his bid within a stipulated period of time and need not follow the auction closely. This type of auction is normally rather slow, but the stipulated period may of course be very short.

The auction by candle

4.20 A variant of the time-interval auction is an auction where the time interval is uncertain. In the 1490s it is recorded that time-limit auctions were held. A candle of one inch was lit and the last bid before the flame went out became the purchaser. Instead of candles sand glasses, or hourglasses, were sometimes used. The candle auction became popular in the 1600s in England and the method is still in use in French wine auctions.[10] The time limit for candle auctions is somewhat uncertain. This uncertainty may have interesting consequences for the bidding strategies.

4.21 The electronic equivalent to auction by candle can be established by using a method of randomly ending the time within which bids are to be submitted. Due to frequent disturbances in communication over the Internet, one has to consider the risk of being shut down. In a way this makes most auctions held over the Internet similar to the old auction by candle.

The sealed-bid auction

4.22 An auction where a bidder can see the bids of earlier bidders is called an open-book auction, as opposed to a closed-book auction with sealed bids. In a semi-open book, bidders know the total volume of bids and the current price, but cannot see the individual bids. Sealed-bid arrangements are equivalent to the time-interval auction with the only difference being that the submitted bids are not made known to anyone until the time limit has passed. This is a common procedure in public procurement.[11] Sometimes the sealed-bid auction is called a 'silent auction' because the bids are provided in writing instead of by open outcry. There are many techniques available for submitting sealed bids electronically over the Internet.

4.23 An example of the sealed-bid procedure is Priceline.com. Priceline.com lets buyers specify what they want to buy and name their price. Priceline.com then

---

[9] Cassady (n 3 above) 74 ff.

[10] B Learmount, *A History of the Auction* (Bernard & Learmount, 1985) 17.

[11] The oldest known sealed-bid procedures are French and German from the mid-nineteenth century (E R Huber, *Das Submissionswesen* (Tubingen, 1885) 3).

forwards the bids to participating sellers who can choose anonymously to accept the request or not.[12]

The sealed-bid auction could be conducted in several stages where the bids are **4.24** not disclosed during each stage but only afterwards. There is an amount of competitive bidding at the next stage, starting from the disclosed bids in the first stage. New stages are added until only two bids remain.

The Yankee method

In the Yankee method,[13] which is a variant of the English auction, several identical **4.25** items are offered simultaneously. Bidding increases incrementally and the items are sold to the highest bidders. If there are 100 items for sale and there are 200 bids, the highest 100 bidders get the items either at the individual price each bidder submitted or all bidders get to buy at the same price as the lowest of the top 100 bids.[14] Sometimes this type of auction is also called misleadingly a Dutch auction.

The multiple-unit auction

A variant of the Yankee method is a process that collects bids from purchasers. **4.26** Each bid specifies a price and a quantity. At the end of the auction, the bids are sorted by price, with the highest price first. Bidders are allocated units in this order until all of the units on sale are accounted for. The last successful bidder will probably get only a fraction of the number desired: a *partial fill*. Either bidders have to agree in advance to accept a partial fill, or the last winning bidder has the option of declining to purchase.[15] In the *single-price* version of the multiple-unit auction, all the successful bidders pay the lowest winning bid price, even if they bid a higher price.[16]

The audible-bid rotation system

In the audible-bid rotation system each bidder bids in turn. When all but one have **4.27** said, 'I pass' the bidding is over.[17] This is suitable for close, small groups of bidders. It is also suitable for the electronic environment. From a technical point of view it requires only a simple email system. It is thus easy to use for parties not wishing to involve third-party auctioneers and where the potential bidders are known beforehand.

---

[12] <www.priceline.com>.

[13] Yankee auction is a trade mark of OnSale (<www.onsale.com>).

[14] See E Turban, 'Auctions and Bidding on the Internet: An Assessment' (1997) *Electronic Markets*, Vol 7, No 4, 7. This method is used in <www.onsale.com> and analysed from a legal point of view by M Korybut, 'Online Auctions of Repossessed Collateral under Article 9' (1999) *Rutgers Law Journal*, Vol 31, No 1, 33–129.   [15] Hall (n 2 above) 44.

[16] ibid, 47.   [17] Cassady (n 3 above) 78.

The reverse auction

4.28 When the *buyer* initiates an auction—instead of the *seller*—it is sometimes called a reverse auction. The buyer expresses an interest in buying a particular item or service and sellers are invited to bid. The seller offering the lowest price is awarded the contract. The reversed auction may be used for all the described types of auctions, with the reverse effect that the Dutch auction becomes ascending in price and the English auction becomes descending in price.[18] The reversed auction is often used in procurement and is well-suited to multi-attributable transactions.[19]

4.29 On rare occasions a reverse auction may be converted into an English auction. This happens, for example, when the bidders/sellers find that they are willing to do something for free and even to pay, which was not expected by the buyer initiating the auction. The typical example is a reversed auction for undertaking to take care of waste where it turns out that the waste has a value. Another example is when undertaking to do a certain service may be of value to the service provider/seller for goodwill reasons.

The double auction

4.30 A double auction is when both buyers and sellers are initiators at the same time. The bids are then matched. The sellers' bids are arranged in descending order and matched with the buyers' bids. In cases where many bids are submitted, it is almost impossible to handle this procedure without the help of computers. In addition, since speed is often required, the electronic environment is particularly appropriate for double auctions.

The continuous double auction

4.31 'Continuous double auction' is another name for exchanges with matching systems where buyers and sellers submit their bids, which are then matched (see para 4.30 above on double auctions). Auctions in stocks can be held continuously or in batches. The latter alternative is best suited for items with low liquidity, where the order flow is too small for continuous active trading.

The exchange

4.32 An exchange in its simplest form is merely a place where buyers and sellers meet in order to negotiate individual deals. An exchange may also be a place where the

---

[18] The FreeMarkets model: the product is a component specified by the buyer, not used by others, and there are several potential suppliers; the buyer arranges for the suppliers to bid against each other in a buy-side or reverse auction.

[19] For a thorough analysis see Bichler (n 2 above) ch 6.

sellers bid against one another to supply an item and buyers bid against one another to obtain an item. The stock markets have been described by some as a 'double' auction because the exchange process is based on competition between sellers as well as between buyers. It is perhaps better characterized as a multiple negotiation scheme in which competitive sellers and buyers attempt to find a mutually satisfactory basis for effecting trades.[20]

In an exchange the actors are informed about other actors' willingness to sell and buy. The transactions are made with full knowledge of the other individuals' preferences. In the London Stock Exchange the orders are matched. In the New York Stock Exchange orders are not matched electronically but meet via open outcry in a standardized manner. In the Nasdaq model the product is standardized, with many buyers and sellers. They meet in an exchange, where both buyers and sellers can post bids and consider bids from others. **4.33**

For an exchange to function well it must have high liquidity, that is to say, a large number of bids to be matched. An auction procedure could be a preferable alternative when there is not enough liquidity.[21] **4.34**

The legal definition of auction

Legislation covering different aspects of auctions can be found in many countries. The following text analyses when there is a transaction covered by law relating to auction. **4.35**

The semantic method

On occasion legislation provides no particular guidance as to what kinds of transactions are covered by the term 'auction'; see for example CISG, Article 2(b) exempting auctions from its scope of application without describing what constitutes an auction. A semantic method of interpretation is often natural and helpful to use. We must then ask what the term 'auction' means and determine whether it has an inner meaning in itself. **4.36**

The historic origin
The oldest known auction is described by Herodotus referring to Babylonian auctions about the year 500 BC. It was an auction of girls for marriage. The prettiest girls were paid for and the men marrying the less pretty girls got paid to marry them. At the time of the early Roman Republic it was quite common with auctions held by the state where the property of severe criminals or war trophies **4.37**

---

[20] Cassady (n 3 above) 13.
[21] See ch 5 for the problems in relation to the definition of an exchange.

were sold.[22] Private auctions were also frequent in early Roman times. Auctions were held in China in 700 AD to sell the belongings of deceased Buddhist monks.[23]

4.38   The first known legislation related to auctions is the French Act of 1556 about 'huissiers priseurs' (bailiff-auctioneers), which gave exclusive rights to certain persons to sell property left by death or taken in execution.[24] Much later, the auction turned out to be an efficient way of helping in the financial re-organization which followed the French Revolution and the massive redistribution of the country's wealth.[25]

4.39   The word auction historically derives from the Latin 'auctio' (from 'augere') which means 'increase'. A definition focusing on a requirement of 'increasing' would exclude the Dutch auction and the reverse auction from the definition of an auction in the legal sense, since bids in such transactions are decreasing. Also the Japanese auction, where bids are submitted simultaneously, is not 'increasing'. Reverse auctions were already being held at the time of the Roman Republic. It is not clear whether the term auction was used in Roman times to cover both increasing auctions and reversed auctions. It is, however, clear that the term auction has long since been used to cover both increasing and decreasing procedures. This shows that the semantic origin of the term auction is not appropriate to be used as a source in defining the term from a legal point of view. The prerequisite of 'increasing' would not only exclude transactions frequently perceived as auctions but also cover transactions that normally would not qualify as auctions, for instance, individually negotiated deals where the price may be increased by offers and counteroffers provided by only two negotiating parties.

4.40   Many languages use a term for auction related to the Latin word, but completely different terms are also in use. In Italian auction is called *incanto*, which means 'increase'. In German it is *Versteigerung*, which also means 'increase'. In German law the term *uneigentliches Versteigerung*, which actually translates as 'unreal auction', is sometimes used for reversed auctions. The difference between *Versteigerung* (increasing auction) and *Meistbietenden oder Wenigstfordernden* (highest bid and lowest bid) is often emphasized in Germany. The French term is *vente aux enchères*. This term is related to increase.[26] *Enchérir* means 'become more expensive' and *enchérissement* means 'increased price'. The Spanish term is *subasta*, which means 'under the sword'. It refers to auctions of war trophies

---

[22] Kindervater, 'Ein Beitrag zur Lehre von der Versteigerung' in Jehring, *Jahrbucher für die Dogamtik des heutigen römischen und deutchen Privatrechts*, VII (1865) 2.

[23] R P McAfee and J McMillan, 'Auctions and Bidding' (1987) 25 *Journal of Economic Literature*, 701.   [24] Learmount (n 10 above) 15.

[25] ibid, 60.

[26] See T Schafft, 'Reverse Auctions im Internet' (2001) *Medienrecht 6* 393–401, with references to BHG GRUR 1986, 622—Umgekehrte Versteigerung, Ernst CR 2000, 304 (305) and Huppertz, MMR 2000, 65 (66).

held in Roman times. The Dutch term is *veling*. The word *veilen* means 'sell'. To have something *veil* means to have it for sale. We see that the origins of the national languages' term for auctions vary and that none of them is particularly helpful in finding a precise legal definition.

The dictionaries

We could search elsewhere than in semantic history for the inner meaning of the **4.41** term auction. In the *Halsbury* dictionary an auction is defined as: 'a manner of selling or letting property by bids, usually to the highest bidder by public competition'. This definition is both too narrow and too vague to be of any assistance in the task of legally defining the term auction. It would be most strange if the term auction did not include the reverse auction, where property is not sold or let, but bought. Also the reference in the dictionary to 'usually' is too vague to provide enough guidance as to what types of transactions are covered by the term.

The German dictionary, *Wahrig Deutsches Wörterbuch* defines *Versteigerung* as: **4.42** '*Verkauf durch Ausbieten zum bestmöglichen Preis*'. This definition also only refers to the English auction with increasing bids and does not cover the reverse auction or simultaneous bidding methods.

The French dictionary *Petit Larousse* defines *enchère* as: '*offre d'un prix* **4.43** *supérieur à celui qu'on autre propose pour l'achat d'une chose à vendre au plus offrant*'. Like the English and German definitions, the French one only refers to increasing auctions and does not mention the reverse auction or the Dutch auction.

It can be concluded that general dictionaries are unable to provide sufficient guid- **4.44** ance in making a legal definition of the term auction.

The sciences

The economists use other definitions. An auction has been defined in economics **4.45** as: 'A market institution with an explicit set of rules determining resource allocation and prices on the basis of competing bids from market participants.'[27] Another definition is: 'any well-defined set of rules for determining the terms of an exchange of something for money can reasonably be characterized as an auction'.[28] These are two of many definitions used in economic literature. It is quite controversial to include a necessary prerequisite of 'explicit set of rules' or 'well-defined set of rules' since it is unclear how the requirements relate to default rules in law and it is unclear how much that needs to be covered by the set of rules.

---

[27] McAfee and McMillan (n 23 above) 701.
[28] P R Wurman, W E Walsh and M P Wellman, 'The Michigan Internet AuctionBot: A configurable auction server for human software agents', Paper presented at the second international conference on autonomous agents (Agents '98) Minneapolis.

4.46   Another problem in using such definitions is that it is difficult to know which definition is authoritative since they may differ between different authors.[29] Furthermore, 'scientific' definitions often serve different purposes from legal ones, ie typically to qualify conclusions made in research.

4.47   Naturally, literature in the areas of economics and sociology is important for lawyers to understand fully the risks and opportunities involved in auctions, but it is not recommended that these definitions be blindly transferred to the legal environment.

Definitions in legislation

4.48   Sometimes the term auction is expressly defined in legislation. In section 57 of the English Sale of Goods Act 1979, in Part VII on sale of goods by auctions, the definition is tied to the 'fall of the hammer or in other customary manner'. Also the US UCC § 2–328(2) specifically regulates auctions with hammer. The English Mock Auctions Act 1961 refers to 'competitive bidding'. In Austria the particular rules on auctions apply to oral proceedings *inter praesentes*, including offer and acceptance among an unspecified or limited group of persons (OR, Articles 229–36).[30] According to Indian law, auction is a sale by competition of bids.[31] In the Spanish *Ley 7/1996 de Ordenación del Comercio Minorista*, Article 56 an auction is defined as: '. . . property offered publicly and irrevocably to the benefit of the person who by bid in a bidding procedure within allowed time limits provides the highest bid.' (my translation).

4.49   Such descriptions in law are helpful, but one is faced with another type of question: what is 'other customary manner' in the English Sale of Goods Act? Is the Austrian regulation applicable by analogy to non-oral proceedings, or should we make a conclusion to the contrary? Are 'oral proceedings' equivalent to electronic means of conveying sound? Do the Indian and English references to 'competition of bids' refer to all transactions where more than one party may express interest in an offer? Does the Spanish regulation exclude transactions where the party putting the object up for auction has a reserve price (ie where the offer is not irrevocable)?

Conclusion of the semantic method

4.50   It is necessary to use the semantic method when analysing which transactions are covered by law relating to auction, but the method is often unsatisfactory. We only get half the solution by carrying out a semantic analysis and the definitions

---

[29] This is illustrated by the following quotation: 'As automated buying software becomes applied to auctions, they will no longer be auctions. They will morph into dynamic pricing mechanism needed to support almost 'perfect competition' and market equilibrium' (P Finger, H Kumar, T Sharma, '21st Century Markets: From Places to Spaces' in *First Monday* (<http://firstmonday.org/issues/issue4_12/fingar/index.html> 8)).   [30] K H Neumayer in Schlesinger (n 1 above) 415.
[31] I C Saxena in Schlesinger (n 1 above) 419.

produce incompatible definitions.[32] We understand vaguely from the semantic approach that an auction involves competition between several interested parties and that sometimes there is a specific moment in time at which the bidding procedure is ended. However we are still uncertain over such issues as whether oral proceedings are required and whether the bids can be of a decreasing nature. The semantic method must be combined with an extended analysis of the purpose and function of the particular legislation related to the auction.

The functional method

When focusing on the underlying purpose of the law and understanding what   **4.51**
interests the law is aimed at protecting, it will become less uncertain to which types of transactions the law applies. Regulations on auctions may have different goals: some are introduced to secure the state's interest in collecting revenues; some to enhance trustworthiness and prevent abuse or fraud; some to prescribe mandatory protective rules as to how a contract in an auction is formed; some stipulate that certain transactions need to be made by auction; and some provide default rules regarding the conditions of sale.

The functional method supplements the semantic approach.[33] It shows that it is   **4.52**
difficult, probably even impossible, to find a definition of an auction in the legal sense that is applicable to all types of legislation. In the following paragraphs, I will examine some of the features frequently associated with the notion of auction so that in an individual case an analysis can be made concerning to what kinds of transactions the relevant auctions legislation is applicable.

The price-setting mechanism

The auction price-setting mechanism is different from the individual negotiation   **4.53**
price setting or the price setting determined by a standardized price list (a fixed or take-it-or-leave-it pricing). It is, consequently, important to understand the differences of price setting in auctions, individual negotiations and standardized price-list transactions.

In the *standardized price-list transaction* the price maker sets a price that   **4.54**
customers are expected either to accept or reject without haggling. Potential buyers, of course, may reject this price simply by absenting themselves. An adjustment must then be made which again puts the price on take-it-or-leave-it terms and, as before, is not subject to negotiation.[34]

---

[32] 'What is and is not an exchange is now unclear', R Lee, *What is an Exchange? The Automation, Management and Regulation of Financial Markets* (OUP, 1988) 1.

[33] See also ibid, 299, 300. A functional approach was used in the German case *Hamburg Urteil 315 O 144/99 Verkundet am 14 April 1999.*   [34] Cassady (n 3 above) 11.

4.55   In the *individual negotiation pricing scheme* either a price is specified which both buyer and seller know is subject to negotiation, or no price is specified and the initial quotation is made by one of the parties, presumably at a level that will provide 'manoeuvring room'. This initial action is followed by one or more counteroffers or compromises, often accompanied by discussion or stratagems designed to gain an advantage for one side over the other. Both buyer and seller make adjustments until an agreed price is reached.[35] There are examples of websites offering different solutions to individual negotiation schemes on the Internet.[36]

4.56   In *auctions* the competitors attempt to outbid one another, thus tending to force the price to, or at least towards, the level of the successful bidder's highest demand price or, in the case of a reverse auction, the seller's lowest supply price. Competitive bidding, in contrast to take-it-or-leave-it pricing, is a flexible pricing scheme by means of which prices are tailored to each transaction. Private negotiations and competitive bidding schemes also differ widely; the former brings the seller into contact only with buyers individually, whereas the latter pits buyers against buyers.[37]

4.57   In some respects auction pricing is a distinctive, possibly even a unique, method of price-setting. Its basic characteristic is the focusing of supply or demand and competition on each transaction. It is true that auctioning is a bidder-set method of pricing, but the bidder who determines the price is in direct competition with other bidders. Moreover, in each transaction the price is set by the successful bidder, who may be quite a different bidder in each individual transaction; and a different price may be set in each transaction even for identical property, depending on how much the highest bidder has to offer in order to acquire the desired item.[38]

4.58   In regard to the types of auction described above we readily see that the English, the Dutch, the Japanese, the time-interval, the auction by candle, the Yankee method, the audible-bid rotation system and the double auction (or exchange) all fit into the description of competitive bidding arrangements and cannot be described as take-it-or-leave-it pricing nor as a price-setting mechanism driven by individual negotiations (private-treaty pricing).

4.59   We see that in practice there are mixtures of haggling, standardized price-lists and auction procedures available in Internet marketplaces and that it then becomes particularly difficult to determine whether the method can be defined as an auction. An example is Chemconnect: a customer locates a sale offer of potential interest with an asking price of, for example, $210 and offers $206 per ton

---

[35] Cassady (n 3 above) 11 ff.
[36] See Hall (n 2 above) *passim*, with reference to many such sites, particularly <Priceline.com>.
[37] Cassady (n 3 above) 12.   [38] ibid, 13.

against, which the seller counters with $208 per ton. The buyer finds this accept-able and pushes the 'accept' button. The offer-bid-accept model is a flexible method. If there are several bidders, they will keep bidding the price up until all but one of them drops out. During the time when bids are flowing in and rising, the seller will not accept any of them. Once the flow stops, if the seller accepts the current bid of the one remaining buyer, the process is the same as a regular English auction, which finishes selling the item to the buyer with the highest value, at a price just above the drop-out price of the buyer with the second-high-est value. If the seller continues to dicker with the drop-out, the seller has a chance of getting a better price. The seller's decision about accepting an offer below the current asking price depends on just what the seller might be able to coax out of the current bidder, but also on what other bidders might come along in the next week or two.[39]

Several competing bidders

The general view is that an auction includes many competing bids. In some cases,   **4.60**
however, only one bid is submitted, and despite the lack of apparent competition an auction may be in existence. The crucial factor is whether competing bids are possible.[40] An important factor in determining whether a procedure constitutes an auction is whether *in practice* it was possible for several bidders to participate. There may be a situation where it was so difficult to participate from a techno-logical point of view that only one bidder could submit bids. In such situations the procedure is better described as 'individual negotiation'.

An auction may exist if no bids are submitted, as long as it was possible to submit   **4.61**
bids. In such instances there is rarely any conflict between the party taking the initiative to the auction (the invitor) and (potential) bidders, but for other types of relationships it may be important in determining whether there is an auction, for instance the relationship between the auctioneer and the invitor, or for tax reasons.

Equal treatment of all bidders

A prerequisite for a well-functioning auction (and exchange) is that all bidders are   **4.62**
treated equally and make bids for exactly the same object. When the bidders are subject to different rules—in the bidding process or in relation to the terms of the final transaction—they are not bidding on the same object. By being treated equally in the bidding process the bidders are able to use strategies based on predictions of

[39] Description from Hall (n 2 above) 63.

[40] From history we know of legislation requiring several bids in order for a sale in an auction to be valid. See the old Russian legislation for the Baltic States from 1864, referred to in T Almén, *Om auktion såsom medel att åvaägabringa aftal* (Uppsala, 1897) 5.

rational behaviour by other participants, ie rational in light of the stipulated rules for the bidding process. Also by identifying the object for the auction—including the terms of the membership terms and conditions of sale—there is a sound basis for a rational evaluation of the object. It is essential that the law relating to auctions protects the principle of equal treatment of all bidders. I would argue that when the law or a contract is ambiguous on this matter, if at all possible it is essential to be able to interpret the legal or contractual provisions in a way that is consistent with the principle of equal treatment among auction participants.

4.63   There might be situations where the bidders are not treated equally. This is, for example, the case when consumer protection law is applicable only to some bidders but not to all. Another example is when bids under private international law are subject to different jurisdictions each of which allocates different levels of responsibility to the bidders.[41]

4.64   There is a danger if the feature of equal treatment is included in the legal definition of an auction. If we say that equal treatment is a prerequisite in the definition of an auction some auctions may be wrongfully excluded from the definition. Equal treatment is important for the auction but it is not a relevant factor to be included as a prerequisite for the existence of an auction.

Commensurability of bids

4.65   To create true competition, the bids must be commensurable (or comparable) in order to achieve certainty among the bidders as to which is the winning bid. This is why bids are normally given in a monetary amount. One could imagine other types of equivalents than money, such as grain or a certain metal. As long as it is possible for several bidders to submit bids in the relevant equivalent, there is competition and thus the basic requirement for an auction is met.[42] New technology makes it possible to compare bids that have been impossible to compare before.[43]

Auctions handled by a third party (not the seller or buyer)

4.66   Auctions may be administered and initiated by either the party wishing to put up an object for auction or by a third party acting as an intermediary. The Internet

---

[41] See ch 6.

[42] Historically it has happened that the bids are provided to be in grain in order for the seller to avoid the risk of inflation.

[43] To overcome these limitations, <Perfect.com> has created a kind of automated request for purchase, in which buyers can spell out quickly what they want—from speed of delivery and length of warranty to quality and reputation. As many as 100 variables are possible. Potential sellers also fill out web forms that describe their wares and indicate ways in which they are willing to adjust their bids to satisfy requests. The technology ranks the best offers, based on the priorities established by the buyer. See also <Tradeextension.com>.

facilitates auctions both with and without an intermediary party. The role of the intermediary may vary from simply passively providing a meeting place, to offering an elaborate technical platform including the rules of the game, and to even taking an active role in the settlement of the deals. Normally it is not important for the definition of an auction whether or not an intermediary is involved.[44]

The fact that an intermediary is present is not enough to establish an auction.[45]   **4.67**
There are many cases where deals are made with the help of a third party but where the price-setting mechanism is based on individual negotiations or on a standardized price-list. Thus, in analysing whether the SplitTheDifference operations (described below) are to be defined as auctions, the fact that a third party is involved is irrelevant.[46]

Similarly, it is irrelevant whether the bidders submit the bids or the bidder only   **4.68**
accepts a suggested bid provided by a third party (the auctioneer).

When the party putting the object up for auction himself acts as auctioneer, there   **4.69**
is a risk of price manipulation, particularly if the other bidders do not know that the auctioneer is the same person as the initiator. Price manipulations may, however, occur whether the initiator acts as auctioneer or not.[47]

Determining the winning bid

The auctioneer fulfils an important personal role in the traditional auction by   **4.70**
determining who provided the winning bid and at what price. In the English auction the auctioneer decides when the bidding has come to an end; in the Dutch auction the auctioneer determines whom of the bidders shouted 'mine' first and at what level; in the Japanese auction the auctioneer determines who provided the highest bid and at what price. In the electronic auction no human intervention is needed to determine the winning bid. In the electronic Dutch auction and the electronic Japanese auction the first 'mine' bid and the highest bid are registered automatically and no auctioneer is needed to make the determination. In English time-interval auctions the winning bid is also determined automatically. If there is no time-limit, the electronic English auction needs either a person determining when the bidding process has come to an end or a technical system declaring that the bidding has come to an end when, for instance, no new bids have been submitted within a certain period of time.

The fact that a determination of the winning bid must be made is an important   **4.71**
feature of the auction. As a consequence of the auctioneer's role in determining the winning bid, he is also liable where he makes a wrong determination. The

---

[44] In Argentina it is mandatory that auctions be conducted by an authorized *martillero* (the holder of the hammer): Ley 20.266 from 1973.

[45] However, in Argentina the auction seems to require a *martillero* (n 44 above).

[46] See para 14.04.   [47] This problem will be discussed in ch 15.

auctioneer may face liability whether the transaction is made in a traditional 'physical' way or electronically. In the traditional auction the human auctioneer may make human errors. In the electronic auction the electronic software program may be defective and award the contract to the wrong bidder.[48] We see that the legal problems are of quite the same nature irrespective of whether the determination of the winning bid is made by a human or by a machine. Consequently, there is no need to include a prerequisite of a human auctioneer in the definition of an auction.[49]

The fall of a hammer—closing a deal

4.72   A symbolic feature of the English auction is the fall of the hammer. By analogy, obviously other tools may be used, eg a shoe or a bell. In the Dutch auction no tool is used other than the bidders' technical device for communicating the 'mine' bid. Instead the first bid in itself constitutes the contract. The importance of the use of a hammer or other tool is not the tool in itself, but that the fall of the hammer makes it absolutely clear at what point in time the deal is closed. It is essential for auctions that there is no uncertainty as to whether a contract is made and at what price it is made.[50] Such certainty can be established by different means. When the technical program produces a distinct event at which the contract is made or formed, who the winning bidder is and at what price, the underlying purpose that was fulfilled by the traditional fall of the hammer is solved technically. An important prerequisite for an auction is that there is a distinct moment in time at which the process is ended. By exactly which means this distinct moment is established is of no relevance for the definition of auction.

Auctions limited in time

4.73   Many auctions are time-efficient. They allow all interests in the object for sale to be concentrated and expressed within a short period of time. This is why auctions are frequently held in relation to the sale of flowers, vegetables, fish and other fresh products. Also traditional 'physical' auctions for antiques need to use a quick selling method, because of the many objects offered for sale. It should, however, be acknowledged that although a traditional auction may seem to be limited in time, it is often possible to submit bids beforehand to the auctioneer. This, in effect, makes the auction more extended in time.

---

[48] For an analysis of these issues see ch 9.

[49] See for example the German case *BGH-Zivilsenats ftd.de, Mi, 7.11.2001*, 17:21, where an Internet auction by mouse clicks led to a contract equivalent to an ordinary auction. See also the German case *Landgericht Wiesbaden Urteil vom 13 Januar 2000 13 0 132/99*: sale of art in an English auction limited in time where the winning bid was the highest bid by the end of the time limit was considered to constitute an auction in the legal sense.

[50] See further chs 7, 8 and 9 on withdrawal, cancellation and mistake.

In the electronic environment the need for a speedy procedure is not always as **4.74** important. Since it is practically feasible to assemble participants for long periods—which was not possible when the bidders had to be assembled at a particular geographical location—it is thus possible to extend the bidding period for a considerable period of time and thereby increase the liquidity by attracting more bidders. For certain types of objects there is still a need for a speedy procedure, such as with fresh products. A speedy procedure is probably also to be preferred when the transactions are so frequent that they can form a basis for a continuous auction (or an exchange). On the Internet we see auctions that are periodically held each day at a certain hour.[51] There are also examples of auctions being held randomly, often in procurement reverse auctions. Some Internet auctions are held in real time.

A difference between speedy and lengthy procedures is that in the latter time may **4.75** be used to plan strategy and to complete a thorough evaluation of the object for the auction. Those who participate in faster types of auctions have no such advantage. Thus, the bidding strategies differ in speedy and lengthy procedures.

We see that time limits may differ in auctions. The length of the procedure is of **4.76** little, if any, importance in defining an auction from a legal point of view.[52] From a bidder's point of view it is naturally important since it affects the bidding strategies. The time factor may also be of relevance in determining the legal responsibilities of the parties involved.

The invitor's lack of control

A common feature of the auction is that the party putting an object up for auction **4.77** (the invitor) is bound to conclude a deal with the bidder providing the best bid. Seen this way, the invitor gives away his right to reject the best bid by entering into the auction. There are possibilities for the invitor to avoid such lack of control. He may either put up a reserve price, which may be openly stated or hidden, or he may bid for the object himself and thereby prevent others from concluding the deal.[53] We see that the invitor's lack of control is sometimes, but not always, present in an auction. It is not a necessary prerequisite for an auction that the invitor has abstained from control, but it is quite a common feature of auctions.

---

[51] MetalSite opens auctions every day at 10.00 (US eastern time).

[52] In the German case *Landgericht Wiesbaden Urteil vom 13 Januar 2000 13 0 132/9*, a procedure whereby an art auction closed at a certain point in time—and not when there were no more bids—was considered to be an auction. The question of limitation in time was also discussed in the German case *Hamburg Urteil 315 O 144/99 Verkundet am 14 April 1999*.

[53] See paras 8.26–8.44 below about restrictions in this respect.

The bidder's lack of control

4.78   The bidder providing a bid in an auction cannot always be certain that his bid will lead to a contract with the invitor. In Dutch auctions the bidder who first submits a bid is in control and knows that he will be the winner. Also in sealed bid auctions the bidder cannot know whether higher bids are submitted. In the other types of auction, the bidder can never be sure whether other bidders will provide more favourable bids. Also in the Dutch auction the bidder lacks control in the sense that he may never know at what point in time other bidders intend to submit a bid. The bidder's dependency on the actions taken by other bidders is a typical feature of an auction.

'Live' auctions

4.79   Traditional auctions require simultaneous participation by all buyers and the seller. Product information has to be available to buyers, prices must be announced, buyer responses collected and new prices disseminated. Previously, such co-ordination required the presence of participants at the same physical location. The Internet allows these same functions to be conducted remotely.

4.80   Anyone who has attended a traditional 'physical' auction is familiar with the particular atmosphere of professionalism, concentration, excitement and control. In some auctions only members are allowed to participate and they are trained to 'read' the behaviour of other participants and adjust their bidding strategies accordingly. It would be rather difficult to transfer such an atmosphere to the electronic environment. However the electronic auction may also create an 'atmosphere' that ensures professionalism, concentration and control. The important factor is not whether the participants of the auction can touch, see, and smell each other—ie that the auction is held 'live'—but that the 'rules of the game' are stable and thus enable the bidders to use efficient bidding strategies. The bidding strategies can also be adjusted to take into account the electronic behaviour of other participants.

4.81   Some traditional 'physical' auctions consist of a combination of present and distant participants in the sense that a bidder not present in the auction submits written bids beforehand. Participants in the auction may challenge written bids. For practical reasons the non-present bidder of the written bid has no opportunity to outbid the oral bids higher than his. Despite this inability of the distant bidders to submit competing bids successively, it is usually considered that the mere fact that written bids and oral bids can be combined does not preclude a procedure from being legally defined as an auction.

4.82   Modern auctions may be combined in the sense that some bidders are physically present and some participate via telephone or a computer. In such procedures all participants may challenge all bids. The fact that the bids are submitted by different media—orally while present, orally by telephone and digitally via the computer—should be of no relevance in defining the procedure as an auction.

The electronic nature as opposed to the 'physical' nature of an auction

There might be some reluctance to apply the rules of physical auctions to elec- **4.83** tronic auctions. One could argue that the rules stipulated for auctions were aimed at and intended only for physical auctions. This is certainly the case, when electronic auctions were not in existence at the time the legislation on auctions was enacted. However, does this fact exclude the ability to apply the law also to electronic auctions? I would argue that it does not.[54]

The legal profession is facing huge problems in transferring traditional 'paper **4.84** concepts' to the electronic environment. The notions of 'document', 'writing', 'signature', 'place' and 'presence' all used to have self-evident meanings. A document was a piece of paper with letters in ink, writing was letters in ink, a signature was something written by the hand of the signer on a paper with a pen, a place was where one had solid ground under one's feet, and presence was a situation where the parties could touch each other if they wanted to. In the electronic environment it is no longer self-evident whether an electronic document is a document; digital letters constitute writing; a name at the end of an email is a signature; cyberspace is a place; and whether parties communicating electronically by oral words in real time are present.

The United Nations have come up with a method called 'functional equivalence' **4.85** for understanding terms in the new electronic setting: see The UNCITRAL Model Law on Electronic Commerce 1996.[55] This method deals with a classic problem in law, and that is interpreting legal texts in new situations. It requires the reader to analyse the formerly self-evident or obvious meaning of the term and seek the underlying purpose of the legal requirement. When this underlying purpose can also be satisfied by electronic means of communication, the legal requirement is met. The method is generally expressed in the Model Law, Article 5: 'Information shall not be denied legal effect, validity or enforceability solely on the grounds that it is in the form of a data message.' Most jurisdictions have in their legal theory methods corresponding to functional equivalence, such as purposive interpretation and teleological interpretation.

---

[54] The German case *BGH Urteil vom 7.11.2001–VIII ZR 13/01* states that declarations of intent made in an online Internet auction are legally binding. Also in the German case *Landgericht Wiesbaden Urteil vom 13 Januar 2000 13 O 132/99* an Internet auction is acknowledged. The relevance of the *örtliche* (earthly or physical) nature of an action was also discussed in the German case *Hamburg Urteil 315 O 144/99 Verkundet am 14 April 1999*.

[55] <www.uncitral.org> see the Model Law with Guide to Enactment.

4.86   The UNCITRAL Model Law on Electronic Commerce has several articles dealing with writing, signature, document, and original in particular (Articles 6, 7, 8, and 9). In relation to these terms, the Model Law has identified what the underlying purposes of the legal requirement might be. The general functional equivalence method introduced in Article 5 can be applied also to other terms that are not specifically dealt with in the Model Law, such as 'place', 'presence' and 'auction'.

4.87   Many rules related to auctions have a fairly clearly identifiable interest to protect. It may be, for instance, preventing the sale of stolen goods, facilitating taxation, ensuring a fair price, or enhancing trust in the auction. These are also interests worthy of protection in electronic auctions. It would be strange if the legal system required that new legislation be enacted, with the precise wordings of the already existing legislation, but aimed specifically at auctions held electronically. It would also be strange if it were necessary specifically to include electronic auctions in the legislative texts, where the law already applies generally to auctions, although not explicitly requiring the auction to be held in a certain place or requiring that the participants were able to touch each other. Those interpreting legal texts with references to 'auction' should instead be ready to apply the law to any transaction that corresponds to an auction, irrespective of by what medium the auction is held.

4.88   Some statutory texts make it almost impossible to apply the traditional rules on auctions to electronic transactions. In Argentina, for example, the legislation requires that bids be submitted orally.[56] In Argentinian literature it is said that the provisions also apply to bids submitted by hand signs.[57] It is rather difficult to decide whether the law applies to procedures under which oral bids are submitted by digitally transferred sound. It is also difficult to know whether bids submitted in real time by text messages are comparable to physical hand signals and thus within the legislation's scope of application.[58]

Open and closed auctions

4.89   In the English auction, the bidders are normally aware of the bids submitted by the other bidders. This is not so in the Japanese auction, in a sealed-bid transaction or in the Dutch auction (although knowledge of other bidders' price levels are revealed to bidders in a second round in the Dutch auction where the first bidder is entitled to take only a part of the offered lot). The knowledge of bids of

---

[56]   Ley 20.266 Art 9(g).

[57]   U T Cortez, *Manual del martillero, apuntes para una reflexion* (Argentina, 1998) 91.

[58]   It is generally stipulated that the Civil Code of Argentina also applies to electronic transactions (see <www.ecomder.com.ar> for information in English). The question of electronic auctions and their relation to the Argentinian legislation has been taken to court, but the case was settled. See <www.lineajuridica.com.ar/arch20010/s24g02.html>.

other participants affects the bidding strategies. From a legal point of view the chosen negotiation strategy is often of little interest so long as it does not include illegal procedures, such as price manipulation, threat, violence or fraud.[59]

Sealed bids (including the Japanese auction)

It is particularly difficult to determine whether sealed-bid schemes are to be clas-   **4.90** sified as auctions. In legal literature the debate on whether sealed-bid procedures are auctions dates a long way back and opinions on the matter differ.[60]

Some might characterize a sealed-bid transaction as an auction because it is   **4.91** intended to achieve the highest price by competitive means. The sealed tender, however, does not involve 'competitive' bidding in quite the sense used in conventional auctions since first, the bidders do not get information about the other bidders' levels of interest; and secondly, the bidder in a sealed-bid situation is unable to adjust his bid to meet the competition from other bids. The common aim of open and sealed-bid procedures is to create competition and the question is whether the competition created in sealed-bid procedures is the type of competition associated with auctions.

The argument that an auction must enable the bidders to outbid each other is often   **4.92** stressed by those who do not characterize sealed procedures as auctions. The bids are *unrelated* in sealed-bid procedures and the special feature of the auction is said to be the *dependency* of the different bids.[61] The same is true for Dutch and Japanese auctions where the bids in each transaction are unrelated. They are not procedures where the bids are given successively, but only on one single occasion.

The bidder submitting a sealed bid in competition with others is acting more   **4.93** blindly than in an open auction. In the English auction the bidders may determine how strong the interest is in the object up for auction by the presence of would-be buyers.[62] In Dutch and Japanese auctions the bidders also submit their bids

---

[59] See ch 15.

[60] Some German scholars, in the past, were of the opinion that it was irrelevant whether the procedure was written or oral (F Regelsberger, *Civilrechtlige Erörtertungen*, I. (Die Vorverhandlungen bei Verträge, 1868) 165; H Thöl, *Das Handelsrecht*, I:1, 2, 5 Aufl (1875) 76.) However other scholars disagreed (J A Seuffert, *De auction* (1854) 6; A Brinz, *Lehrbuch der Pandekten*, 2 Aufl (Hersogt von Ph. Lotmar, IV) 329; O Wendt, *Lehrebuch der Pandekten* (1888) § 201, 496; O Stobbe, *Handbuch ders deutchen Privatrechts*, III (1878–1885) 91; Schott, *Der Obligatoriche Vertrag unter Abwesenden* (1873) 148 note 256.) In Argentina, sealed-bid auctions are forbidden, unless they are expressly permitted in law (Ley 20.266 Art 19).

[61] In the US case *Boatmen's National Bank v Eidson*, 796 SW 2d 920 (Mo Ct App, 1990) the Missouri Court of Appeal of the Southern District found that a foreclosure sale of farm machinery was not an auction where it was made to the highest bidder under sealed bids solicited by newspaper advertisements and where 82 bids where submitted. The court found that the sale was not an auction, reasoning that 'competitive bidding refers to the basic concept of an auction, that is, knowledge of the highest bid with an opportunity to bid higher'. From Korybut (n 14 above) 64.

[62] Cassady (n 3 above) 13.

blindly, since they have no knowledge about the other bids. In continuous Dutch auctions, where only a small lot is taken by the first bidder, transparency is in a way created by the successive transactions. This can also be so in Japanese auctions. The non-transparency in sealed-bid transactions, Dutch and Japanese auctions influences the bidding strategies.

4.94   This is indeed a strong argument for not including such procedures in the definition of an auction. However I am against making such a distinction, because it would be difficult to determine which types of Japanese and Dutch auctions actually involve bids that are related to each other. An alternative would be to exclude all Dutch and Japanese auctions from the definition of an auction. I do not generally favour this alternative either, since the participants in Dutch and Japanese auctions normally perceive the procedure as competitive and name the method an auction.

4.95   It has been argued that a sealed-tender scheme is to be distinguished from an auction because of the considerable time interval between when the bids are registered and when the award is made.[63] As argued in paragraphs 4.73–4.76, I do not find the length of time of the procedure relevant in defining an auction.

The nature of the obligations

4.96   A particular feature related to auctions is that one of the obligations is fixed—the object put up for auction—and the other obligation is not fixed but depends on the bids. The possibility of negotiating the respective obligations of the parties is thus limited and can only be made one-sidedly. This is a feature that appears in many types of transactions to a greater or lesser degree and cannot serve as a helpful characteristic in distinguishing auctions from other types of transactions.

Final remarks as to the legal definition of auction

4.97   As said already at the outset of this chapter, the question of how to define an auction in the legal sense cannot generally be solved.[64] The analysis made here merely points out some of the problems. The lowest common denominator is the price-setting mechanism. The price in an auction is established only for the isolated deal—lasting and relevant only for the single transaction.[65] Furthermore, the price in an auction is determined in competition—at least on one side there is

---

[63] Cassady (n 3 above) 12.

[64] Of the same opinion is T Schafft, 'Reverse Auctions im Internet' (2001) *Medienrecht 6* 393–401 at 395.

[65] This single transaction may, however, involve many future transactions between the initiator and the winning bidder if the object put up for auction is for instance successive delivery of goods or services.

opportunity for more than one person to express interest in the object offered. Thus, the price in an auction may never be fixed beforehand. At the outset, the definition of an auction needs to meet these two basic requirements. Beyond this, several aspects could be taken into account narrowing down the concept of an auction.

The analysis made here shows that the legal definition of auction may differ **4.98** depending on the legislation and what functions the relevant legislation fulfils. It is not possible, nor advisable, to give a single legal definition of the term auction. It is impossible to provide a definition of an auction and to describe an appropriate method of making the definition that would be accurate for all jurisdictions and for every type of legislation. The aim of this study—which is international in nature and not based on national rules—is not to produce such an answer. My aim has merely been to direct attention to how difficult it may be to define an auction in the legal sense. The above analysis of some of the factors that may be relevant can be used as a guide in coming up with a definition in a particular case under the appropriate legislation.

In providing a legal definition of an auction it is important to consider the under- **4.99** lying purpose of the particular legislation that refers to the notion of auction. This is sometimes easy. For example the English legislation which stipulates that objects for sale in an auction must be presented in a catalogue, aims to prevent the transfer of stolen goods and fraud. In determining what procedures are subject to this legislation it is of less relevance whether the other bidders knew of the submitted bids and whether there was an opportunity to outbid other bidders. Thus, the legislation ought to apply to the English, Dutch, Japanese and sealed-bid auctions.

It can generally be said that the opportunity to collude or use other means of price **4.100** manipulation are particularly important in determining the application of legislation aimed at enhancing trustworthiness and preventing abuse or fraud. For default rules particularly applicable to auctions it is possible to have a less restrictive interpretation of the notion of auction. Lastly, for legislation stipulating that certain transactions need to be made by auction the aspect of adequate competition is of particular importance.

According to German law, some types of auctions may only be held when the **4.101** authorities have granted permission.[66] It is not always apparent what interests legislation requiring a licence is aimed at protecting and, consequently, it is difficult to say what elements are relevant in defining the legislation's scope of application. It may be that the legislation is aimed at ensuring that the auctioneer does not manipulate and fool bidders, but treats them equally and provides adequate

---

[66] See the German cases *Landgericht Hamburg Urteil 315 O 144/99 Verkundet am 14 April 1999* and *Landgericht Wiesbaden Urteil vom 13 Januar 2000 13 O 132/99.*

information about the objects put up for auction. If so, the relevant features in the definition of an auction probably would be that there is competition and a speedy procedure that does not provide the bidders with sufficient time for thoughtful consideration.

4.102   According to the US UCC, Article 9, repossessed collateral must be sold by auction. The underlying purpose of this requirement is that the secured party may purchase his collateral only if it is sold on a recognized market or the type that is the subject of widely distributed standard price quotations. Thus, in order to know how to apply Article 9 to electronic auctions one must understand the underlying purpose and take into account to what extent the auction was accessible to the secured party. This has been analysed in depth by Michael Korybut.[67]

4.103   In the following discussion I will cover many transactions and refer to them as auctions. I am doing so in the interests of demonstrating efficient norm design for many different types of transactions, irrespective of whether they all qualify as auctions in every legal sense.

---

[67]   Korybut (n 14 above).

5

DEFINITION OF THE TERM 'EXCHANGE' IN LAW

Introduction

Like the term 'auction', the term 'exchange' is difficult to define. It is uncertain **5.01** to what extent the transactions must be centralized to the marketplace and how the bids are to be qualified as two-sided. Furthermore, it is unclear if an exchange requires that the transactions are carried out continuously and whether there is inherent in the term a special form of price discovery. In this chapter I will analyse the semantic and functional methods in relation to the term in order to come up with some sort of definition and thereby gain knowledge about what applicable national laws mean when they use the term.

The semantic approach

The dictionary approach is just as problematic in relation to the term 'exchange' **5.02** as was described in relation to the term 'auction'.[1] Lee found in a survey that all the general dictionaries examined had more than one definition, so that there is no single exclusive meaning of the word. Furthermore, the terms used in the definitions were vague (such as an exchange being 'centralized' on a market or marketplace). In the specialist dictionaries Lee found the same incoherent picture

---

[1] In *Board of Trade of the City of Chicago v SEC* 883 F 2d 1270 (7th Cir, 1991) the Court of Appeals confirmed that the wording of the definition of an exchange is not 'crystal clear'.

and vague terms, for instance there were many references to 'physical' location while there was also a note that the exchange might operate electronically. The specialist dictionaries often referred to such matters as authorization, ensuring fairness, fast price disclosure, and that an exchange provide liquidity—all such definitions run the risk of becoming circular.[2] The survey clearly shows how little help the dictionaries are in finding a legal definition of an exchange.

5.03   The term is sometimes defined in legislation. The US Securities Exchange Act 1934 defines an exchange as:

> any organization, association, or group of persons, whether incorporated or unincorporated, which constitutes, maintains, or provides a market place or facilitates for binding together purchasers and sellers of securities or for otherwise performing with respect to securities the functions commonly performed by a stock exchange as that term is generally understood, and includes the market place and the market facilities maintained by such exchange.

An exchange's facilities are defined as:

> (its) premises, tangible or intangible property whether on the premises or not, any right to the use of such premises or property or any service thereof for the purpose of effecting or reporting a transaction on an exchange (including, among other things, any system of communication to or from the exchange, by ticker or otherwise, maintained by or with the consent of the exchange), and any right of the exchange to use the property or service.

This definition contains many complicated elements. For instance, a facility for binding together purchasers and sellers could include many types of transactions, as does the broad definition of an exchange's facilities. The vague qualification 'stock exchange as that term is generally understood' clearly points to the problems. Another difficulty with the definition is that it seems to cover all exchanges of securities over the Internet, no matter to what jurisdiction it claims to belong.[3]

5.04   There have been discussions in the US as to whether the present definition of exchange in legislation should be modernized and improved. The suggestions for new or revised definitions all pose new problems. It seems impossible accurately to capture the whole notion of an exchange in a legislative definition.[4]

The functional approach[5]

5.05   On a functional analysis, the exchange is a provider of 'trading systems' and a forum for executing trade. 'In relation to exchanges opinions differ as to what the

---

[2] For a full understanding of the complications, see R Lee, *What is an Exchange? The Automation, Management and Regulation of Financial Markets* (OUP, 1988 appendix 2) 322, 323.

[3] The SEC did not think that Instinet fitted within the statutory scheme contemplated for exchanges, although it clearly had the aim of providing a platform for the buying and selling of stocks: SEC Release No. 34–26708 (18 April 1989).   [4] Lee (n 2 above) ch 12.

[5] The detailed problems in relation to the definition of an exchange in US financial markets are analysed in ibid, 280–300.

relevant attributes and functions of exchanges should be, and *unless the reason for identifying which institutions should be specified exchanges are made explicit, the selections of which attributes or functions should be deemed conclusive is either arbitrary or a matter of preferences.*[6] The SEC has tried to use a functional approach to determine whether a particular trading system should be registered as an exchange by analysing whether registration would further the purposes of the legislation. There are, however, substantial difficulties in doing so, since the legislation pursues many goals, some of which clash or conflict.[7]

Centralization

An exchange is frequently said to carry the characteristic feature of centraliza-   **5.06** tion. That is to say, that all or most of the trade is allocated via the exchange. The exchange's function is to channel most transactions related to a certain object via the exchange. This is an important feature in distinguishing an exchange from a mere broker. In the US the distinction between a broker and an exchange has caused many problems, since the requirements of accreditation differ between the two. Lee argues, and I agree, that it is not possible to retain this distinction in the future due to the development of automated trading systems.[8] The questions usually asked in order to ascertain whether centralization is present do not make sense in a world where marketplaces (exchanges) may exist parallel to and compete with each other. Furthermore, the requirement of centralization does not function well in areas outside the financial markets of trade where the object may derive from many different sources, eg commodities, services and manufactured goods. There are a number of relevant questions in relation to centralization. Do all orders compete against each other on a particular trading system? Is price priority obtained on the system? Are participants required to deal on the system if they deal in the assets traded on the system? Does a trading system need to have a physical location or floor to allow transactions?

Two-sided quotes

An exchange is often characterized as *double* in the sense that both buyers and   **5.07** sellers submit bids in parallel. This is different from the typical auction where a single invitor initiates the transaction by placing an invitation and the bidders then actively provide bids in competition (in the English auction the invitor is the seller and in the reverse auction it is the buyer). This may at first appear to be a clear difference as compared with the auction. There are, however, difficulties in making the distinction. First, there is a time factor, which becomes more practically important in the new electronic trading systems. When the bidding process

---

[6] ibid, 2.   [7] ibid, 280.   [8] ibid, 279.

is not restricted in time and the invitor is allowed to withdraw his bid/offer, it is difficult actually to determine whether the initiative derives from only one side. If the marketplace typically only allows one side (the buyer or the seller) to initiate transactions, it is more likely that it is an auction—and not an exchange.

5.08 Another problem is when an intermediary matches bids without actually putting them *on the floor* but instead silently matches them *back stage*. Formerly, when an exchange transaction necessarily was limited in time, the distinction was easy to make. Now the technology makes it possible to expand the transactional process. The clear distinction between bids submitted in a marketplace to be matched against other bids and bids submitted to an intermediary who undertakes to match the bids *at his office* is blurred. The *on-the-floor* prerequisite of an exchange is thus more difficult to apply in the electronic environment.

Regular and continuous basis

5.09 Most persons would instinctively perceive an exchange as a lively place with many and quick transactions. The traditional exchange took place in a particular location and within a limited time span. This was necessary since the bidders were asked to appear physically in a certain location. In modern trading systems it is not necessary—and to a larger extent less preferable—to limit the transactions in time. It has been possible to expand the transactional time span due to the fact that bidders no longer need to appear in a physical location. The new technology makes it possible to create marketplaces where the pace is much slower than in traditional exchanges. This is so for exchanges in relation to objects where the transactional speed used to be higher. The new technology also makes it possible to use the exchange for objects where the transactions are not dense enough for them to function in a traditional physical exchange. Thus, the regularity and continuity can be vastly expanded in time. Consequently, the exchange is difficult to distinguish from an ordinary marketplace, such as a fair or a traditional shop.

The bidders' expectation that they may regularly execute their orders

5.10 High liquidity leads to the participants' expectation that they can readily, if not immediately, execute their orders because of the presence of regular or continuous two-sided quotations. The notion of liquidity—which is essential for a well-functioning auction or exchange—involves two elements:[9]

---

[9] The concept of liquidity is very elusive and will not be analysed in depth here. See M O'Hara, *Market Microstructure Theory* (Basil Blackwell, 1995) 216–23 and R A Schwartz, *Equity Markets: Structure, Trading and Performance* (Harper, 1988) ch 11.

(a) *immediacy*, which refers to the time needed to execute an incoming order;
(b) *depth (resilience)*, which refers to the possibility of executing a market order without affecting the price.[10]

Where there is lack of immediacy and lack of depth, it is not an exchange. Such procedures are more likely to constitute auctions. This is, however, a matter of degree. How immediate need a procedure be in order to qualify as an exchange? Also how much must an order influence the price for the marketplace not to be deep (resilient) enough to qualify as an exchange? Naturally, it is not possible to determine the exact borderline between auctions and exchanges in this respect. In a complex determination facts such as the levels of immediacy and depth may be important elements.

Trade execution

A system that does not provide trade execution is not an exchange. However, **5.11** execution facilities, automated or not, are not a sufficient requirement for a trading system to qualify as an exchange.[11]

Transparent prices

Passive-pricing trade execution mechanisms are often not classified as **5.12** exchanges. Open disclosure of the price at which deals are concluded is a feature that basically distinguishes exchanges from other trading systems. The fact that a trading system does engage in price discovery, however, is not conclusive that the system should be classified as an exchange.[12]

Final remarks as to the legal definition of 'exchange'

The question of how to define an exchange in the legal sense cannot be solved **5.13** generally. The analysis made here merely points to some of the problems.[13] Different types of regulations need different definitions. It is not possible, nor advisable, to give a single legal definition of the term 'exchange'. It is impossible to provide a definition of an exchange and to describe an appropriate method of making the definition that would be accurate for all jurisdictions and every type of legislation. The aim of this study is not to produce such a definition. My

---

[10] The more depth, the less volatility. This is why the variations in the prices become smaller in efficient Internet marketplaces as compared to the high fluctuations in traditional auctions and exchanges with less liquidity (R Laulajainen, *Financial Geography—a Banker's view* (Göteborg, 1998) 137).   [11] Lee, (n 2 above) 284.
[12] ibid.
[13] The detailed problems in relation to the definition of an exchange in US financial markets are analysed in ibid, 280–300.

aim is merely to direct attention to how difficult it may be to define an exchange in the legal sense. The above analysis of some of the features that may be relevant in making a legal definition can be used as a guide in making a definition in the particular case under the actual relevant legislation.

5.14 When the national legislation applicable to an exchange is aimed at preserving general trust in the marketplace—which is for instance particularly important with respect to stock markets and markets in other financial instruments—the important feature in defining an exchange is centralization, ie that the actors' ability to conduct their transactions in another marketplace is limited and thus the dominating marketplace/exchange needs to be governed by protective legislation. Another important factor for such legislation appears to be the immediacy and depth (resilience). When the national legislation merely provides default rules in private law particularly aimed at transactions by exchange, it is of greater interest to analyse to what extent the bids in the marketplace are provided by both sellers and buyers in parallel (two-sided quotes) when determining the legislation's scope of application.

THE APPLICABLE LAW

Introduction

Historically, the question of applicable law has not caused many problems in rela- **6.01**
tion to marketplaces, since the auction and/or exchange have been geographically
limited with all participating parties being physically present at the place where
the deals are made. Because of the internationalization of auctions and exchanges
the question of which law is applicable becomes of greater practical importance.
When an electronic auction or exchange is held over the Internet the question
arises as to whether all states' regulation applies, or only one, or only some. In
this chapter I will describe some of the principles of private international law and
point to how difficult they all are to apply to Internet auctions and exchanges.[1] I
will also examine to what extent the parties may designate the applicable law by
contract.

The equal treatment concern

A particular feature to bear in mind in relation to auctions and exchanges is the **6.02**
need to treat all participants equally.[2] It is absolutely essential that all participants
submit their bids under the same conditions. In contrast to individual negotiations, the parties' economic strength, connections, gender, nationality and ethnic

---

[1] Note that the question of which law is applicable may be determined differently in different
states. This particular feature of private international law will not be analysed to any depth in this
study. [2] See paras 4.62–4.64 on equal treatment.

origin are effectively of no relevance. The same opportunity for closing a deal applies to all participants in the marketplace and they are all acting under the same rules. By being treated equally in the bidding process the bidders are able to use strategies based on a prediction of rational behaviour by the other participants, ie rational in relation to the stipulated rules for the bidding process. When the bidders are subject to different rules in the bidding process or in relation to the terms of the final transaction, they are not bidding on the same object. Also by identifying the object for the auction (including the terms of the contract), there is a sound basis for a rational evaluation of the object. Furthermore, the bids may not be compared and ranked if they are not wholly equivalent. When different laws apply to different bids it becomes practically impossible to compare them (they are incommensurable).[3] Thus, it is against the whole idea of an auction or an exchange to have different laws applicable to different participants.

6.03 The importance of equal treatment is relevant not only in deciding the applicable law, but also in determining the relevant forum. It is essential that all bidders are acting with equality when it comes to the forum for solving conflicts. Hence, in auctions and exchanges the same rules in relation to the forum should apply to all bidders.[4]

6.04 The need for equal treatment of all bidders in a marketplace is of fundamental importance and is not only relevant in relation to the question of the applicable law or the question of the forum. I will often refer to this chapter in the following discussion.

Lex loci contractu

6.05 According to most jurisdictions, the applicable law to auctions and exchanges has traditionally been determined according to the principle of *lex loci contractu*. In other words, the applicable law is the law of the state where the auction is physically held. This has been the case also when bidders of foreign nationality participate in the auction or exchange. Furthermore the principle has been upheld when bids have been submitted from abroad by for instance using an agent or when communicating by telephone.

6.06 In electronic Internet auctions it is sometimes difficult to determine where an auction or exchange is held (there is no physical locus). One could say that the locus is the state from which the marketplace is administered. However, the place of administration is not always easy to identify in the Internet environment. It becomes more and more common for Internet marketplaces to be administered from many states and with different functions possibly being fulfilled in different

---

[3] See above para 4.65 on commensurability.   [4] See ch 18 below on dispute resolution.

places. Not even the seat of the company operating the marketplace is always a crucial factor, since the ownership of the marketplace may be split in many parts that are owned by companies in different states.

A solution to the problem of where an auction or exchange takes place could be **6.07** to make a rather mechanical examination of where the electronic messages are when they become legally relevant. If they are considered effective when they have reached the marketplace, the marketplace is not dispersed in cyberspace but actually assembled in the place where the marketplace's server is located. It is often stated in legislation relevant to electronic commerce at what point in time an electronic message is considered to have been dispatched or to have reached the addressee.[5] However I have not found any legislation generally stipulating at what place an electronic message has legal effect. Furthermore messages in electronic auctions and exchanges will be sent by and to the invitor, bidders and operators, thus it is not one place where the messages will become legally effective but many, depending on who of the involved parties is the sender or addressee. Consequently, it is extremely difficult—if not impossible—to establish the *loci contractu* for Internet auctions and exchanges.

The centre of gravity test

Against the principle of *lex loci contractu* stands another international private law **6.08** principle for contracts: the centre of gravity test. Under this principle, the presumption is that the applicable law is the law of the state of the party performing the obligation, which is characteristic of the contract.[6] It should be emphasized that there may be three different situations:

(a) the relationship between the participants and the marketplace: the gravity test typically leads to the law of the marketplace;
(b) the relationship between the buyer and seller in auctions initiated by the buyer, typically the law of the invitor-seller;
(c) the relation between the buyer and seller in reversed auctions, typically the law of the bidder-seller.

The centre of gravity principle is not always suitable for auctions and exchanges. The consequence of this principle in reversed auctions is that the bidders are acting under different jurisdictions and that different rules apply for the bidders. This is against the fundamental idea of the auction and exchange in which bidders should act under true equality. Also in non-reverse auctions it may become difficult to use the centre of gravity principle. When many invitors-sellers act in the marketplace

---

[5] UNCITRAL Model Law on Electronic Commerce, Art 15 and UETA, s 15; see also para 8.79 below.
[6] Convention on the law applicable to contractual obligations (80/934/EEC), Article 4(2).

the bidder-buyers must constantly keep track of the sellers' nationality and adopt their valuation of the objects accordingly. In line with these concerns we see many exemptions in private international law under which the gravity principle is not applicable to auctions.

6.09 The 1980 Convention for the International Sale of Goods (CISG), which is based on the centre of gravity principle and applies the law of the seller, makes an exemption and is not applicable to auctions (see Article 2(b)).[7] One reason why CISG does not apply to auctions is that it would cause huge problems as to which is the applicable law. According to CISG, Article 1, the convention is applicable when both parties have their place of business in different states. For auctions and exchanges this would lead to uncertainty as to what law is applicable (CISG or the national law on formation of contracts and sales) until one knows whether the winning bidder has its place of business in the same state as the party taking the initiative in the auction. This, in turn, would cause different rules to apply for different participants, something that earlier has been described as against the fundamental premises for an auction.

The country of destination principle

6.10 Within the area of consumer law a comparatively new principle of private inter-national law is emerging. The purpose is to protect the consumer and allow him to rely on the consumer protection granted to him by his domestic law. The principle may be partly found in the Rome Convention, Article 5 according to which the gravity principle is kept—typically, the law of the seller—with the exemption that a consumer may under certain conditions rely on the protective consumer law in his home country.[8] It should be noted that the law of the country of destination is only applicable in part under the Rome Convention, Article 5.

6.11 The principle of the country of destination poses fundamental problems in rela-tion to auctions and exchanges, due to the need already described to treat all participants equally. In an auction some bidders may act as consumers while others may not. Consumer protection law is in many states different from the general law applicable to business bidders, for instance by providing generous opportunities for consumers to cancel contracts, limiting the caveat emptor rule, or allowing claims against not only the counter-party but also against the auction-eer. In addition to the problem that participants may consist of both consumers and businessmen, there is also the problem that the participating consumers may come from different states. Consumer law is not internationally harmonized. The

---

[7] See <www.uncitral.org>.

[8] Convention on the Law Applicable to Contractual Obligations, opened for signature in Rome on 19 June 1980 (80/934/EC).

EU Directives aiming at harmonizing consumer law are all of a *de minimis* nature, ie they can be implemented differently in different member states as long as they at least grant the consumers the rights described in the Directives.

Some consumer protection regulations exempt auctions from their scope of appli-   **6.12** cation. One such example is Directive 97/7/EC on the protection of consumers in respect of distance contracts.[9] Transactions made in financial exchanges are sometimes exempted from consumer regulations either explicitly or by the fact that the definition of a consumer does not include financial activities as being made in a consumer capacity.

As described above, it is essential that the bidders be treated equally. In deter-   **6.13** mining the applicable law for a transaction made in an auction or exchange where a consumer is acting, it is necessary that the same law applies to all bidders. One cannot isolate the individual relationship between the invitor and the bidder, but must also recognize the nationality and status of all participating bidders. If a particular consumer protection law is deemed applicable in a certain relationship, the very same law must apply to all bidders irrespective of whether they act as consumers or not and irrespective of their home country.

Private international law and party autonomy

In short, it is difficult to know which law applies to Internet auctions and   **6.14** exchanges. Nowadays, consequently, it is more important than ever to establish the rules of the marketplace specifically so as to reduce the need to resort to national law which involves the difficult issue of which law is applicable. It is not the aim of this study to report and analyse the national default rules of auctions and exchanges in every jurisdiction. The aim is instead to explain the appropriate rules to be contained in the membership terms and conditions of sale depending on which interests the marketplace wishes to emphasize. The more elaborate and extensive the membership terms and the conditions of sale, the less need there is to resort to national law and the fewer problems there will be in the area of private international law.

In private international law the parties are to a large extent able to agree on the   **6.15** applicable law.[10] There are, however, limitations as to party autonomy in private international law. These limitations are mainly that some states require a connection to the law chosen as the applicable law, a restricted ability to choose the applicable law in consumer transactions, and the doctrine of *lois d'application nécessaire* (or *ordre publique*).

---

[9] Although some states have chosen to make the cancellation period also applicable to Internet auctions, see below p. 111, note 35.
[10] Convention on the law applicable to contractual obligations (80/934/EEC), Art 3.

6.16 The doctrine of *lois d'application nécessaire* and *ordre publique* restricts the ability freely to choose the applicable law in cases where the content of the chosen law would be against national public policy. This, in effect, will probably not cause many practical problems between the parties, since the rules of serious marketplaces are unlikely to conflict with fundamental public policy in national law. However, a particularly problematic area with respect to violating fundamental national public policy is sale restrictions for offensive goods, such as drugs, arms and pornography. This problem is dealt with below.[11]

6.17 Beyond the area of contract law as between the parties in a marketplace, national legislation often contains quite heavy regulation of exchanges in financial instruments. The same is also true in regard to product liability and anti-trust. These regulations are typically not within the scope of party autonomy. In other words, the parties may not avoid the relevant burdensome regulations by designating the applicable law in their contract.[12]

International instruments advisable to refer to as a supplement to national law

6.18 In deciding the applicable law in a choice of law clause, it should be emphasized that one law may be applicable to the formation of contract, another law may be applicable to the deal between seller and buyer, and a third law may be applicable as between the marketplace operator and the participants. For instance, CISG, Part III is an appropriately functioning system to use as the applicable law for the sale transaction, even though auctions are excluded in CISG, Article 2. The only part of CISG that is not well-suited for auction transactions is Part II on formation of contract.[13]

6.19 As a general point I would like to recommend strongly that the marketplace in its membership terms and conditions of sale makes a reference to the UNIDROIT Principles of International Commercial Contract (UPICC).[14] This instrument covers a large area of contract law and is particularly designed for international transactions. The result for the legal infrastructure of a contract when there is a reference to UPICC is that three 'layers' of law are established: the first level would be the specific membership terms and conditions of sale. If they do not provide an answer to a certain question, UPICC would apply as the second level. Only in the situations where UPICC do not cover the issue in dispute will it be necessary to refer to national law, as the third and final layer.

---

[11] See ch 12.

[12] See for example R Lee, *What is an Exchange? The Automation, Management and Regulation of Financial Markets* (OUP, 1998) 133 ff, on English law in relation to German transactions.

[13] See ch 8 below on withdrawal.

[14] To be found at <www.unidroit.org>; see also <www.unilex.info>.

The recommended choice of law clause to use in order to refer to UPICC is:[15] **6.20**

This contract shall be governed by the UNIDROIT Principles (1994) [except as to Articles . . .], supplemented when necessary by the law of [jurisdiction X].

It is recommended that one and the same national law cover both the relationship between the marketplace operator and the participants, on the one hand, and the relationship between the individual participants. It is not recommended that the law of the seller regulate the relationship between the buyer and seller, since this may lead to different bidders or different transactions being subject to different laws, which is against the equal treatment concern.

Conclusion

This chapter has pointed to some of the fundamental problems related to deter- **6.21** mining the applicable law in relation to electronic auctions and exchanges. Unfortunately, it is not possible to provide any resolution of these problems. There is undoubtedly a great need for the international community to provide certainty in this area. Until such certainty is established by conventions on private international law—which is unlikely to be for some considerable time yet—it is wise to limit the practical problems. This can, to some extent, be done by referring explicitly to the applicable law in the contracts between the participants and between the marketplace and the participants in the conditions of sale and in the membership terms. Furthermore, it is recommended that the auction or exchange stipulates from where the transactions are administered and conducted and, naturally, ascertains that this stipulation is in line with where the transactions are actually administered and conducted.

[15] For alternative references, see <www.unidroit.org>.

7

MEMBERSHIP TERMS AND CONDITIONS OF SALE

Introduction

Most jurisdictions allow marketplaces extensive freedom to set their own rules **7.01** and conditions. A few jurisdictions have restricted the auction participants' ability to agree freely on the terms. An example is French law, which stipulates a procedure for some types of auctions that cannot be departed from by the parties' agreement.[1] A marketplace must consider to what extent mandatory national law

---

[1] P Bonassies, in R B Schlesinger, *Formation of Contracts, A Study of the Common Core of Legal Systems,* Vol 1 (NY, 1968) 413. It is only in private auctions held in a private residence that general contract law applies.

restricts the ability to agree freely on membership terms and conditions of sale by either adhering to mandatory national law or denying access to participants protected by mandatory law.

7.02 The rules may stipulate how *the contract is formed*, for instance to what extent invitations and bids are binding and may be withdrawn. Furthermore, they may concern *the contractual obligations between the seller and buyer*, for instance regarding the time of performance and liability for defective quality. The rules may also determine *the obligations between the participants and the market-place*, for instance regarding access.

7.03 We see that the actors may have different roles. They may be invitors, bidders, buyers, sellers or operators. It is possible for one person to play many roles in parallel. For instance, a buyer that initiates an auction (hereafter the initiator of an auction will be called 'the invitor') may also function as the operator. The contract thus should have rules that regulate the responsibility for the different roles. It should be observed that there could be three contractual relationships:

(a) the participant's contract with the marketplace/auctioneer on the one hand (what I call 'membership terms');

(b) the participants' relationship (also normally regulated in the membership terms);

(c) the seller's contract with the buyer (what I call 'conditions of sale': note that what I say about such conditions also applies when there is not a transaction for the sale of goods, but instead a contract for the sale of a service or an intangible).

In order to avoid the use of too many documents, these different types of terms may be included in one contract, but the person drafting the contract should be aware of the fundamental difference between the terms depending on what relationship they intend to regulate.

7.04 When the invitor operates an electronic auction, there will normally not be a multi-party contractual relationship, but a one-to-many contractual arrangement, ie the participants will have a contractual relationship with the invitor/marketplace operator, but not with each other. However, it is advisable for the contract to make a clear distinction between on the one hand the terms of the auctions that regulate how a deal is concluded and, on the other hand, the terms related to the relationship between the invitor and the successful bidder (the buyer and the seller). Although uncommon, it may be that in marketplaces operated as a one-to-many transaction, the contract may also regulate the relationship between the bidders. If so, it becomes a many-to-many contractual relationship (or a multi-party contract).

7.05 The question as to how the conditions of sale are incorporated, interpreted and adjusted according to mandatory regulations will depend on the applicable national law. An explicit reference to the applicable law is advisable. Outside the area of mandatory consumer law, such references are normally acceptable.[2]

This chapter is focused on the written text of the membership terms and condi-   **7.06**
tions of sale. In designing both the membership terms and conditions of sale, the person drafting the contract must be also aware of the need to cover issues relevant to the technical structure. Later I will describe how the technology used interacts with the written contractual agreement.

The multilateral nature of the membership terms

In a closed Internet marketplace, the operator can make certain that the same   **7.07**
membership terms and conditions of sale bind all participants. All participants thus adhere to the same rules. These contracts become multilateral in the sense that they regulate not only the relationship between the participants and the marketplace operator, but also the relationship between individual participants. This is so even though the contracting parties may appear to be only two. There are usually only two parties signing the contract, ie the marketplace operator and an individual participant. However, the membership terms can be—and are advised to be—construed in such a way that a new participant becomes bound in relation to all earlier and later participants.[3]

Traditionally, when thinking of a contract, a two-party relationship comes to mind.   **7.08**
Persons not being parties to the individual deal who have claims against these two parties have to base them outside the law of contract, mainly in tort or property law. In a multilateral contract the participants are connected and their relationships are regulated by the multilateral agreement. When parties to a multilateral contract have claims against each other these can be based on the multilateral contract. A multilateral contract can cover aspects that a contract between only two parties cannot. For example, A, B and C can agree that B's claims are to have a higher priority than C's where A goes bankrupt. Furthermore the multilateral contract can contain provisions concerning to what extent C has a claim against A when A has caused C losses due to wrongful information submitted to B. Both these examples are normally determined by national property law and tort law, respectively. In a multilateral contract with hundreds or thousands of participants, some of the traditionally non-contractual legal relationships can be governed by contract. It should be noted that of course persons who are not parties to the multilateral contract are not affected by them but have to base their claim or defence with reference to the applicable non-contractual law. The multilateral contract is in a way similar to a

---

[2] See on the applicable law ch 6 above.
[3] See for a reference to arbitration H H. Perritt Jr, 'Jurisdiction in Cyberspace' in B Kahin and C Nelson (eds), *Borders in Cyberspace* (MIT, 1999) 187.

company, where a mixture of company law and 'contractual agreement' (the articles of association) bind the owners. The participants are connected to each other by the membership terms and agree in this contract to undertake obligations in regard to other participants and also to recognize rights against each other.

7.09   Issues that are usually covered by tort law, procedural law and property law are transferred to contract law by using the technique of a multilateral contract. This is especially important in light of the international nature of Internet marketplaces. Contractual parties may to a large extent choose the applicable law for their contractual relationship.[4] To agree on the applicable law, however, is not possible for potential disputes outside contract law. In a multilateral contract the participants may to a larger extent choose and predict the applicable law by regulating issues regarding property rights and damages as between participants in the marketplace. Most importantly, the marketplace can design an efficient and tailor-made solution to the potential problems of a property law and tort law nature among its participants.

Incorporation of membership terms and conditions of sale

Incorporation in physical auctions

7.10   In traditional auctions the conditions of sale are normally posted up in the auction room. The conditions are not specifically brought to each participant's attention. The conditions are only available for the participants to read where they wish to do so as the participants of the auction should be aware of the existence of conditions of sale. It should be noted that they are deemed incorporated without explicit acceptance by the participants.

7.11   We see a parallel to standard terms in other types of transactions. The standard terms need not be read in each transaction, and despite the fact that the parties have not read them and that the terms, consequently, do not correspond to any actual intention of one party, the standard terms are deemed incorporated. The explanation is of a pragmatic nature. It would be too costly (from a transaction cost point of view) to require the standard terms to be read and understood in each individual case. This formalistic approach to incorporation is in most jurisdictions compensated for by a dynamic approach, under which standard terms prescribed by only one party must not be unexpectedly burdensome or unfair to the other party.[5]

---

[4] See ch 6 above.

[5] In some jurisdictions unfair terms are openly set aside or adjusted (for instance according to the Scandinavian Contract Acts, Art 36), in other jurisdictions the contract is interpreted or construed in favour of the disadvantaged party. See Council Directive 93/13/EEC of 5 April 1993 on unfair terms in consumer contracts, Art 3.1.

Some jurisdictions require that the auction contract be made in writing. Normally **7.12** such formal requirements are not relevant for the validity of the contract, but only have the effect that each party is entitled to demand a written contract (*ad probationem*).[6] For Internet transactions, electronic documents normally constitute writing and, consequently, a written contract can be entered into by web technique.[7]

Incorporation of standard terms in Internet marketplaces

Applying the rules on incorporation to the electronic transaction is not complic- **7.13** ated. However, the available technology will probably lead to the effect that it is not enough merely to have the standard terms readily available on the marketplace's website. Many jurisdictions are likely to require that the participants be expressly informed about the existence of the membership terms and conditions of sale. Sometimes it may be required that special attention is brought to surprising or burdensome terms. Furthermore, it may even be required that the participants actively accept the membership terms and conditions of sale.

From a strictly legal point of view the conditions of sale are readily available **7.14** when placed on the website of a marketplace. This is quite similar to a situation in traditional auctions where the conditions of sale are posted on a wall in the auction premises. The reason why it may not be enough to make the membership terms and conditions of sale available on the website is that it is quite easy technically to determine that the participants are notified expressly about the existence of the terms and conditions. It is recommended that a marketplace should introduce procedures whereby each participant expressly accepts the membership terms and conditions. This is a requirement of notification and actual acceptance that is not always present in relation to incorporation of traditional 'paper' membership terms and conditions of sale. I believe, however, that the law in the future will require contracting parties to make use of the available technology. When it is technically easy to ensure explicit acceptance of the terms and conditions and it can be done without great cost and unnecessary waste of time, the legal systems are likely to require that such technology be used.[8] See below regarding the need to direct special attention to surprising or burdensome terms.

National law on incorporation of standard terms often contains protective provi- **7.15** sions for consumers, requiring that standard terms in consumer contracts be incorporated in particular ways to ensure that the consumer actually has an opportunity to read and understand the terms. National law sometimes does not provide

---

[6] This is so in Spain, see J Ataz López, *Régimen Juridico General del Comersio Minorista (McGraw-Hill/Interamericana de España*, 1999) 678.

[7] See paras 4.83–4.88 above.

[8] G E Maggs, 'Internet Solutions to Consumer Protection Problems' (1998) *South Carolina Law Review*, Vol 49, No 4.

the same level of protection and requirements for incorporation of standard terms for business-to-business transactions. Consequently, it may be important for a marketplace operator to identify whether the person applying to become a member of the marketplace is a consumer and act accordingly depending whether the applicant is a consumer or businessman. There are two problems here. First, in electronic transactions it may be difficult to determine the status of the applicant, whether a consumer or a businessman. Secondly, in an international setting the definition of consumer varies across different states and sometimes even varies within a particular state's different statutes and regulations; this makes it difficult to have the same procedure for incorporation of standard terms for all nationalities of applicants.

7.16 Due to the importance of equal treatment of all bidders in auctions and exchanges it is essential to ascertain that all participants are bound by the same contractual terms and that the standard terms are accurately incorporated. The new technological means of communication are likely to lead to the gradual disappearance of the traditional division between consumer transactions and business-to-business transactions. For both types of transactions it is important that the contracting party's attention is brought to the following: (1) that standard terms exists; (2) that he gets an opportunity to read them; and (3) that he becomes specifically aware of surprising and/or burdensome terms. In designing the technical structure for incorporation of standard terms, a marketplace should ensure that these three features are appropriately communicated. The problems of special form requirements in some national laws for consumer transactions and ways of defining and identifying consumers to whom such form requirements apply remain for the time being greatly problematic in practice. The present differences in consumer law make it almost impossible to design a marketplace for international business-to-consumer transactions.

7.17 In traditional paper transactions the conditions of sale can be deemed incorporated by usages or custom that the parties have established among themselves or by implicit understanding.[9] It is unlikely that this will apply to electronic auctions and exchanges. The reason is that in multi-party relationships there is little room for development of practices between individual parties or for implicit rules.[10]

7.18 From a technical point of view there are a number of alternatives available as how to design the procedure of incorporation of standard terms.

(a) The applicant could be required to read the text of the membership terms and conditions of sale and certify that he has read and understood them. In this alternative the text is shown on the applicant's screen and there is no way of concluding the application unless the whole text has been scrolled through

---

[9] UPICC, Art 4.3(b) (<www.unidroit.org>).
[10] See paras 6.02 and 6.03 on equal treatment.

and actively accepted (by, for instance, clicking OK in a box stating that 'I have read the membership terms and conditions of sale and I accept them').

(b) The applicant could be provided with an opportunity to read the membership terms and conditions of sale, but the technical design is not such that the applicant necessarily has to read or scroll through the texts. He may choose to read them by clicking on a link to the text. The applicant must actively accept the terms by clicking in a box on the screen.

(c) The applicant could be provided with an opportunity to read the membership terms and conditions of sale and the application could state that they are incorporated, but the applicant does not have to read them or scroll through them, nor must he actively accept them.

Naturally, there are many combinations available of these three main alternatives to incorporation of standard terms in the electronic setting. In choosing the appropriate means of incorporation for an Internet marketplace, I would like to recommend the first of the above three alternatives. Since the terms are incorporated only once in connection with the access procedure and intended to apply for all future transactions made in the marketplace, the extra time that this alternative entails is not a major obstacle. The benefit of choosing the first alternative is that at least in business-to-business transactions it is fairly likely that all national jurisdictions will deem the incorporation procedure sufficient.

The problem of incorporation of terms is closely connected to interpretation of **7.19** the terms. Even when the membership terms and conditions of sale taken as a whole are deemed incorporated, there is a risk that certain clauses are not properly incorporated. Surprisingly burdensome or unusual terms may need special attention in order to be incorporated. In the traditional paper transaction, case law in different jurisdictions shows that courts sometimes are reluctant to enforce surprisingly burdensome or unusual clauses in standardized contractual texts. Also the membership terms and conditions of sale for Internet auctions and exchanges are standardized and may thus require that special attention be directed towards unusual or burdensome clauses. This is particularly so when all or some of the participants are consumers. Particular attention could be drawn to surprising or burdensome terms by, for instance, repeating such clauses and having the applicant specifically accept these terms by individually clicking an acceptance box in relation to each such burdensome or surprising term.

Interpretation of membership terms and conditions of sale—*rigor commercialis*

In auctions and exchanges all participants can be well-informed about the **7.20** membership terms and conditions of sale and, consequently, adhere to them and not be surprised by them. This transparency legitimates or justifies a *rigor* *commercialis* approach under which the terms are interpreted objectively according to the wording of the text with the main focus on the functioning of the marketplace as a whole.[11] In the interpretation of individual contracts not only the wording of the texts as such but also the expectations and understandings of the parties are usually of relevance.[12] To what extent such personal factors are relevant may differ in different jurisdictions. For auctions and exchanges based on multilateral contractual relationships and where the importance of equal treatment of all bidders is crucial, it is essential that the contractual text has a 'life of its own'. It would be devastating if the same contractual term was interpreted in one way as between participants A and B and in a different way in the relationship between participants A and X. Consequently, no relevance should be given to the subjective intention and understanding of the individual parties. The *rigor commercialis* approach has three effects:

(a) it makes individual silent or implicit conditions irrelevant. A merger clause, stipulating that the membership terms or conditions of sale completely embody the terms, is likely to be upheld;[13]

(b) the *rigor commercialis* approach reduces the need to resort to concepts of fairness. The harshness of the rules in an individual case is justified by the efficiency for the marketplace as a whole. Disturbances in the basic foundation ('the rules of the game') will create uncertainty among the participants and thus hinder the efficiency of the marketplace to the detriment of all future transactions;[14]

(c) membership terms and conditions of sale that are expressly agreed on by the participants are likely to be interpreted objectively and without much attention being given to the individual participant's perception of the meaning of the terms.

7.21 Once the aspect of *rigor commercialis* is taken into account, interpretation of Internet membership terms and conditions of sale is similar to any other interpretation of contractual texts. Ambiguities must be resolved by:

• the nature and purpose of the contract;
• the meaning commonly given to terms and expressions in the trade concerned;
• usage and custom;
• good faith and fair dealing; and
• reasonableness.[15]

Interpretation of the membership terms and conditions of sale also should acknowledge the close relationship with the technological aspects of how transactions are made in the marketplace. As will be described in paragraphs 7.34 to

---

[11] See ch 3 above.   [12] UPICC, Art 4.1(1), 4.2(1) and 4.8(2)(a) (<www.unidroit.org>).
[13] UPICC, Art 2.17 (<www.unidroit.org>).   [14] See ch 3 above.
[15] UPICC, Art 4.3 and 4.8 (<www.unidroit.org>).

7.41 below, it is advisable for the person drafting the terms and conditions to 'synchronize' with the technology and to include in the terms and conditions the norms prescribed by the technology. In interpreting the terms and conditions one should strive towards finding a harmony or balance between the technological structure and the wording in the texts. Furthermore, it is essential to take into account the basic features of the auction or exchange: mainly that all bidders should act under equal conditions and that there must be confidence in the marketplace, specifically that promises are kept and that norms or rules are strictly followed.

7.22 A special problem or concern in the interpretation of membership terms and conditions of sale in international Internet marketplaces is that contractual terms may be set aside due to national mandatory law; this is particularly so in relation to consumer contracts. Furthermore, there is in some states national legislation on the interpretation of non-individually negotiated terms. This may mean that different interpretative methods are used depending on the nationality of the participants; this in turn leads to unequal treatment of the participants in the marketplace.[16]

Incomplete contracts and gap filling

7.23 Conditions in traditional auctions are often fragmentary in nature. In traditional auctions the many contractual gaps are filled out by default rules in national law and usage or custom. In traditional business-to-business auctions and exchanges the participants are familiar with the procedures of the marketplace and the usage is common knowledge to them. Often persons acting in the marketplace are only accepted after a long period of training during which they become acquainted with the usages, customs and practices of the marketplace. These are an important source of law in traditional auctions.

7.24 Gap filling with the help of usage is more difficult in Internet marketplaces. This is because of continuing changes in procedures and the wide variety of ways of operating. Since there is hardly any gap filling by usage possible in the electronic environment, there is a greater need for detailed membership terms and conditions of sale.

7.25 In the future, definite understood usages and customs may develop. It is perhaps not surprising in these times of great change that they have not yet emerged. It is hard to predict with any certainty that such usages and customs will develop in such a way for Internet marketplaces that they could serve as a source of law.

---

[16] In the German case *BGH Urteil vom 7.11.2001–VIII ZR 13/01* the question of *Inhaltskontrolle* was briefly discussed.

Some believe that Internet transactions will be individually tailored for each specific type of business to such an extent that no general usage will evolve. Usage consists of people's actual behaviour. In the electronic environment the flexible technological solutions allowing some types of behaviour and preventing others will probably partly overtake the role of traditional usage in law.

Changes in the conditions of sale or membership terms

7.26 Membership of an Internet marketplace may be limited to only one single transaction. However, it is more common that participants regularly carry out transactions in the Internet marketplace and that membership is intended to last for a long period of time and over many transactions. The membership terms and conditions of sale need to be flexible and easy to change. The reasons for changes are several. Improved technology may affect the way transactions are made. Furthermore, it may turn out that a particular risk allocation ought to be distributed differently. To allow for this flexibility it is necessary to make it possible to change and adapt the membership terms and conditions of sale.

7.27 Due to the basic principle that promises are to be kept, it is always difficult to make changes in contracts. It is therefore important to describe how changes are to be implemented. The membership terms or conditions of sale should address how changes are to be made and the effects when a participant does not accept the change.

7.28 The terms should stipulate who is entitled to take the *initiative to make a change*. Normally, this would be the operator of the marketplace. Sometimes, it should be possible for the participants to submit suggestions as to how the procedures in the marketplace could be improved.

7.29 Different from the right to take an initiative in suggesting a change is the *power actually to make a change* in the contract that is binding on all participants. Normally, the operator of the marketplace will give itself the power to introduce and effect changes. In sensitive marketplaces it could be advisable to have a procedure of general approval (for instance, that at least 50 per cent of the participants should vote in favour of the suggested change). It could also be a good idea to give any participant who does not accept the change, an opportunity to cease being a member and bound by the membership terms. Another alternative is to require express acceptance as a condition of allowing a participant further access to the marketplace.

7.30 Due to the need to treat all participants equally it is not advisable to allow participants to choose whether they wish to adhere to the old or new regime.[17] It is normally essential that all participants are acting under the same conditions.

---

[17] See paras 4.62–4.64, and 6.02 and 6.03 above.

Changes in the membership terms or conditions of sale should be *brought to each* **7.31**
participant's attention and expressly accepted to make sure that they are deemed
incorporated in the legal sense. In relation to changes it is necessary to take into
account what was said in paragraphs 7.10 to 7.19 above concerning incorporation
of membership terms and conditions of sale. Another important factor in making
changes is that participants are informed well in advance whenever there is a need
for them to change their business operations because of the change. Membership
terms may be deemed unfair if the participants are not allowed such a period to
adapt. Some national jurisdictions may put such unfair contract clauses aside or
adopt them but order that the participants be given compensation.[18]

Another way of creating flexibility in the membership terms and conditions of **7.32**
sale is to make them valid only for a limited period of time. At the end of each
period the contractual relationship is terminated and the marketplace operator is
free to change the terms. When choosing such a solution it is important to bear in
mind that the contract needs to be terminated at the same date for all participants,
for instance, on 15 May at 12.00 pm, in time zone x. This may create confusion
for participants becoming members of the marketplace only a short time before
the contract period is ended. Furthermore, this solution is cumbersome in that it
involves requiring all participants to take the time to renew their membership.

A not uncommon way of allowing flexibility in contracts is to include renegotia- **7.33**
tion or hardship clauses. This is, however, not an option available for Internet
marketplaces. The multi-party nature of the relationships does not make such
procedures possible, as they are mainly appropriate for individual negotiations.

When introducing changes it is important to check carefully that there are *no*
retrospective effects. Transactions carried out under the old regime must be
clearly separated from transactions made under the new regime. Since the participants' bidding strategies are highly dependent on the 'rules of the game' retrospective changes may be devastating for trust and confidence in the marketplace.

The relationship between conditions of sale and technological solutions

The conditions of sale and membership terms function as manuals of behaviour **7.34**
for the participants. In the conditions the procedures are described and the participants get to know what happens when they do not follow the 'rules of the game'.
In the traditional world it was generally possible to break the rules and when such
breaches were detected certain consequences and sanctions were enforced. In the
Internet environment technique may make it impossible to commit some types of

---

[18] See UPICC, Art 3.10(3) on gross disparity (<www.unidroit.org>).

breaches. In such situations behaviour is not primarily guided by the conditions and terms but by the technical structure of the marketplace. Lessig has provided an interesting description of this relationship between law and technology in his book *Code and Other Laws of Cyberspace*.[19] He does not examine Internet marketplaces in particular but provides other examples of this major change in how citizens' behaviour can be monitored and steered.

7.35   It is crucial for an Internet marketplace to establish harmony or balance between the technology, on the one hand, and the conditions of sale and membership terms, on the other hand. This may seem obvious advice. In practice, however, it is not uncommon that the communication between persons responsible for technical solutions and persons responsible for drafting the membership terms and conditions of sale is not adequately synchronized or co-ordinated.

7.36   If, for example, it is technically impossible to withdraw a bid in the auction, this should also be reflected in the membership terms and conditions of sale. It is recommended that such a rule be 'repeated' in explicit wordings even when it is self-evident from the technical structure that withdrawals are not allowed. If there is disharmony between the technical design and the content of the terms and conditions, there is a risk that a participant may use 'offline' means to make a withdrawal, by sending a fax to some participants or an email to all participants. If the terms and conditions do not stipulate anything about withdrawals being forbidden, it is ambiguous to what extent such 'offline' behaviour has legal effect.

7.37   There are other reasons for synchronizing the legal and technical design. It gives the potential participant in the marketplace a deeper understanding of the risks and opportunities. Some participants may prefer to learn about the rules of the marketplace by 'hands-on' experience and put an emphasis on becoming familiar with the 'demo-version' of the marketplace. Other participants may prefer to learn about the rules of the marketplace by reading the manuals and the membership terms and conditions of sale. It is important that these different categories of participants receive a similar picture as how to behave in the marketplace.

7.38   Furthermore, well-synchronized legal and technical designs may be important to a potential judge or arbitrator who may find it less difficult to apply written membership terms and conditions of sale as a source of norms than he would a technical (implicit) structure.

7.39   The same correlation between the technological and legal design appears when the technology does not deter prohibited behaviour. If, for example, an invitor is not allowed to submit bids, but is still technically able to do so, it is essential that the membership terms clearly state that such behaviour is forbidden. The best solution is, of course, to synchronize the technological design with the legal

---

[19] Basic Books, New York, 1999.

design in such a way that what is not allowed in the membership terms or conditions of sale is also impossible to carry out due to technological barriers.

It is normally difficult to make it technically impossible to cancel settled deals, **7.40** and thus the terms or conditions ought to have a clause regulating to what extent cancellation is allowed and the effects of breach of this clause. The participants should also be informed about this at a proper time before making a forbidden cancellation by, for instance, information boxes appearing on the screen.

The particular problems related to withdrawal and cancellation are described in **7.41** chapter 8: the examples provided here are only given in order to illustrate the relationship between legal and technical design.

The membership terms and conditions of sale as a means of avoiding disputes

The question of incorporation is not only a legal question as to whether the member- **7.42** ship terms and conditions of sale have become part of the contract where there is a dispute. The incorporation of the terms and conditions should be examined also from a less legalistic and more pragmatic perspective. The terms provide the rulebook and manual for how transactions are to be conducted in the marketplace. It is essential that the terms be introduced to the participants so that they know how to behave and are aware of the consequences of different actions. The more familiar the participants are with the rules, the less likely it is that disputes will occur.

The relevant questions to ask are: **7.43**

(a) How are the membership terms and conditions of sale incorporated in order to make the participants act in accordance with them?
(b) How are the membership terms and conditions of sale incorporated in order correctly to influence the expectations of the participants, so that future disputes can be avoided?

Naturally, the legal rules related to incorporation are aimed at securing these interests. However, it might be advisable to take additional measures to the legal minimum requirements for incorporation. Here, again, we see the close relationship between the membership terms and conditions of sale and the technological structure. The more 'instructive' the technology is, the less education the participants need. When the technology lets a participant act against the rules, it is more important to direct his attention to the written rules. The means of doing so vary. Electronic apprenticeship or online tutorial—where the applicants show in demo-versions that they master the procedures—may be alternatives.[20] Another alternative is to require

---

[20] See paras 18.01–18.04 below about how participants can be required to become familiar with the procedures in the marketplace before being accepted as members.

the participants to pass a test. A third alternative is to make the applicant scroll through a question form in order to establish that he has understood the terms. A fourth solution is to let information boxes appear directing attention to particularly important clauses in the membership terms and conditions of sale and require the applicant expressly to approve each such box.

7.44 It is interesting that disputes rarely occur in physical marketplaces based on auctions or exchanges. The explanation is that the participants are well acquainted with the 'rules of the game'. These rules are efficiently implemented by ensuring that the participants are aware of them. Some traditional non-Internet auctions and exchanges require that the brokers be licensed. In some exchanges a licence is only given after an examination showing that the applicant has understood the conditions of sale. In other marketplaces a long period of apprenticeship or participation in tutorial schemes is necessary in order to be licensed. Furthermore, the whole atmosphere at the non-Internet marketplace reinforces the 'rules of the game'.

7.45 It is essential that Internet marketplaces create the same awareness of the rules of the game and an equivalent to the atmosphere discouraging disputes in the physical marketplace.[21] In the Internet marketplace the equivalent to this atmosphere is the technological structure, which 'automatically' shows the participants how they may act and how they should not act. This illustrates how important it is to synchronize tightly the legal and technological structure in Internet marketplaces.[22]

Particularly about the conditions of sale

7.46 The conditions of sale need to be fixed beforehand in auctions and exchanges. They cannot be negotiated after a deal is closed because of the need for equal treatment of the bidders and for the offered bids to be commensurable.[23] The invitor may be allowed to decide the conditions of sale himself and attach them to the object put up for auction. The terms decided by the invitor thus acquire a 'take-it-or-leave-it' character. Naturally, it is important that the invitor does not set unreasonable terms, but uses a balanced set of norms.

7.47 The marketplace may wish to restrict the invitor's ability individually to decide the terms of the sale in order to ensure that the terms are well-balanced and do not tend to harm the general confidence in the marketplace. This can be achieved

---

[21] At *FruitLine.com* new participants get personal training carried out on the site.

[22] Traditional marketplaces that have become electronic can sometimes benefit from the traditional non-litigious atmosphere and successfully preserve that atmosphere; Norex appears to be such an example (see <www.norex.com>) and below p. 125.

[23] See paras 4.62–4.64, and 6.02 and 6.03 above.

by indicating in the membership terms different types of recommended conditions of sale or by providing limits within which the invitor may decide the terms. A helpful instrument in this respect is the e-version of the ICC Model Sale Contract for manufactured goods.[24]

For marketplaces with a highly specialized type of transaction it is often recom-   **7.48**
mended that the membership terms provide that all transactions are made under the same conditions of sale. The reason for such a scheme is to avoid the bidders being burdened with the task of examining the terms for each transaction. Also in this respect the e-version of the ICC Model Sales Contract for manufactured goods may serve as a useful instrument.[25]

Issues to be addressed in the conditions of sale or membership terms

Below is a checklist of issues that may be resolved in the conditions of sale and   **7.49**
membership terms.[26] Naturally, this list is not exhaustive, nor does it list all alternative solutions. In the following discussion some of the issues will be examined in depth. In this context it should be noted that it is not always in the interest of the marketplace operator to include a maximum exclusion of liability. In order to attract liquidity and trust, it may be wise to undertake some liability in different respects.[27]

General information

The name and address of the auctioneer/operator.   **7.50**

Access terms (chapter 16 below)

Who may give invitations at the site (qualifications required)?   **7.51**
Who may bid at the site (qualifications required)?
To what extent is it allowed to bid through an agent?
When can a participant be expelled from participation in an individual transaction?
When can a participant be wholly expelled from doing transactions in the marketplace?

---

[24] See Paction at <www.iccwbo.org>.   [25] See <www.iccwbo.org>.
[26] The list is much inspired by B W Harvey and F Meisel, *Auctions Law and Practice* (2nd edn, OUP, 1995) ch 6.
[27] M R Geroe, 'Agreements between an Electronic Marketplace and Its Members', (Fall 2001) *The International Lawyer*, Vol 35, No 3, 1069, provides an extensive list of recommendations as to how the marketplace operator may exclude its liability.

When is a participant liable to pay a fee or fine to the marketplace?

What are the rules relating to collusion such as auction rings (chapter 15)?

Contractual relationships

7.52 Does the auction lead to a contract between the seller and buyer directly; or with the buyer and the marketplace, on the one hand, and with the marketplace and the seller, on the other hand?

How are the membership terms or conditions of sale changed (paragraphs 7.26–7.33)?

Terms on formation of contract (the bidding procedure)

7.53 How to provide an offer.

When to provide an offer.

How to provide a bid.

When to provide a bid.

The time the auction is held.

The time the auction lasts (if being a time-interval auction).

The opportunity to inspect the object before the auction is held.

To what extent the operator has the right to offer goods owned by him.

The amount the bid covers (can a bidder choose to buy only a part of the lot?) Is a bid only for a single object even if more than one is included in the lot?

The right to withdraw and revoke a bid (chapter 8).

The right to cancel a completed deal (chapter 8).

The right of the invitor to state a reserve price: no such right/a duty to disclose the reserve price/a duty to disclose that a reserve price exists/no duty to disclose the existence of an allowed reserve price (chapter 8).

The right to withdraw an offered lot (chapter 8).

The right for the invitor to bid anonymously or by disclosing his identity or not at all (chapter 8).

The right for the operator to advance bids at his discretion (chapter 15).

The right for the operator to advance bids on behalf of the invitor (chapter 15).

If a bid may be rejected when the advance is too small.

Any stipulation of the bids being automatically increased or decreased by a certain amount.

How the 'winning' bidder is determined (chapter 10).

What the winning bidder should pay (chapter 10).

Who pays what fees to the operator, including responsibility for taxes related to the auction (chapter 10).

Consequences where necessary permissions are not granted (chapter 11).

Terms of the sale

The passing of the title to the goods (chapter 13).   **7.54**
Payment conditions: when, how and where, deposit requirements, liability for
taxes, effects of failure of compliance (chapter 13).
The quality of the goods: grading standards, goods sold 'as is', 'in perfect condition', 'with all faults and errors of description', 'as and where they lie', with
express warranties.
The liability of the operator for defects (chapter 16).
Claims must be submitted: when and where and how and what is the effect of a
late or wrongful claim.
Delivery of the goods: transport from where and to where at the expense and
responsibility of whom.[28]
Assumption of risk: from when? The fall of the hammer, the storage of the goods,
the delivery of the goods.[29]

Dispute resolution (chapter 18 below)

Dispute resolution regarding the formation of contract—possibly a regulation as   **7.55**
to how and when a dispute results in putting the lot up for sale again plus the duty
to pay fees to the operator in such a case.
Dispute resolution regarding the contract for sale.
Dispute resolution in conflicts between the participant and the marketplace operator.

Applicable law

References to applicable law and international instruments, such as UPICC,   **7.56**
INCOTERMS, UCP and other standard terms (chapter 6 above).

Other

The buyer's liability to remove (fetch) the goods within a certain period of time.   **7.57**
Collusion/collaboration between participants (chapter 15).
To what extent information not widely spread can be taken advantage of, for
example insider problems (chapter 14 below).

---

[28] See INCOTERMS at <www.iccwbo.org>.   [29] ibid.

Summary

7.58 The person drafting the membership terms and conditions of sale, should observe:

(a) the fundamental difference between rules for the marketplace and the participants, and the rules between the participants;

(b) the difference between rules related to formation of the contract and the rules related to the sale;

(c) that he cannot rely on usage or custom to fill out the gaps in the contract, but must strive to include explicitly all rules in the membership terms and conditions of sale;

(d) that the membership terms and conditions of sale constitute a multi-party contract under which the participants become bound towards each and every participant;

(e) that the conditions of sale and membership terms become part of the contract by having the participant actively accept them;

(f) that the membership terms and conditions of sale describe how changes are to be implemented;

(g) that changes in the conditions of sale or membership terms are expressly accepted by the participants;

(h) that the participants are trained and become familiar with the rules of the game;

(i) that the legal and technological designs are synchronized.

8

WITHDRAWAL AND CANCELLATION OF INVITATIONS AND BIDS

Introduction

A basic problem in contract law is the question of how a contract is formed. There **8.01** are two main different theories on formation of contract. One is found in the Anglo-American jurisdictions, mainly characterized by the parties being simultaneously bound at a crucial moment—in 'normal' cases when the acceptance is put in the postbox. Before this crucial moment the offer can be withdrawn or revoked without any consequences, since none of the parties are bound. According to German legal tradition the contract is concluded in two steps. One party is unilaterally bound by his offer during a period of time and the offeree becomes bound by his acceptance. When each party is bound by a corresponding promise a mutually binding contract is formed. There are many variations to these two main types of mechanisms for formation of contracts and to some extent the parties may deviate from the law by agreeing on other ways of concluding the contract.

8.02   Cancellation and withdrawal are closely related. Withdrawal is when one of the parties withdraws his invitation or bid. Cancellation takes place after the contract is concluded and is where one party effectively cancels both the invitation and the bid. Generally, the chances to cancel are more limited than the chances to withdraw. In practice, it is sometimes unclear at what point in time a contract is actually concluded. The distinction between cancellation and withdrawal thus becomes blurred.

8.03   It is rare to find specific legislation in relation to cancellation of deals concluded by auction. Legislation related to withdrawal and cancellation is often of a non-mandatory nature and may be deviated from in the conditions of sale (see above). Because there are different rules in different jurisdictions regarding formation and cancellation of contracts, it is particularly important to have express terms in electronic marketplaces where there are participants from many states. Furthermore, it is important to stipulate clearly what actions give rise to a contract and to what extent cancellation of contracts is permitted, since general national contract law is often not very certain in this respect. This chapter intends to show when it is efficient or inefficient to allow withdrawal and cancellation in relation to auctions.

Fitting the actions in auctions into the concept of offer and acceptance

8.04   There are many examples of cases showing how fruitless it is to try to apply the theories of offer and acceptance to auctions. It is always difficult to establish what constitutes a promise as opposed to, for example, merely an invitation to start negotiations, which may eventually lead to a promise. It is particularly difficult to determine whether an offer to put an object up for auction or a bid in an auction can be withdrawn or is binding (irrevocable) and when it can be withdrawn, for how long or until which stage in the auction process. Trying to define the offer by the auctioneer as an offer in the legal sense or to determine whether it is simply an invitation to deal sometimes becomes overly technical.[1] The disadvantage of legal technicalities is that such analyses tend to move the focus away from what would be the most appropriate solution.[2]

---

[1] The problems in Spanish law are presented in L Díez-Picaso, *Fundamentos del derecho civil patrimonial* (Madrid, 1986) part 1, 216. See for English law *Barry v Davies (trading as Heathcote Ball & Co)* [2000] 1 WLR 1962; comment by R Fletcher, 'An Offer you Can't Refuse' (2001) *Business Law Review*, 162. For German law see T Stögmöller, 'Auktionen im Internet', *K&R Heft* 9/1999, 394 with references, and a reply to this article by H Russmann and T Reich, 'Internet als gewerbeordningsfreier Raum?' *K&R Heft* 3/2000.

[2] P K Howard, *The Death of Common Sense—How law is suffocating America* (NY, 1994).

In states where there is no explicit law regulating the withdrawal of bids in **8.05** auctions, usage becomes an important source of law. In the absence of definite usage, one has to resort to general legislation on contract law. This frequently leads to a problem in establishing which action in the auction transaction constitutes an offer and which action constitutes an acceptance.

Unfortunately, it is difficult for a court to do anything more than try to mould the **8.06** offerings and bids in auctions into the established legislative 'boxes' of offer and acceptance. There is a more liberal approach to be found in UPICC, Article 2.1 and Principles of European Contract Law (PECL), Article 2:101 referring to 'sufficient agreement',[3] which invites the court to let go of the formalistic concepts of offer and acceptance in favour of finding the efficient and appropriate solution. However, regrettably, this is not likely to be a freedom the courts are willing to take on. Courts in many countries have tended to prefer a technical legal analysis and thereby avoid having to address the more intellectually challenging question of the consequences for the individual deal and the market as a whole.[4] Experience shows that lawyers arguing cases in court tend not to follow the more liberal approach, but instead refer to the concept of offer and acceptance, which in turn limits the judge's ability to give reasons for his decisions based on the concept of 'sufficient agreement'.

Bearing in mind the difficulties of applying the concept of offer and acceptance **8.07** to auctions and exchanges, the parties are advised to stipulate clearly in the conditions of sale and membership terms to what extent the invitations and bids are binding, can be withdrawn and cancelled. In fact, lack of specific legislation relating to auctions could be seen as beneficial, since it places an incentive on the parties to stipulate the solution that is most appropriate for their type of auction and marketplace.

In order to avoid the conditions of sale or membership terms being interpreted in **8.08** light of the concept of offer and acceptance, it is generally advisable not to refer to the terms 'offer' and 'acceptance' in the legal sense, but instead to say directly to what extent different messages may be withdrawn, revoked or cancelled. The words used could be something other than the technical legal terms 'offer' and 'acceptance', for example 'initiating bid' or 'invitation' and 'bid'.

---

[3] PECL, Art 2:101(1): Conditions for the Conclusion of a Contract. A contract is concluded if: (a) the parties intend to be legally bound, and (b) they reach a sufficient agreement without any further requirement.

[4] Examples of such cases of a theoretical-formalistic nature are the British Guiana case *Demerara Turf Club v Wight* (1918) AC 605; the Indian case *Jorvarmull v Jeygopaldas*, AIR 1922 Mad 486; the English case *Warlow v Harrison* (1858) 120 ER 920 and 925; and the US case *Zuhak v Rose* 264 Wis 2d 286, 58 NW 2d 693, 37 ALR 2d 1041 (1953). See also the Commentary to PECL, Art. 2:201 where the transactions in an auction are squeezed into the concept of offer and acceptance, despite the availability of referring to 'sufficent agrement' in PECL Art. 2:103 (O Lando and H Beale (eds), *Principles of European Contract* Law (Kluwer Law, 2000) 160. It is even worse to try to define the bid as a binding offer (or acceptance) in the legal sense conditioned by no other higher bids being put forward.

8.09 In regard to the borderline between withdrawal and cancellation we often come across analyses of a technical legal nature. The question as to when a contract is concluded is decided on a formalistic basis, instead of addressing the question of to what extent the reliance of the non-cancelling party needs to be protected. For auctions it has been particularly difficult to know whether the deal is concluded at the time of the fall of the hammer, at the time of the shouting of 'mine' in the Dutch auction, or at the stipulated time limit or at the time of confirmation in time-limit auctions. Sometimes the crucial moment does not correspond to the fall of the hammer. In a US case the court found that the seller had reserved the right to confirm or disaffirm the sale made by the auctioneer.[5] This case shows how important it is to regulate specifically in the conditions of sale or membership terms when each party is bound and to what extent it may or may not cancel the deal.

The promise principle and its importance in the individual deal and for the marketplace as a whole

8.10 The basic principle of contract law is that promises are binding. The underlying rationale is that a society functions best when people are able to trust each other's promises. It is generally important that invitations and bids in auctions are not withdrawn.[6] The marketplace is dependent on participants trusting and relying on invitations and bids. Such trust makes it worthwhile to invest the time and make the preparations to take part in the auction. If it would be generally highly uncertain whether an invitation actually would lead to an auction, many would refrain from participating, which would be to the detriment, not only of the individual deal but also for the marketplace as a whole.[7] If the situation is analysed by only examining the relationship between two individual participants—as opposed to analysing the problem from the point of view of the whole marketplace—it is often difficult to see the reason why a party taking the initiative for an auction (normally the buyer in English auctions and the seller in reverse auctions, hereinafter called the 'invitor') or the bidder should not be allowed to withdraw before any individual contract has been formed. To provide the full picture, I will analyse below the consequences of withdrawal both for the individual parties and for the marketplace as a whole.

8.11 The traditional national rules on formation of contract mainly deal with balancing the interests of the market as a whole and the interests of the individual party.

---

[5] *Continental Can Co v Commercial Waterway District No. 1* 56 Wash 2d 456, 347 P 2d 887, 354 P 2d 25 (1960).

[6] R E Hall, *Digital Dealing: How e-markets are transforming the Economy*, 2001, at <http://www.stanford.edu/~rehall/LinoleumReport.pdf> 54. See for another opinion M R Geroe, 'Agreements between an Electronic Marketplace and Its Members', (Fall 2001) *The International Lawyer* Vol 35, No 3, 1069 at 1080.   [7] Hall (n 6 above) 9.

As explained earlier in chapter 3, modern technology makes it practically possible to make a distinction between, on the one hand, the interests in the individual deal and, on the other hand, the interests of the marketplace as a whole. The mutual interest is that promises are kept, but the consequences of a broken promise can be tailored to meet the differing interests. In the individual deal the main interest is to compensate a party who has suffered economic loss due to the broken promise (reparation, compensation for reliance). For the marketplace as a whole it is important to prevent breach of promises by creating general disincentives for participants to break their promises and to bar from participating those persons likely to harm the marketplace by not standing by their promises (a prophylactic prevention).

Withdrawal by the invitor

The general problem

The question examined here is to what extent it is appropriate to allow the invitor to withdraw his invitation at different stages in the process. At paragraphs 8.45–8.62 below I shall examine the effects when bidders in auctions and exchanges withdraw their bids.   **8.12**

When an invitation is announced that an object will be put up for auction it is intended to create interest in the individual auction transaction and in the marketplace generally (when many objects are offered at the same occasion). When an invitation is withdrawn trust in the marketplace may be harmed since participants get an impression that other participants are not serious and do not consider the matter thoroughly enough before making an invitation. From an individual point of view, the announcement may cause potential bidders to prepare and take action in order to be able to take part in the auction. A withdrawn invitation may thus lead to individuals incurring wasted costs.   **8.13**

In most jurisdictions the auctioneer can stipulate in the conditions of sale or membership terms whether the initiative for an auction is a binding offer or merely an invitation to deal.[8] The default position in different jurisdictions varies as to whether invitations may be revoked without an express condition that it is revocable.[9]   **8.14**

---

[8] Some countries seem to make it mandatory that offers are irrevocable: see the Spanish Ley 7/1996, *de Ordinacíon del Comercio Minorista*, Art 56 No 1.

[9] In France it is presumed that the offer cannot be revoked if not specifically so stated by the auctioneer (R B Schlesinger (ed), *Formation of Contracts, A Study of the Common Core of Legal Systems*, Vol 1 (NY, 1968, 82). According to US law (A E Farnsworth, *Contracts*, 2nd edn (Little, Brown & Co, 1990) 142 with reference to UCC 2–328(3)) the seller who offers something for sale is *in dubio* not obliged to accept the highest bid, but may reject all bids. The auctioneer's proposal is not a legally binding offer, but each bid is an offer that the auctioneer may accept or reject. In a German case the offer by the invitor was not merely an invitation to treat but constituted a legally binding offer when the auction rules stated that the highest bid would be accepted (*BGH Urteil vom 7.11.2001–VIII ZR 13/01*).

The individual perspective

8.15   From an individual point of view a withdrawn invitation in an electronic auction rarely causes any significant harm to potential bidders. The cost of participating is low since no travel is needed. The potential bidders rarely have to make any technical preparations, since this is normally a procedure connected to being initially accepted as a participant in the marketplace. The time wasted is in many cases limited and since all negotiations run the risk of not leading to a final contract anyway, there is usually no compensation for negotiation costs (unless the invitor acted with the intention of deceiving the bidders: UPICC, Article 2:17). All these factors point towards permitting withdrawal of invitations in the membership terms up to the time when a deal is concluded (see below on cancellation) and that potential bidders should not be entitled to any compensation when an invitation is withdrawn.

8.16   It may be somewhat different in situations where the bidders need to make extensive preparations, for instance when the invitation to build a house is provided in a reversed auction and the bidders are required to calculate and submit bids for construction costs. When the marketplace involves such transactions, the invitor could be allowed to withdraw the invitation under the membership terms but the terms should stipulate that the potential bidders are entitled to compensation. The compensation could take the form of liquidated damages (specifying a fixed amount). Alternatively, the conditions of sale could provide a method of calculating the compensation.

8.17   When bidders are entitled to compensation it is important to identify clearly which potential bidders are entitled to compensation. A well-known problem related to compensation for withdrawn invitations is how to limit the group of persons entitled to compensation. Is the invitor liable to compensate all potential bidders? If so, it could be an unreasonably burdensome liability. From an evidentiary point of view it is difficult to show *causality*—that the withdrawn invitation actually damaged an individual potential bidder. Furthermore, the *amount* of damage is difficult to establish. It is, consequently, advisable that the membership terms clearly stipulate which participants qualify for compensation and what such a participant must have done in order to be entitled to damage where there has been withdrawal of an invitation that under the terms is not permitted to be withdrawn. The membership terms should furthermore provide that there be liquidated damages for those participants entitled to compensation.

The perspective of the marketplace as a whole

8.18   Even though individual bidders are not much harmed by a withdrawn invitation, the withdrawal may cause harm to the marketplace as a whole. When invitations are withdrawn frequently, bidders may lose trust and decide not to waste their time in that marketplace in the future. A single withdrawal may also harm the marketplace, ie when that particular object was used to draw attention to the marketplace (a withdrawal may then cause irritation among the participants).

The marketplace could consider creating a general disincentive against with- **8.19** drawals by charging a fee for each withdrawal, to be paid to the marketplace. This fee could be higher for every withdrawal which a particular participant makes. Such a rule would emphasize the importance of commitment in making invita- tions in the marketplace. This is an example of how it is in the interests of the marketplace as a whole that promises are kept and how the effects of such broken promises mainly serve as a disincentive rather than provide economic compensa- tion for individual participants. For marketplaces where withdrawals of invita- tions are directly harmful to trustworthiness, withdrawals could be forbidden either by making withdrawal technically impossible or by stipulating in the conditions of sale or membership terms that invitations are binding and may not be withdrawn.

When an auction is operated by the invitor (mainly in procurement transactions), **8.20** it is well advised not to withdraw its invitations, so as not to upset the bidders. When the invitor in such marketplaces finds it important to be able to withdraw invitations, it should be clearly communicated to the bidders that withdrawals could be made, so that they are not unpleasantly surprised and accordingly become less inclined to participate in future auctions set up by the invitor.

Consequences when withdrawal constitutes breach

When withdrawal is forbidden under the membership terms it is advisable to **8.21** implement technical procedures making it impossible for invitors to withdraw their invitations. When such technology is not used it is necessary to stipulate consequences or sanctions where withdrawals of invitations are made in breach of the membership terms. There should also be explicit information available making it clear that withdrawal is not permitted.

Withdrawal of invitations before the bidding has started
When an invitation is withdrawn before the bidding process has started no one in **8.22** particular incurs any losses. The reason why such withdrawals may not be accepted is normally that they cause harm to the marketplace as a whole. Thus, the most efficient approach is normally not to provide a remedy to individual participants, but instead to provide liability for payment of a fee to the market- place operator.

Withdrawal of invitations when the bidding process has started
It is more difficult to find the appropriate consequence or sanction when an invi- **8.23** tation is withdrawn during the bidding process. The highest bidder at the time of

withdrawal might in such a situation feel that he is harmed by the withdrawal, since he did not acquire the object put up for auction. Consequently, it may appear logical to provide him with a claim for specific performance (that is to say, to allow him to get the object for the bid he had submitted at the time of withdrawal). However, had the invitor not breached by making a withdrawal, other bids could have been submitted, higher than the last bidder's at the time of withdrawal. If specific performance were to be granted, the highest bidder at the time of the interruption of the auction would receive a windfall.[10] Because of this windfall argument, it is rarely appropriate only to compensate the highest bidder at the time the invitation is withdrawn.

8.24   I would like, once again, to stress how important it is to use technology that makes it impossible for the invitor to withdraw during the bidding process when the membership terms stipulate that withdrawal of invitations is forbidden. When the technology does not prevent forbidden withdrawals, the most appropriate course is often to stipulate that the invitor acting contrary to the membership terms may face denial of access or have to pay a fee to the marketplace.[11] In some marketplaces it could be appropriate also to allow all participating bidders to recover their reliance expenses (preferably in the form of liquidated damages).

Conclusion in relation to wrongful withdrawals of invitations

8.25   Often the best way of coming up with a solution that encompasses, on the one hand, the needs of the individual invitor and, on the other hand, the interest of the marketplace as a whole is to have two rules. One rule would allow the invitor to withdraw in relation to the bidders and the other rule would create a disincentive for the invitor by making him obliged to pay a 'withdrawal fee' to the marketplace. The membership terms could also stipulate that invitors who repeatedly withdraw and thereby cause considerable harm to the marketplace as a whole could be expelled from the marketplace.

The invitor submitting bids

8.26   A withdrawal may consist either of an actual withdrawal or where the invitor himself bids and thus acquires the object. When the invitor outbids the other bidders, he achieves the same result as if he had withdrawn the invitation. In such situations no individual participant is economically harmed, since individual bidders can never be sure of acquiring an object put up for auction. However, where an invitor knows that he will probably bid for the object and himself invites participants to spend time and effort in negotiations that he knows or suspects will not lead to the formation of a contract he is possibly behaving in a

---

[10]   I R Macneil, in Schlesinger (n 9 above) 396.   [11]   See ch 16 below.

way that could amount to bad faith. This is generally not accepted in national law
(see UPICC, Article 2:15). According to the English Sale of Goods Act 1979,
section 574(4) the seller may not bid himself without disclosure. The rationale is
to minimize the risk of price manipulation.[12] It could be argued that auctions held
in Internet marketplaces generally should implement a corresponding rule.

In traditional auctions it is frequently expressly provided what the consequences **8.27**
are when the invitor himself bids for an object. Generally, disincentives for such
behaviour are created by the invitor having to pay the auctioneer a fee even
though the object is not sold to anyone. A similar solution could be used in the
electronic auction or exchange. The accumulated small costs of each participating bidder are from a transaction cost efficiency point of view best collected by
the auctioneer (the operator of the marketplace). Furthermore, it serves as an efficient disincentive on invitors to put up objects for auction without announcing an
explicit reserve price.

Often in electronic auctions and exchanges it is not possible for the participants **8.28**
to know who submitted the winning bid. Consequently, the bidders rarely know
when the invitor himself gets his object back. In some commercial sectors the
invitor's bid may not be harmful to individuals or the marketplace as a whole. For
such cases there is no need to implement technology and/or legal rules preventing bids from the invitor or providing for legal sanctions against such behaviour.[13]

In a second-price sealed-bid auction it is particularly important that the auction- **8.29**
eer/operator is neutral and independent of the invitor and is trusted by the bidders.
Otherwise, if the auctioneer lets the invitor peek inside the order book and place
a bid, the invitor can force the price up to the price bid by the winning bidder. All
the invitor has to do is to place a bid just below the winning bid. That price will
become the auction price under the second-price rule. Bidders will not bid their
true values unless they really trust the auction organization and believe it is independent of the invitor. Consequently, when the invitor runs his own auction, it
should not be a second-price auction, or otherwise there should be some assurance that the invitor/operator will not submit bids.[14]

In conclusion, in designing the rules concerning the invitor's participation in the **8.30**
bidding, it must be carefully considered whether it is appropriate to allow it.
When it is decided that the invitor should not be allowed to submit bids, it is
suggested that the disincentive take the form of a fee to the marketplace (or in
serious cases, access denial), and not damages to the bidders.

---

[12] In large worldwide marketplaces there are practical obstacles to enforcing such national rules
(see ch 2 above).
[13] See on hidden identities of participants, paragraphs 14.28–14.33 below.
[14] Hall (n 6 above) 41.

Reserve price and auction 'without reserve'

8.31 Frequently, the invitor is unwilling to sell or buy the object put up for auction at any price. In such situations the invitor often stipulates a reserve price. It is common for websites to feature a secret reserve valuation specified in advance but not revealed to the bidders until after the auction.[15] This section will examine whether the existence of the invitor's reserve price ought to be disclosed to the bidders and, if so, whether it is advisable to disclose the specific price level. Furthermore, this section will analyse the effects of using the phrase 'without reserve'. Lastly, there will be recommendations as to the use of reserve prices in electronic auctions and exchanges.

Must the existence of a reserve price be disclosed to the bidders?

8.32 As mentioned above, it may sometimes be harmful to the bidders when the invitor himself submits bids. When the invitor is already aware at the outset of the auction that he has a price limit, he may mislead bidders into undertaking costs in participating by not explicitly disclosing that such a limit exists. In effect, the existence of a hidden reserve price is to a great extent similar to the situation where the invitor is bidding. The only difference is that hidden reserve prices do not entail a risk of price manipulation. It has been shown that many buyers try to avoid auctions with hidden reserve prices, as it is upsetting to win an item only to be told that the winning bid was not high enough.[16] As was concluded above, whether it is appropriate to allow hidden reserve price differs in different marketplaces—it is not really possible to provide a single recommendation suitable for all marketplaces.

8.33 In national law we sometimes find that hidden reserve prices are not accepted.[17] Spanish law upholds a rule that invitations are irrevocable and that the invitor is bound to sell to the highest bidder.[18] Even though national legislation restricting the possibility of using hidden reserve prices is difficult to enforce in transactions made in a non-national Internet marketplace, it is probably wise to comply with such legislation nevertheless. It can generally be recommended that marketplaces have rules under which the invitor must disclose to the bidders that there is a reserve price.[19]

---

[15] M Bichler, *The Future of e-Markets, Multidimensional Market Mechanisms* (CUP, 2001) 135, with a reference to D Lucking-Reiley, 'Auctions on the Internet: What's Being Auctioned and How?', available at <www.vanderbilt.edu/Econ/reiley/cv.html> (1 February 2000). See also H Jungpil, 'The dynamics of mass online marketplaces: A case study of an online auction' <http://misrc.umn.edu/wpaper/default.asp> 317–24 at 322.

[16] Lucking-Reiley (n 15 above).

[17] It was held obiter dicta to be the law in an English case that an invitor was bound to sell to the highest bidder when he had not stated a reserve price: *Warlow v Harrison* (1857) 8 E & B 647. This opinion was later vindicated in *Barry v Davies* (*trading as Heathcote Ball & Co*) [2000] 1 WLR 1962.

[18] Ley 7/1996, *de Ordenacíon del Comercio Minorista*, Art 56.

[19] See concerning an exception for the Dutch and Japanese auctions, paragraph 8.43 below.

The *consequences* of lack of disclosure of a reserve price need not necessarily be   **8.34**
that the invitor is bound to honour the best bid. An alternative is to entitle the invitor to reject the deal and instead pay a fee to the marketplace. The reason why
there is no need for a remedy to the individual highest bidder is that this bidder
can never be sure of winning the auction and has not had any time to rely on the
deal provided that the notice that no deal is concluded is communicated immediately after the close of the auction. However, when the invitor is the one arrang-
ing the auction, ie when the invitor and the marketplace operator are the same
person, it is more appropriate that the consequence of a hidden reserve price is
that the invitor must conclude a contract with the best bidder. This is because it
is not enough disincentive to the invitor that he has to pay a fine to himself in his
capacity as a marketplace operator.

Can the limit of a reserve price be hidden?
A requirement that the existence of a reserve price be communicated to the   **8.35**
bidders does not necessarily mean that the amount be specified. Often invitors are
unwilling to disclose their minimum limits, since this may induce the bidders not
to deviate too much from that limit. In exchanges the limit is frequently stipulated
openly and made known to the whole marketplace. In auctions, however, the limit
is frequently hidden. In order to make certain that the invitor sticks to his original reserve price, the marketplace may provide an opportunity for the invitor to
disclose the reserve price limit to the marketplace operator, without it being
disclosed to the bidders.

Each marketplace must determine to what extent it is important to provide an   **8.36**
opportunity for the invitor to hide the limit of the reserve price. When such an
opportunity is available, it may be left to the invitor to decide before closure
whether he is willing to conclude a deal. An alternative is that the invitor provide
the limit secretly to the marketplace operator and that deals are automatically
concluded when the highest bid exceeds the reserve price limit and, respectively,
does not automatically result in a deal when the reserve price limit is not
exceeded. In exchanges where bids are matched the reserve price issue must be
determined during the bidding process and not later.

The meaning of the phrase 'without reserve'
It is difficult to interpret the meaning of making an invitation in an auction 'with-   **8.37**
out reserve'. Does a statement 'without reserve' amount to a promise to sell to the
highest bidder or may the invitor refuse to sell to the highest bidder?[20] Under US

---

[20] The former uncertainty in English law in this respect has recently been resolved in *Barry v
Davies (trading as Heathcote & Co)* [2000] 1 WLR 1962 commented on by Fletcher (n 1 above),
establishing that the auctioneer cannot refuse the best bid in an auction announced as 'without
reserve'. See also Schlesinger (n 9 above) 408–9; B W Harvey and F Meisel, *Auctions Law and
Practice* 2nd edn (OUP, 1995) 29 ff.

law, the highest bid must be accepted in auctions that are announced as 'without reserve' (UCC 2–328(2)).[21] However, in the US the existence of a reserve price has been interpreted generously. In one case a bank's announcement that it would sell to the 'highest, best and last bidder' was not sufficient to constitute an auction without reserve.[22] Also under German and Swiss law, an auction 'without reserve' imposes a duty on the invitor to sell to the highest bidder.[23]

8.38   A related question is whether the invitor may withdraw his invitation before the auction has come to an end, when the auction is held 'without reserve'. Under the US UCC § 2–328(3) goods put up without reserve cannot be withdrawn (this is, however, a default rule, which can be deviated from in the conditions of sale or membership terms).

8.39   Auctions held 'without reserve' may also have implications as to the invitor's ability to submit bids (see above).

8.40   It is not advisable simply to state that the auction is held 'without reserve' since the meaning of this expression is difficult to interpret. It is better directly to clarify either that the invitor has a right to refuse the most favourable bid, or that he is bound to accept it. By using such straightforward language it is not necessary to use the concept of 'without reserve'. As said above, it should also be made explicit in the conditions of sale or membership terms whether the invitor may withdraw his invitation before the auction has come to an end and whether the invitor is allowed to submit bids. The implemented technology should also address this issue, preferably making it impossible for the invitor to deny a deal when the intention is automatically to produce a contract with the best bidder.

Advantages and disadvantages of allowing reserve prices in auctions and exchanges online

8.41   It is impossible to provide a single solution as to whether it is advisable to allow reserve prices in electronic auctions and whether the reserve price should be disclosed or allowed to be hidden. The answers vary depending on the type of transaction. In the following paragraphs, different types of auction methods will be analysed in relation to the reserve price.

8.42   **The English auction, the time-interval auction, the auction by candle, the sealed-bid auction, the Yankee method, the audible-bid rotation system, and the reverse auction**   In these types of auctions the initial invitation often conveys information about the invitor's reserve price. This is, however, not always the case. When an initial invitation price is stated before the bidding

---

[21]   Farnsworth (n 9 above) 142. Macneil (n 10 above) 394.

[22]   *Sly v First National Bank*, 387 So 2d 198 (Ala 1980).

[23]   K H Neumayer in Schlesinger (n 10 above) 417 with references. See also the German case *BGH Urteil vom 7.11.2001–VIII ZR 13/01.*

process has started, this often serves as an indication to the potential bidders as to whether it is worth the effort to participate in the auction. As long as it is clear from the conditions of sale or the membership terms whether there may or may not be a reserve price and to what extent the invitor is allowed to submit bids, there is no general efficiency argument pointing in either the direction of allowing, or forbidding a hidden reserve price or bids by the invitor. However, when the bidders have extensive costs in determining what bids to submit, it is generally advisable not to allow hidden reserve prices or bids by the invitor. When the use of hidden reserve prices or bids by the invitor causes costs for the marketplace itself, or disturbs the flow, a disincentive may be established by charging the invitor a fee when he chooses to introduce a hidden reserve price or to submit bids himself.

The Dutch and Japanese auctions   The characteristic feature of Dutch and **8.43**
Japanese auctions is that the bidders are unaware of the price levels which are of interest to the other bidders. When the invitor in the Dutch auction wishes to impose a reserve price, he will simply tell the auctioneer beforehand not to go further down than the reserve price. In the Japanese auction the invitor may participate and provide the minimum limit as a security that it is not sold at a lower level. Normally, I see no reason why the existence of a reserve price or the limit of a reserve price must be disclosed to the bidders before the object is put up for the Dutch or Japanese auctions. I also see no reason why the invitor should be denied the opportunity to bid himself. Only when the object put up for the Dutch or Japanese auctions needs to be thoroughly examined or analysed by the participants, is it advisable to restrict the invitor's ability to hide the existence and the level of a reserve price and his ability to submit bids.

The exchange   In the continuous double auction (or exchange) the bidders **8.44**
normally submit reserve prices and openly state the limits. It is only rarely that the bidders are prepared to provide open bids to be matched freely. The systems are normally technically set up in such a way that it is impossible to submit bids without a limit. It is quite another matter that buyers and sellers may instruct their brokers to buy or sell at certain maximum or minimum levels but the bids submitted by the broker in the exchange constitute in themselves reserve prices. Due to the rapid price variations that often take place in exchanges, it is highly advisable openly to disclose the reserve prices in order to enable the participants to assess quickly and predict the levels of supply and demand and proceed with their strategic bidding accordingly. Participants in exchanges ought not to be restricted in submitting bids for selling and buying simultaneously, unless there is a risk that such behaviour may be used to manipulate the price-setting mechanism in the marketplace.[24] When a participant in an exchange has submitted a reserve price,

---

[24] See ch 15 below.

he ought to be entitled to withdraw his bid as long as the bid has not been matched. As will be examined below (see paragraphs 8.61–8.62) there is no reason not to allow such withdrawals as long as it does not influence the price-setting mechanism.

Withdrawal by the bidder

8.45   In the following paragraphs I will examine the dangers in allowing bids to be withdrawn in different types of auctions. The purpose is to find the most appropriate solution for each type of auction.

8.46   As a basic position I take the view that withdrawals of bids should be allowed. The reason is that when it becomes obvious at an early stage that one party is not interested in closing a deal the relationship is only likely to lead to dispute and conflict. However, for situations where the individual parties are substantially harmed because of a withdrawal, there can be consequences: either specific performance or economic compensation. When the marketplace as a whole is affected negatively by withdrawals, it is important to determine appropriate consequences that prevent withdrawals.

Withdrawal of bids in the English auction, the auction by candle and the time interval auction

8.47   In an auction where ascending bids are provided, a bidder might wish to retract his bid before the fall of the hammer or, in electronic auctions, before the highest bid is accepted in any other way than by the use of a hammer. In traditional auctions such a withdrawal is made by the bidder shouting, 'I retract', or something similar. When the bid is given in writing or by telephone before the auction starts, the bid can often be retracted either orally at the auction or in writing or by telephone before the bidding has started. When a withdrawal is made at this stage, no individual participant has yet had the opportunity to rely on the bid and a withdrawal, consequently, causes no harm to any individual participating in the auction.

8.48   The retraction of bids may interrupt the 'flow' of the auction. Many auctions are held at great speed and it takes time to handle a withdrawal from a practical point of view (even if automatic processes can be designed to handle withdrawals swiftly). Furthermore, other bidders may be disturbed by a withdrawal. When it is a 'slow' auction some potential bidders may leave the auction when a high bid is submitted and these potential bidders may not become aware that the high bid was later withdrawn. Bid shielding may be particularly harmful. This occurs when two bidders conspire to place one bid high enough to scare other bidders off and one bid lower than the fair market value, and then the higher of the two withdraws at the last minute, thereby defrauding the invitor of the value of the object as determined by open, competitive bidding.[25]

These examples show that withdrawals may give rise to anxiety and uncertainty **8.49** in the marketplace. In extreme cases and in marketplaces where withdrawals become frequent, there is a risk that the trustworthiness is so damaged that the marketplace no longer attracts participants. However, a single retracted bid every now and then ought not to induce any real problems in English auctions, auctions by candle and time-interval auctions.

The marketplace must decide what the consequences should be when a bid is **8.50** withdrawn. A solution may be to let the second best bid provide the new base for further bidding. However, this is only an advisable solution when it can be ascertained that (1) the second best bidder is still active and has not left the bidding process as a result of the higher bid provided by the withdrawing bidder; and (2) the second best bidder cannot typically be presumed to have undertaken other transactions based on the presumption that he will not be bound in the auction. For all the mentioned types of auctions the system must require that the second best bidder confirm that he is still ready to stand by his bid. When the second best bidder is not willing to stand by his bid, a domino effect may result. When procedures of confirmation are cumbersome and effectively slow down the transaction and disturb the flow, it may be advisable not to permit bids to be withdrawn in English auctions, auctions by candle and time-interval auctions.

It is recommended that marketplaces using the types of auctions mentioned above **8.51** introduce some consequence, sanction or penalty for withdrawals, in order to prevent the bidders from submitting bids which they might later regret. It could be a fee to be paid to the marketplace. The fee need not be excessively high. The only situation where a fairly large fee is advisable is when the auction continues for a long period of time and there is a risk that potential bidders will leave the auction when a high bid is submitted and later withdrawn. In extreme cases, a particular bidder who frequently withdraws bids could be expelled from further participation.[26]

National legislation appears to be generous in allowing the retraction of bids. **8.52** According to the default rule in US UCC § 2–328(2), the bidder is allowed to retract his bid before the auctioneer announces completion of the sale.[27] Under English law a bidder may retract his bid up until the fall of the hammer.[28] Due to the concerns expressed above, a marketplace is, for many types of auctions and exchanges, advised to contract out of such default law and to restrict the ability to withdraw bids.

---

[25] See para 15.16 below about bid shielding.   [26] See ch 16 below.

[27] Farnsworth (n 9 above) 142.

[28] *Payne v Cave* (1789) 100 ER 502 and Sale of Goods Act 1979, s 57(2) referred to in Harvey and Miesel (n 20 above) 30.

Withdrawal of bids in the Dutch and Japanese auctions

8.53   In the Dutch auction a contract is concluded at the moment when the first bidder shouts 'mine' (or presses a button). Thus bids cannot be withdrawn in the legal sense. Instead it becomes a problem to what extent the bidder may cancel the deal.[29]

8.54   In traditional Japanese auctions the auctioneer had to determine which bid was the highest by looking at the hand signals of the bidders. Therefore the auction-eer's decision to sell to a certain bidder corresponded to the fall of the hammer in the English auction. In the electronic version this determination is made auto-matically. In the electronic version the Japanese auction is concluded automatic-ally by the highest bidder. As with Dutch auctions, there cannot be any withdrawals in the legal sense in Japanese auctions where the bid concludes the deal, thus we instead face a problem of cancellation.[30]

Withdrawal of bids in sealed-bid auctions

8.55   Withdrawing sealed bids within the timeframe during which bids are to be handed in seems to be without difficulty. There is no convincing argument why a sealed bid should not be allowed to be withdrawn before the time for submitting bids has ended. The invitor or the other participants in the auction have not relied on the withdrawn bid. Since it was sealed there could not have been any such reliance. In addition the marketplace as a whole is not disturbed. Withdrawals of sealed bids might cause the auctioneer to incur some administrative costs, but they appear to me to be too small to be of any importance generally. It is recommended that the technique used in sealed-bid auctions makes withdrawals possible and that no legal sanctions follow from a withdrawal.

8.56   After the bidding period has ended, there might be a time gap before the invitor actually assesses the bids and chooses to conclude a contract—presumably with the bidder who provided the best bid. Also during this period I can see no reason why the bid should not be allowed to be withdrawn providing that the bidder has not received information about whether his bid was the highest or not.

Withdrawal of bids in audible-bid rotation systems

8.57   Withdrawals of two types exist in the audible-bid rotation system. The bidder may want to withdraw his bid, and a participant having said 'I pass' may want to start bidding again.

8.58   In the audible-bid rotation system a contract is automatically concluded at the moment when one of the last two remaining bidders says, 'I pass'. Thus, this

---

[29] See paras 8.63–8.78 below.   [30] See paras 8.63–8.78 below.

second last remaining bidder cannot withdraw his 'I pass' message. If the last remaining bidder changes his mind and wishes to withdraw his previous bid, it becomes a question of cancellation, for which see below. It is, however, not always the case that the contract is concluded automatically when the second last remaining bidder says, 'I pass'. When the invitor has made a hidden reserve price or retained his right to accept the result of the audible-bid rotation procedure, a contract is concluded first after such acceptance is given. The marketplace should explicitly regulate to what extent the winning sole remaining bidder is allowed to withdraw his bid during the time the invitor considers whether to accept the bid.

A participant announcing that he passes ought to be allowed to take part again. I **8.59** can see no reason why such a reopened participation would cause any problems to the individual participants or to the marketplace as a whole as long as the participants' strategies can be adjusted accordingly.

There may be problems in relation to a bidder withdrawing his bid in the audible- **8.60** bid rotation system. If this bid has caused participants to pass and leave the auction, the price-setting mechanism is destroyed. Furthermore, when a bid is withdrawn the second best bid prevails and this bidder may have announced that he passes due to the high bid from the bidder now wishing to withdraw. These concerns also apply to the English auction, for which see above. However, since the audible-bid rotation system is often a slower process involving fewer particip- ants than other types of auctions, it may be relatively easy to ascertain whether the second best bidder still stands by his bid. Thus, it is often less inappropriate to allow withdrawals in audible-bid rotation systems than in English auctions, auctions by candle, and time-interval auctions.

Withdrawal in the double auction and exchange

As long as the bids from the seller and the buyer have not been matched in an **8.61** exchange, there is no problem in allowing a bid to be withdrawn. Bids waiting to be matched may influence the price-setting mechanisms when the marketplace discloses the level of such bids. In exchanges there is a risk that high offers in price or large offers in quantity may affect the balance between supply and demand. If such high or large offers are withdrawn, the invitors and bidders concluding deals before the withdrawal of the high or large invitation will have acted with inaccurate information about the amount of supply and demand. The participants affected by the withdrawal are participants making deals that do not relate to the lot that was actually withdrawn. It is difficult to identify these partic- ipants and to determine to what extent the prices were actually influenced by the withdrawn offer.

It is in practice difficult to ascertain the appropriate persons to compensate and the **8.62** amount of compensation. Thus, it is advisable to forbid withdrawals of invitations when the transactions made in an exchange are sensitive and easily influenced by changes in the amount of supply and demand. However, since there is a great risk that manipulative bids intended to unduly influence the market are actually accepted, there is often enough disincentive against abusing the right to withdrawal without having to forbid withdrawals.[31]

Cancellation by either party after the auction has ended

8.63   As said above, it is often difficult to determine at what point in time the participants in an auction or exchange should be allowed to change their minds and withdraw or cancel their offers, bids and deals. Cancellation may entail severe consequences for the individual party as well as for the marketplace as a whole. Lawyers are usually well-aquainted with the principle that promises must be kept and cannot be cancelled (*pacta sunt servanda*). To understand fully how a well-functioning marketplace ought to be legally designed, this principle will not be treated as an axiom. Instead, I will analyse to what extent it is important that promises are kept in electronic auctions and exchanges. Whether to allow cancellations or not is a question that should be analysed in relation to each type of marketplace.

8.64   Cancellation is sometimes divided into two categories; cancellation and cooling-off periods. Particularly within the realm of consumer law consumers are often granted a mandatory right to cancel a contract within a short period of one or two weeks after the conclusion of the deal. This is so, for instance, according to the Distance Selling Directive.[32] In practice, it is not uncommon that businesses voluntarily allow their contracting parties a cooling-off period. The following investigation will indicate to what extent it is appropriate to allow for cancellation in Internet auctions and exchanges. Focus will be on cancellations in close connection with the concluded deal (cooling-off), but many of the conclusions are equally applicable to cancellations taking place after a longer period of time.

Effects of cancellation for the individual deal

8.65   Where an object for sale can be easily resold without any substantial extra costs, cancellation can be allowed. Websites selling new manufactured goods to consumers often allow the consumer to cancel the deal. Indeed some national legislation even has mandatory provisions allowing consumers a cancellation period.[33] Cancellation in such transactions can be handled relatively smoothly

---

[31]   See ch 15 below on price manipulation.

[32]   Council Directive (EC) 97/7 on the protection of consumers in respect of distance contracts.

[33]   For instance, Council Directive (EC) 97/7 (n 32 above) prescribes a cooling-off period to be implemented in the member states' national law. However, the Directive makes an exemption for auctions.

since the objects for sale are not exposed to rapid price variations and can be offered again without any significant losses.

When a cancellation period is granted in business-to-business transactions, the **8.66** goods cannot be transported to the buyer before the end of the cancellation period. Otherwise the seller takes the risk of having to pay for the transport to and from the cancelling party. This leads to a slower process. In some transactions the positive aspects of allowing cancellation outweigh the negative aspect of the slower process. Generally, I am of the opinion that the need for fast transactions will be an ever more important feature of trade and that, consequently, only short cancellation periods, if any, should be allowed in the conditions of sale or membership terms. An alternative is to commence immediate transportation and require that the cancelling party cover the wasted transportation costs and secure payment for this responsibility before cancellation is executed.

In other types of auctions an extensive ability to cancel would be highly cumber- **8.67** some to handle in practice. In art auctions dealing with unique objects a rejected painting often cannot be resold until several years later. The market reacts with suspicion when the same object is offered again too soon—the object is 'burnt'. It is not recommended that cancellation be allowed for such transactions.

Naturally, cancellation becomes particularly difficult to handle when the object is **8.68** exposed to rapid price fluctuations, such as with commodities and financial instruments. In markets with high volatility it is of the utmost importance to protect the individual's ability to profit from speculation in the volatility. When cancellation is allowed in such markets there is a substantial risk that the deal will be cancelled because one of the parties has made a bad investment. Such possibilities destroy the speculative element. The good investment made by the other party must generally be protected by the rules of the marketplace. Thus, cancellations in deals made in marketplaces with high volatility, are normally not acceptable from an individual point of view.[34]

In the area of consumer law, there is often generous mandatory legislation **8.69** enabling the consumer to cancel contracts. Sometimes auctions are excluded from the mandatory right to cancellation and sometimes not.[35] When individual consumers are abusing their mandatory right to cancellation, the marketplace can use access restrictions to bar them and thereby prevent future disturbance to the price-setting mechanism. When the marketplace is particularly anxious not to allow cancellations, it might be necessary generally to restrict access for consumers from states with mandatory cancellation rights.

---

[34] See similar aspects in ch 9 below on cancellation due to mistakes.

[35] Auctions are exempted from the cancellation right in Council Directive (EC) 97/7 (n 32 above). In implementing the Directive Sweden and Finland, for instance, have not made an exemption for electronic auctions and thus allow a mandatory two-week cancellation period for bids in electronic auctions. I have been critical of this implementation: C Hultmark, 'Ny distansavtalslag' (2000–01) *Juridisk Tidskrift* 48–62.

Effects of cancellation for the marketplace as a whole

8.70 In analysing the appropriate and efficient right to cancellation in relation to auctions it is not only of interest to measure the damage a cancellation may cause the individual deal. The effects are not limited to the buyer and seller but influence the whole marketplace; the confidence in it, the price levels, and the strategies used by invitors and bidders.

8.71 There is a substantial risk that the price-setting mechanism is destroyed when cancellations are permited. If there is a right to cancel, the bidders take no risk in submitting high bids, since the transaction may be cancelled if the bidder later decides not to honour the deal. The prices are thus triggered to become higher in the English auction and lower in the reverse auction, without accurately reflecting the true market values. If this becomes frequent, the whole process is at risk. For this reason, it is necessary to take a much firmer view on cancellations than withdrawals. These two ways of avoiding a contract—withdrawal and cancellation—may seem quite similar at the outset, but have wholly different implications. It is crucial that the rules of the marketplace support the price-setting mechanism of the auction as an institution and that the rules safeguard the auction from the risk of price manipulations and the risk of loss of trust and confidence in the auction procedure.

8.72 As we have seen, cancellation leads to more problems in relation to some auctions than others. Generally, all auctions allowing cancellation run the risk that the bidders do not carefully consider their bids as they know that they may always change their minds later. Such feelings of non-commitment may destroy the whole auction mechanism. If submitting a high bid does not incur any liability, prices may be increased without thoughtful consideration, thereby forcing the bidder who is genuinely interested in the invitation to pay more for it, since he has to outbid the less serious bidders.

8.73 As mentioned earlier, it is particularly important for marketplaces with high volatility to allow speculation. When the participants are unable immediately to rely and make transactions based on concluded deals, the marketplace is likely to lose the necessary trust and the participants will not be as willing to make transactions, and this in turn will lower the necessary liquidity of the marketplace.

8.74 Another disadvantage of allowing cancellation is that the flow of the process may be disturbed. This is particularly obvious in relation to Dutch auctions.

Sanctions against cancellations

8.75 In electronic auctions two main types of sanctions may be used to prevent cancellations: (1) damages between the seller and buyer; or (2) fees/access denial in the relationship between the participant and the marketplace. One could introduce a regime whereby the buyer is allowed to cancel the deal with the seller and at the same time is expelled from the marketplace. An alternative way of creating a disincentive for cancelling deals is to allow the cancelling party to participate in the marketplace but 'punish' him by requiring him to compensate the other party with large (punitive) damages. Either the sanctions are aimed at the individual parties, or the sanctions are of 'public-law nature' where a fee is paid to the marketplace operator as a representative of the whole market.

When the feature of flow is crucial or when there is high volatility in the market **8.76** it is particularly important that a marketplace provide harsh sanctions for cancellation. The technology could make it impossible to communicate cancellation. Another alternative is to require that a participant that cancels pay a high fee to the marketplace operator. A third alternative is to make the participant who cancels liable to compensate the other party with the difference between the amount at which he provided his bid and the amount the offered lot was actually sold/bought for. This third alternative is a traditional way of using private law as a means of preventing cancellations, which are mainly harming the marketplace as a whole.

In other marketplaces, where there is low volatility and the 'flow' is less sens- **8.77** itive, more generous opportunities to cancel concluded deals could be implemented. In order to create a disincentive for cancellations, but not a draconian effect, there could be a minor fee payable to the marketplace operator.

In marketplaces with high liquidity (ie many transactions continuously made) **8.78** cancellation may be allowed but only on the precondition that the cancelling party be required to compensate the other party with the difference in price between the time of conclusion of the contract and the time for cancellation. This solution is efficient from a total transaction cost point of view since it often limits unnecessary transportation costs. However, it is recommended that such a right of cancellation be allowed only within a limited amount of time. An interesting feature of the continuing double auction (the exchange) is that there is often a marketplace readily available. This makes it easy to calculate the losses incurred by a cancellation. Computers may even be used to calculate automatically the sum that has to be paid where there has been cancellation. High liquidity in the market can, however, be put forward as an argument against allowing cancellation, since a buyer wishing to cancel the deal may himself quickly resell the goods. Similarly, when the seller wishes to cancel the deal, he may quickly buy substitute goods in the market with high liquidity.

Sent, dispatched, received

A general problem in electronic commerce is to determine at what exact moment **8.79** a message is sent, dispatched and received. Often the time the message is sent, dispatched or received has significant legal consequences. It is recommended that the conditions of sale or membership terms define these terms. In national law, the US Uniform Electronic Transaction Act (UETA) has carefully considered the definition of these terms in relation to electronic communication.[36] The drafting of conditions of sale and membership terms can benefit from copying UETA in this respect.

UETA, section 15: Time and Place of Sending and Receipt

(a) Unless otherwise agreed between the sender and the recipient an electronic record is sent when it:

  (1) is addressed properly or otherwise directed properly to an information processing system that the recipient has designated or uses for the purpose of receiving electronic records or information of the type sent and from which the recipient is able to retrieve the electronic record;

  (2) is in a form capable of being processed by that system; and

  (3) enters an information processing system outside the control of the sender or of a person that sent the electronic record on behalf of the sender or enters a region of the information processing system designated or used by the recipient which is under the control of the recipient.

(b) Unless otherwise agreed between a sender and the recipient, an electronic record is received when:

  (1) it enters an information processing system that the recipient has designated or uses for the purpose of receiving electronic records or information of the type sent and from which the recipient is able to retrieve the electronic record; and

  (2) it is in a form capable of being processed by that system.

(c) Subsection (b) applies even if the place the information processing system is located is different from the place the electronic record is deemed to be received under subsection (d).

(d) Unless otherwise expressly provided in the electronic record or agreed between the sender and the recipient, an electronic record is deemed to be sent from the sender's place of business and to be received at the recipient's place of business. For purposes of this subsection, the following rules apply:

  (1) If the sender or recipient has more than one place of business, the place of business of that person is the place having the closest relationship to the underlying transaction.

  (2) If the sender or the recipient does not have a place of business, the place of business is the sender's or recipient's residence, as the case may be.

(e) An electronic record is received under subsection (b) even if no individual is aware of its receipt.

---

[36] See for a comment on UETA, A Boss, 'The Uniform Electronic Transaction Act in a Global Environment' (2001) 37 *Idaho Law Review* 275–342. See also <www.uetaonline.com>.

(f) Receipt of an electronic acknowledgment from an information processing system described in subsection (b) establishes that a record was received but, by itself, does not establish that the content sent corresponds to the content received.

(g) If a person is aware that an electronic record purportedly sent under subsection (a), or purportedly received under subsection (b), was not actually sent or received, the legal effect of the sending or receipt is determined by other applicable law. Except to the extent permitted by the other law, the requirements of this subsection may not be varied by agreement.

MISTAKE IN EXPRESSION

Introduction

Many users of electronic means of communication are aware of the speed with **9.01** which Internet transactions are made. It is likely that many are also aware how easily something can go wrong. The 'send' button is clicked on too early, the 'Yes, I accept' box is clicked on by mistake and a kilogram of peppers is ordered instead of one single pepper. Worse things may happen. One of my students working in a bank office once ordered 10,000 Ericsson shares (at an approximate total cost of 3,000,000 Swedish crowns) on the Stock Exchange instead of ordering Ericsson shares to the value of 10,000 Swedish crowns (approximately 1,000 euros).

The problem of mistake has a long legal history. It has been difficult to strike the **9.02** balance between, on the one hand, the interest of a mistaken party not to be bound by unintended expressions of promise and, on the other hand, the interest of a party relying on a promise to be able to act upon it. In electronic auctions and exchanges it is important to consider how the risk of mistakes is best allocated between the operator, the party taking the initiative to put an object up for auction (the invitor) and the bidder.

9.03 Two of the main features of electronic communication are speed and automation. Both these features increase the risks of making mistakes that cannot be easily corrected before they reach the addressee. Discussions in the legal literature and initiatives by legislative bodies indicate that electronic commerce might provide good reason for adjusting the present distribution of liability in connection with mistake and considering more the mistaken party's need for protection.[1]

9.04 As an introduction to and illustration of the problem of mistake I would like to mention 'sniping'. This occurs in auctions where the software provided by the marketplace enables the bidders to submit bids at the very last second. Late bids prevent the prices from being pushed upwards and also enable bidders to win the auction. This is a story on sniping found on the Internet:

> . . . In due time, I did receive my book. In fact, purchasing online has become my preferred method of making purchases. I even purchased an automobile—slightly used—on eBay, the online auction house. There was great trepidation there, you can be assured! It turned out to be a great car, and an even better story, since the price was only £51! Of all the purchases I've made, the car seemed to promise the greatest legal implications: I was in the US; the car was in England. I had no opportunity to inspect the car prior to bidding on it. I used what is called 'sniping' software to bid on eBay, something that is permitted and 'legal' by eBay, but which is a great irritation to would-be buyers who are 'sniped'. You enter your highest bid into the program, which is online, and tell it the item you wish to bid on. The program searches eBay, and obtains the particulars regarding the item. The program makes a record of the time the auction ends, down to the second. As the user, I can set it to bid any time before the close of the auction, down to 10 seconds. In this case, I set it to bid 30 seconds before the auction's close. For experienced bidders, it is common to wait until the last possible moment to bid on an item. This hopefully precludes someone from driving the price up. Bidding 'manually', however, leaves you to the vagaries of the Internet—your connection could fail or simply be slow or your timing may be off. Someone else may be parked on a T-3 line and he will eat you alive! Sniping brushes the manual bidders aside, since the sniping computer, not you, does the bidding. I have never failed to successfully bid on anything using sniping. It worked for the car as well.

Sniping is difficult when a mistake occurs. The mistake can consist of an automatic bid being submitted too late (when the auction is over), or of a bid being submitted that is too high, or of a bid being submitted too early.

The problem in theory

9.05 Contract law in most jurisdictions is based on the theory of intention and reliance. A contract is formed and the parties are bound by it because they *intended* to be bound and both *expressed* this intention. Under this theory a contract ought not to be formed when one of the parties in fact did not wish to be bound, but by mistake expressed such a wish, since there is a lack of mutual consent. However, the party

---

[1] See for references the references to be found in the footnotes to this chapter generally.

relying on the mistaken party's expression of intent could deserve protection, and in certain circumstances the mistaken party can be held responsible for his mistaken expression of intention. All jurisdictions strive towards finding a balance between the interest of the mistaken party only to be bound by his true intention, and the interest of the relying party to be able to rely on expressions of intention.[2]

The general problem in practice

Traditionally, the risk has been placed on the party making a mistake, the ration-ale being that such a rule creates an incentive to act carefully and prevents mistakes from being communicated. Another explanation for the rule is that the party to whom the mistake is communicated should be protected since it has no means of discovering the mistake. At the outset it may seem unfair to hold someone to a mistake. However, a party relying on the mistake incurs a loss and should be enti-tled to compensation. This is particularly the case when there was no mistake, but merely a change of mind. In practice, it is often hard to know whether a party who claims that it has made a mistake really did so or only changed its mind.[3] In this regard, there are two major problems. First, how can it be established that it was a mistake and not merely a change of mind? Secondly, the suitability of allocating the risk for mistake on the relying party depends on the type of contract and on how soon the mistake is discovered and brought to the other party's attention, ie to what extent the other party had reason to rely and act on the mistake. **9.06**

For some types of contracts, it is in practice not critical if a party changes his mind and wishes to cancel a contract or withdraw an invitation or bid. The basic principle that promises are to be kept (*pacta sunt servanda*) is not crucial for all types of contracts, particularly not when notice of the mistake is provided at an early stage. In other words, when a party makes a mistake and soon afterwards informs the other party about it, the other party does not necessarily incur any losses; this is for example the case with the sale of consumer products such as cars, bikes and kitchen appliances. For such situations, it may seem unreasonably harsh to hold the promisor to his mistaken expression. **9.07**

For other types of contracts it is absolutely vital that the parties be able to trust expressions of promises. This is the case, for example, in auctions and exchanges and for the sale of products exposed to rapid price variations, such as financial instruments and commodities. If there was an opportunity to escape from such contracts by referring to a mistake, parties would be tempted to refer to a mistake when they in reality only made a bad bargain, ie the buyer could **9.08**

---

[2] H Zweigert and H Kötz, *An introduction to comparative law*, 3rd edn (Clarendon Press 1998) 31.

[3] E A Farnsworth, *Changing your mind—the law of regretted decisions* (Yale UP, 1988) *passim*.

claim that he made a mistake when the price falls after the purchase. If such contracts were not upheld due to mistake, the party relying on the promise would incur losses; this is not a proper risk allocation since he was not at fault and had no means of protecting himself from the mistake made by the other party.[4]

9.09 A third type of contract is where an object that is not exposed to rapid price variations causes a party to bind himself to other contracts—with sub-contractors, or suppliers—or in other ways involving taking passive actions, such as not committing himself to another contract due to the first contract making him 'fully booked'. For such transactions also it is recommended that there be a restriction on the ability to escape from contract for mistake.

9.10 It is difficult to uphold a strict division between contracts that are sensitive to mistakes and contracts that are not. Every marketplace needs to determine specifically how to allocate the risk for mistakes.

The problem in electronic commerce

9.11 Electronic communication can be conducted by persons typing messages on their computers in emailing or chat groups, or by an individual communicating with an automated system (such as for instance a website), or by two automated systems communicating (such as for instance in an EDI relationship). Individuals, as well as computer systems, can make mistakes. The individual may slip on the keyboard or with the mouse and click the 'Yes' box instead of the 'No' box, or click on 'send' before the message is intended to be sent, or the figure '4' may be typed instead of '2', or an extra '0' may be typed inadvertently. Furthermore, computer systems may communicate mistakes due to being wrongly programmed or fed with inaccurate information.

9.12 In the 'good old days'—when we mainly communicated by paper messages—many mistakes could be corrected by informing the addressee about the mistake before he received the message containing the mistake, by for instance telephoning before the addressee read the message. The addressee was thus prevented from relying on the mistake. Such a means of correction is rarely possible in the electronic environment since the addressee often receives the message with maximum speed and the addressee acts on it automatically and immediately.

9.13 Two of the main features of electronic communication are speed and automation. Both these features increase the risk of making mistakes that cannot be easily corrected before they reach the addressee and before the addressee takes actions in reliance on the mistake.

---

[4] Furthermore, the whole market will be harmed if there is uncertainty as to the binding nature of offers and acceptances.

General solutions on mistake—a short comparative survey

National law prescribes different rules in relation to mistake. The basic rule is **9.14** normally that the mistaken party is held liable for his mistake. The consequences of liability for mistake vary, as do the exemptions from the rule.

Exemptions

When the party who received the expression of intent understood that it contained **9.15** a mistake in expression, the mistaken party is normally not held liable for it. This rule is clearly aimed at individual transactions. In computerized communication it is difficult to transfer the concept of 'understanding'. One could program a system to identify extreme situations as being improbable (ie as a result of a mistake). When such a system is implemented—or should have been implemented—the party receiving the information could be deemed to have understood that there had been a mistake. It is naturally advisable to use a system that is able to identify strange and unusual messages.

Some jurisdictions do not require actual knowledge (or understanding) of the **9.16** mistake, but stipulate that it is enough that the receiving party *ought* to have understood that there had been a mistake. In practice, this amounts to a lesser burden of proof on the party claiming that knowledge of the mistake was present. The allocation of burden of proof (and how heavy this burden is) varies in different states. In Germany, for instance, the burden of proof is allocated to the mistaken party and is quite heavy.

Another exemption from liability on the mistaken party is where he notifies the **9.17** other party about the mistake so early that the other party has not yet had the opportunity to rely on it. If such notice is provided before the relying party's course of action is influenced (*re integra*), there is no liability on the mistaken party.[5]

Effects of liability for mistake

When the mistaken party is liable for a mistake, national law provides for differ- **9.18** ent effects or consequences. He may be bound by the contract, liable to compensate for the losses due to the false reliance by the other party, and he may be bound but in practice allowed a generous opportunity to cancel the contract. Knowing that there are different effects in different legal systems, it is strongly advisable in international transactions to agree beforehand in the membership terms on the consequences of liability for mistake.

[5] The Swedish Contract Act, Art 39.

Solutions in law to mistake in the electronic environment

9.19 Discussions in the legal literature and recent initiatives by legislative bodies indicate that there may be reason for electronic commerce to adjust the present distribution of liability in connection with mistake and take the mistaken party's need for protection more into account. This trend of imposing less liability on the party making mistakes in expression ('input errors') can be found in the E-Commerce Directive, Article 11(2) under which the:

> service provider shall make available effective and accessible technical means allowing the person communicating with the service provider to identify and correct input errors prior to the placing of the order.

This protection can be contracted out of in business-to-business transactions, but is mandatory for consumers.

9.20 The US Uniform Electronic Transaction Act (UETA) goes even further in protecting the mistaken party. Section 10(2) on 'Effect of Change or Error' provides:

> If a change or error in an electronic record occurs in a transmission between parties to a transaction, the following rules apply:
>
> (1) If the parties have agreed to use a security procedure to detect changes or errors and one party conformed to the procedure, but the other party has not, and the nonconforming party would have detected the change or error had that party also conformed, the conforming party may avoid the effect of the changed or erroneous electronic record.
> (2) In an automated transaction involving an individual, the individual may avoid the effect of an electronic record thus resulting from an error made by the individual in dealing with the electronic agent of another person if the electronic agent did not provide an opportunity for the prevention or correction of the error and, at the time the individual learns of the error, the individual:
> > (A) promptly notifies the other person of the error and that the individual did not intend to be bound by the electronic record received by the other person;
> > (B) takes reasonable steps, including steps that conform to the other person's reasonable instructions, to return to the other person or, if instructed by the other person, to destroy the consideration received, if any, as a result of the erroneous electronic record; and
> > (C) has not used or received any benefit or value from the consideration, if any, received from the other person.
>
> (3) If neither paragraph (1) nor paragraph (2) applies, the change or error has the effect provided by other law, including the law of mistake, and the parties' contract, if any.
> (4) Paragraphs (2) and (3) may not be varied by agreement.

The US Act indeed turns the traditional rule of mistake in expression upside down. It used to be that a mistaken party was bound by his mistake. Under UETA the burden is now shifted to the party relying on the mistake. The purpose is to create a strong incentive for website operators to introduce 'are-you-sure?' boxes in order to slow down the transaction and thereby reduce the risk of mistakes in Internet transactions. When such a security procedure is implemented on the website, the party making the mistake has to bear the risk. It is important to note that this provision is mandatory and parties may not deviate from UETA, section 10 (not even in business-to-business transactions; also note the rule is not applicable to transactions subject to rapid price variations, UETA, section 10, Comment 6).[6]

The UNCITRAL Model Law on Electronic Commerce also addresses the prob-   **9.21** lem of mistake, in Article 13 dealing with the attribution of data messages.[7] This article is relevant to the problems discussed here but is difficult to interpret and understand. According to the *Guide to Enactment*, the intention of the article is not to interfere with the legal consequences determined by applicable rules of national law.[8] However at the same time paragraph (5) stipulates that the

---

[6] A Boss, 'The Uniform Electronic Transaction Act in a Global Environment' (2001) 37 *Idaho Law Review* 68–70.

[7] (1) A data message is that of the originator if it was sent by the originator itself.

(2) As between the originator and the addressee, a data message is deemed to be that of the originator if it was sent:
  (a) by a person who had the authority to act on behalf of the originator in respect of that data message; or
  (b) by an information system programmed by, or on behalf of, the originator to operate automatically.

(3) As between the originator and the addressee, the addressee is entitled to regard the data message as being that of the originator, and to act on that assumption, if:
  (a) in order to ascertain whether the data message was that of the originator, the addressee properly applied a procedure previously agreed to by the originator for that purpose; or
  (b) the data message as received by the addressee resulted from the actions of a person whose relationship with the originator or with any agent of the originator enabled that person to gain access to a method used by the originator to identify data messages as its own.

(4) Paragraph (3) does not apply:
  (a) as of the time when the addressee has both received notice from the originator that the data message is not that of the originator, and had reasonable time to act accordingly: or
  (b) in a case within paragraph (3)(b), at any time when the addressee knew or should have known, had it exercised reasonable care or used any agreed procedure, that the data message was not that of the originator.

(5) Where a data message is that of the originator or is deemed to be that of the originator, or the addressee is entitled to act on that assumption, then as between the originator and the addressee, the addressee is entitled to regard the data message as received as being what the originator intended to send, and to act on that assumption. The addressee is not so entitled when it knew or should have known, had it exercised reasonable care or used any agreed procedure, that the transmission resulted in any error in the data message as received.

(6) The addressee is entitled to regard each data message received as a separate data message and to act on that assumption, except to the extent that it duplicates another data message and the addressee knew or should have known, had it exercised reasonable care or used any agreed procedure, that the data message was a duplicate.

See <www.uncitral.org>.

[8] *Guide to Enactment* 48: see at <www.uncitral.org>.

addressee is entitled to act on the assumption that the data message corresponds to 'what the originator intended to send'. As far as I understand, this is a rule on mistake 'interfering' with applicable rules of national law. Read together with paragraph (4), I come to the conclusion that the addressee may rely on an electronic message as long as he is acting in good faith and is unaware of any mistake. However, as soon as the addressee receives notice of the mistake, he is no longer entitled to rely and act on it. The effects of admitted action and reliance are not clear. It is uncertain whether an acceptance sent by the addressee during the period of time when he is entitled to act on the assumption that the message (in this example, an offer) was correct results in a binding contract or only in compensation for damage.[9] Despite the problems in interpreting Article 13, it is worth noting that UNCITRAL addressed the problem of mistake in electronic communication as early as the beginning of the 1990s. Article 13 in the Model Law illustrates how difficult it may be to find a satisfactory solution to this problem.[10]

9.22 Principles of European Contract Law (PECL) are more traditional in their approach to mistakes and provide that the mistaken party bears the risk for mistakes in expression.[11] Those drafting PECL had probably not identified the new trend in regard to mistakes in the electronic setting. Principles of European Contract Law leave only a limited opening for the risk to shift to the service provider (the website holder), by the reference to 'the mistake was caused by information given by the other party'. It could be argued that the inappropriate design of the website caused the mistake. However, it would have been preferable for PECL to have addressed this question more explicitly.

---

[9] Boss, (n 6 above) 49, 50.

[10] A newly initiated project in the UNCITRAL Working Group on Electronic Commerce deals with the question of mistake in automated trasactions: see Working Paper 96.

[11] Article 4:103 (formerly Art 6.103): Mistake as to facts or law

(1) A party may avoid a contract for mistake of fact or law existing when the contract was concluded if:

    (a) (i) the mistake was caused by information given by the other party; or

        (ii) the other party knew or ought to have known of the mistake and it was contrary to good faith and fair dealing to leave the mistaken party in error; or

        (iii) the other party made the same mistake, and

    (b) the other party knew or ought to have known that the mistaken party, had it known the truth, would not have entered the contract or would have done so only on fundamentally different terms.

(2) However a party may not avoid the contract if:

    (a) in the circumstances its mistake was inexcusable, or

    (b) the risk of the mistake was assumed, or in the circumstances should be borne, by it.

Article 4:104 (formerly Art 6.104): Inaccuracy in communication

An inaccuracy in the expression or transmission of a statement is to be treated as a mistake of the person who made or sent the statement and Art 4:103 applies.

A conclusion as to the new trend

It has been shown here that there is a strong tendency towards making mistakes **9.23** more excusable in the electronic environment than in the paper world. The rationale is that mistakes happen more easily in electronic transactions and that there are, in practice, very few opportunities to use faster means of communication to reach the addressee with a message of correction. Below I shall analyse whether electronic auctions and exchanges are also likely to be influenced by this trend from electronic commerce for greater protection of mistaken parties.

Mistakes in auctions and exchanges online

In auctions and exchanges, whether electronic or physical, we often find harsh rules **9.24** against a participant making mistakes.[12] Contrary to the general trend that mistakes have become more excusable in the electronic environment, I argue that it is necessary for electronic auctions and exchanges to maintain strict rules on mistakes particularly in regard to mistakes in expression and mistakes in assumption, holding participants responsible for their own mistakes. The reason for this view comes from the consequences for the individual deal and for the marketplace as a whole.

However, we also find that a strict rule may be combined with less rigid behav- **9.25** iour by the marketplace participants. An interesting case to illustrate this is the Norex Exchange, a Scandinavian exchange in the equity market. According to its rulebook parties who agree within ten minutes that a mistake has occurred may cancel a deal with the help of the marketplace operator.[13] If the parties do not agree, the liability falls on the mistaken party. One would have imagined that such agreements would take place only rarely. Who would want voluntarily to cancel a favourable deal protected by the rulebook simply because the other party claims to have made a mistake? It turns out in practice, however, that parties often agree to cancel deals due to mistakes. The operator believes that the reason is that there is an unspoken practice to accept mistake as an excuse, perhaps because of the participants' realization that next time it might be the party favoured by the present mistake that makes the mistake.

---

[12] The risk of errors and misinterpretations in out-cry or signalled bids are considerable. The auctioneer may hear wrongly, misinterpret a sign and miss bids: R J R Cassady, *Auctions and Auctioneering* (University of California Press, 1967) 59.

[13] Article 5.7.1 : 'Both On- and Off-Exchange Trades may be cancelled by the Norex Exchange(s) upon request by the Members involved in the relevant Trade. The Members must submit a cancellation request by fax or email on a special form, except for Off-Exchange Trades on Copenhagen Stock Exchange and Iceland Stock Exchange where the Members are required to use the external trade cancel transaction. Such a request has to be submitted within ten (10) minutes after the Trade has been registered in the Trading System. Cancellation of Trades in the Post-Trading Session may only take place during the first ten minutes of the session.' See <www.norex.com.>

9.26   Another interesting feature of the Norex Exchange is that the marketplace operator may cancel a deal whenever it is apparent that a participant has made a
mistake. Article 5.7.3 provides:[14]

> The Norex Exchange(s) may, where so required to ensure the integrity of the Market or in
> other extraordinary situations, cancel a Trade that is the result of:
>
> (i)   an indisputable error or unfortunate mistake which is caused by a technical or manual
>   error at the Exchange(s), Member or Member's clients; or
> (ii)   an, in the opinion of the Norex Exchange(s), indisputable substantial breach of a
>   material provision of law, regulations or the Norex Member Rules; or
> (iii) technical disruptions in the Trading and/or clearing System(s) beyond the Member's
>   control.

The Norex Exchange's rulebook is an example that goes against the general basic
rule on mistake in most legal systems. It is also contrary to my general recommendation that marketplaces with high volatility need strict rules on mistake. It
should be noted that only *apparent* errors might lead to cancelled deals. In practice, only mistaken bids that vary greatly from the current prices are likely to be
corrected by the marketplace operator. Furthermore, there is with this solution
little opportunity for a party to go back on a deal claiming that he made a mistake
whereas he in fact only made a bad deal that he later regrets.

The consequences of mistakes for the individual deal

9.27   The transactions in an auction or exchange are always speculative in nature. Also
transactions that we have come to consider as not being speculative (typically business-to-consumer transactions) contain an element of speculation when made in
exchanges or auctions. The price-setting mechanism, as described above, is such
that there are always variations in each deal. For such markets to function well there
must be strong disincentives on going back on a deal which later turns out to be a
bad bargain. Furthermore, there is an obvious risk that a party who has made a bad
bargain claims that he has made a mistake (in expression or assumption) when in
fact he has only changed his mind. Even when it can be established with certainty
that a party has made a mistake, the effects if the deal were void because of the
mistakes would be unreasonably harsh on the party relying on the mistake. Thus it
is necessary for the marketplace to protect the individual party relying on a mistake.

9.28   We learn from national law that there are two main ways of allocating the risk
for mistakes to the mistaken party. Some states have a 'pure' legal rule stating
that a party making a mistake is responsible for it and must bear the consequences. Other states use the concept of limiting the possibility of claiming a
mistake by imposing a heavy burden of proof on the mistaken party that he made

---

[14] <www.norex.com>.

a mistake in expression. Such a rule with a heavy burden of proof will in practice lead to the same effect as a 'pure' legal rule. I would recommend in electronic auctions or exchanges that there be a rule in law rather than a rule of evidence, but this is really only important from a theoretical point of view.

In combination with the legal regulation on allocating responsibility for mistakes, **9.29** the marketplace is advised also to use technological means for preventing mistakes, for which see below.

The consequences for the marketplace as a whole

The second reason why mistakes should not be made excusable in an auction or **9.30** exchange is the *non-individual* nature of the transaction. A fundamental assumption for most legislative rules on mistake is the close relationship between the contracting parties and thus their knowledge and insight about the other party's actual intentions and assumptions. We frequently see under national laws on mistake that the mistaken party is not bound by his mistake in expression when the other party knew (or ought to have known) about the mistake. In marketplaces where many buyers meet many sellers it is usually not feasible to take into account the knowledge of certain individual participants about other certain participants' implied intentions and inclinations. The reason is twofold:

(a) the need for equal treatment of all participants cannot be satisfied when individuals are better or worse off depending on how much they know about other participants;[15] and

(b) mistakes influence the whole marketplace and the behaviour of all other participants.

It is not feasible—nor sensible—to isolate the individual relationship between two participants when their deal depends on how all other participants (which could be five or thousands) behave and what they knew or understood about the mistake. Were individual knowledge of the actual (but implied) intentions of some of the participants relevant, the bidders would not be treated equally. It would consequently be devastating were individual knowledge of certain bidders' preferences to be of any relevance in allocating liability for mistake.

Electronic auctions and exchanges should design their rules on mistake in such a **9.31** way that makes it irrelevant what some participants know about other participants. From an individual perspective such a rule may appear unreasonably harsh on the party making a mistake. Some jurisdictions may be inclined to deny such a clause effect for unfairness or because it would be denying a party that was aware of the mistake the right to rely on it (promissory estoppel). To achieve the goal of creating a hard and enforceable rule on mistake, it is advisable for the

---

[15] See paras 4.62–4.64 and 6.01–6.04 above.

marketplace expressly to explain in the membership terms the reasons why knowledge of an individual participant is irrelevant.[16]

The importance of using technological means to avoid mistakes

9.32 The hard and unforgiving rule (*rigor commercialis*) on mistake that I have argued is necessary for electronic auctions and exchanges, can be balanced by technological means. The marketplace is advised to design the way transactions are made in such a way as to prevent mistakes from occurring. This could be done in different ways:

9.33 **Fixed bidding levels** in English auctions and audible bid-rotation systems prevent too many zeros from being included in a bid (or too few zeros in the reversed auction). The equivalent in the Dutch auction are the fixed levels of decreasing offers. In the Japanese auction, in sealed-bid auctions, auctions under the Yankee method and in exchanges it is difficult to introduce a similar preventive technical solution. It could also be difficult to have fixed bidding levels in English auctions with time limits and auctions by candle, since this might detrimentally affect the bidding strategies.

9.34 **Question boxes requiring a confirmation** that the bidder really wants to commit himself to the bid he made could provide another solution. This could be introduced in English auctions, Japanese auctions, time-limit auctions, auctions using the Yankee method and sealed-bid auctions, where the request of confirmation could be made to each individual bidder before the result was made known to all participants. The use of confirmation boxes, however, does not function well in marketplaces where the transactions are made very fast. The basic idea behind confirmation boxes is to slow down the speed so as to ascertain the bidder's intention to be bound by what he has just expressed. Naturally, it is not an appropriate concept when the marketplace is anxious to increase the speed. Each marketplace should consider to what extent confirmation boxes are acceptable and efficient for its particular type of transaction. In exchanges where split-second-time speed is not needed such confirmation boxes could also fulfil the function of preventing mistakes.

9.35 A third alternative is to use **technical systems that become accustomed to each participant's individual behaviour**. When a bid is inconsistent with the normal practice of a particular bidder, a confirmation box (or 'are-you-sure?' box) could appear. Such a scheme would require the transactions to be slow enough for some participants to have the time to make the confirmation. On the individual level, it could be advisable to introduce systems under which the individual participants

---

[16] See paras 7.20–7.25 above on interpretation of conditions of sale and membership terms. In a US case of unilateral mistake the mistaken party was not entitled to avoid the contract. 'Were we to hold otherwise we would materially weaken the purpose of the bidding procedure on public contracts' (*Triple A Contractors v Rural Water Dist*, 226 Kan 2d 626, 603 P 2d 184 (1979) referred to in A E Farnsworth, *Contracts*, 2nd edn (Little, Brown & Co, 1990) 694 note 2.

program their maximum/minimum levels to the system and prevent bids outside this range from being communicated to the marketplace.

A fourth way of preventing mistakes in Internet marketplaces is to provide **a panic button**, that is to say, a command whereby the bidders are able immediately to retract their transaction. In marketplaces where split-second time is not necessary, it could be advisable to have a postponement period of a couple of seconds or minutes, before the bid is communicated into the marketplace's order system. When the bidder hits the panic button during the postponement period, nobody has had the opportunity to rely on the bid and it may, consequently, be withdrawn without causing any problems. **9.36**

It is crucial that techniques for preventing mistakes are used in the marketplace. Only by using such techniques can the harsh rules on mistake be legitimized or justified in the eyes of the participants, and also be of help to a judge or arbitrator faced with the task of enforcing a contract which may appear utterly unfair in the individual case. By showing how mistakes are difficult to make in the marketplace—and, consequently, how careless the party making the mistake must have been—it becomes easier to justify that a mistake is not an excuse for the mistaken party. **9.37**

Apart from the need to legitimize the hard rules with technical means, it of course benefits everybody when as few mistakes as possible are made in the marketplace. The methods described above prevent input errors. **9.38**

The drawback of using techniques for preventing mistakes is that they are time-consuming and may cause irritation for the participants as well as affect their bidding strategies. The problem is that the more speculative and volatile a marketplace is, the more important speed is. This, in turn, has the effect that the more important it is for mistakes not to be excusable, the less time there is available to prevent mistakes from occurring. **9.39**

There are techniques by which the individual participant can choose confirmation boxes not to appear. It is probably attractive for professional participants, who are familiar with marketplace procedures and well aware of the risks of making mistakes, to have such an opportunity to gain speed by not being forced to go through prevention procedures. I am, however, inclined to recommend that a marketplace require all participants fully to comply with such technical procedures. This recommendation is based on the need to put all participants on an equal footing and treat them equally when it comes to the speed in transactions and also to create legitimacy for the strict rules on mistake in individual cases. **9.40**

Mistakes relating to the understanding of terminology

Focus so far has mainly been on mistake in expression. Other types of mistakes include misunderstandings in relation to the meaning of terms used in the **9.41** marketplace. The need to standardize the products in exchanges leads to a need to set up standard terminology. It is vital that all participants be familiar with the terminology used. Misunderstandings are much more likely in electronic marketplaces than in traditional marketplaces because of high specialization and the global nature of an electronic auction or exchange. The conditions of sale or membership terms should, I suggest, specify and set out the meanings of the standardized common terminology. It is, furthermore, advisable that before being admitted to use the system and submit bids, the participants pass a simulation test in order to familiarize them with the terminology.[17] Naturally, problems may arise when a participant's system is not synchronized with the system and terminology used in the marketplace.

9.42   There could also be problems in integrating different marketplaces, since they may be using a different ontology (the standard way of expressing terms so that computers can understand them). These have to be reconciled so that a participant in one marketplace can understand the products in another. There is also the potentially huge problem of integrating two different sets of business procedures. These problems are of a technical nature and may to some extent be resolved by EAI technique (which stands for 'enterprise application integration'). When (or if) the technology fails it needs to be supplemented by regulations in the membership terms or conditions of sale allocating the risks in such situations.

The liability of the marketplace for mistakes

9.43   In marketplaces where mistakes occur due to ambiguous procedures, a claim may be directed towards the marketplace operator. An English case about a traditional auction serves as an interesting illustration of the problem. *Friedrich v A Monnickendam Ltd* (1973) 228 EG 1311 concerned a major jewellery auction held in Geneva. The auction was conducted in French (due to a requirement in Swiss law) and many of the bidders were English-speaking. The auctioneer's French was not good and a genuine mistake occurred whereby the bidder believed that a lot had reached 190,000 Swiss francs, when it had in fact reached 290,000 Swiss francs, an extravagantly high price. Under Swiss law the buyer was entitled to avoid the contract on the grounds of mistake. In this case the negligence of the auctioneer (ie that the auctioneer ought to have understood that a mistake was made) was considered. Lord Denning said: 'There was concurrent negligence on the part of the auctioneer. He should have known that the bid of 290,000 Swiss francs was not such a sum as Mr Monnickendam the expert diamond-cutter would knowingly bid. The auctioneer should therefore have assured himself by the clearest words in English that Mr Monnickendam appreciated that the figure was 290,000 Swiss francs.'

---

[17] See ch 16 below.

It is not likely that the same type of mistake as in this English case would be made   **9.44**
in the electronic environment, but one could imagine ambiguity in the currency
or measure of length, size, weight, capacity or dimensions. The English case is
interesting as it points to the duty of the auctioneer to provide an environment
where mistakes are prevented.[18] The case also illustrates that the membership
terms should regulate the liability of the marketplace operator in regard to participants making or relying on mistakes.

Conclusion

Most electronic auctions and exchanges need to have strict rules in their condi-   **9.45**
tions of sale or membership terms, making the mistaken party bound by his
mistake irrespective of what the individual participants know about other participants' mistakes. Furthermore, mistakes should be prevented by technological
means under which they can be avoided before the deal is concluded. Harsh
default rules in the membership terms and conditions of sale do not preclude the
marketplace from allowing parties to agree that the marketplace operator can
cancel deals if a mistake has been made. To introduce this possibility is likely to
contribute to an increased sense of loyalty among the participants and stronger
'social pressure' in the marketplace.

[18] There is a similar Swedish case from the past where the bidder believed that bids should be
made in the currency *riksdaler riksmynt*, but they were supposed to be in the currency *riksdaler banko*
(NT 1864 s 720).

DETERMINATION OF THE WINNING BID AND THE PRICE

Introduction

At first sight it may appear quite simple to determine which bid is the winning **10.01**
bid, how bids are to be matched and what the purchase price is. However, this is
not necessarily simple. This chapter will illustrate some particularly difficult situations and provide recommendations on how to avoid uncertainty by express
regulation in the conditions of sale or membership terms.

The winning bid

There are different methods in use as to how to determine the winning bidder in **10.02**
auctions and exchanges. It is particularly difficult to establish the winning bidder
when the bidders are allowed to submit combinations of bids that are not exactly
the same. Modern technology makes it possible to compare bids that are
combined in complicated ways, and it is then necessary to explain how the
winning bid is determined.[1]

Here are some illustrations of the problems in relation to determining the winning **10.03**
bid.

(a) In the Japanese auction there may be several bidders submitting bids at the
    same level. Who is then proclaimed 'the winner' and what price must that
    winner pay?
(b) In time-interval auctions and auctions by candle the bids often increase in
    number as the time is about to end. It may happen that two similar (winning)

---

[1] See <Tradeextension.com.>

bids are submitted simultaneously. In electronic transactions there are techniques available that make it possible to split seconds and thereby reduce the
risk of simultaneous bids. However, in auctions with many participants
simultaneous bids may still occur.

(c) In Yankee auctions it is not altogether obvious whether the winning bidders
are to pay the amount corresponding to their individual bids or the price
equivalent to the lowest of the winning bids. In <Onsale.com> the bids are
first ranked by price. If there are competing bids at the same price, larger
quantities win over smaller ones. If bids are for the same price and quantity,
earlier bids win over later bids.[2]

(d) In many types of auctions there may appear to be uncertainty as to how each
bid is raised (or lowered in reverse auctions). The increment of each bid is
often predetermined, for instance, when in the English auction the bidder
does not provide a bid and an amount, but only indicates that it is willing to
make a bid, which is raised by a predetermined amount. A quite similar problem is when it is required that a higher bid must be raised with a minimum
amount. In a US case the auctioneer sold to the second highest bidder because
the highest bidder's raise was too small.[3]

The examples show that it may be difficult to identify the winner in auctions and
exchanges. The designers of trading systems may think that this is not a problem
but that the solution is inherent in the system. From a legal point of view,
however, it is highly advisable to state the matter explicitly and regulate the
method for determining the price in the conditions of sale or membership terms.

10.04 Another problem is that nowadays it is possible to submit bids by the use of
different media. Does the Internet auction also accept bids written on paper?
What about bids made orally by telephone or bids made by email and not submitted to the operator's website? The conflicts that may arise from ambiguity in this
respect may be serious since they lead to uncertainty as to who is the best bidder.
Four different conflicting interests appear:

(a) the best bidder of the prescribed bid may claim that he is entitled to the object
put up for auction at his price;

(b) the best bidder of the non-prescribed form may wish to claim that he is (or is
not) entitled to the object;

(c) the invitor may wish to get the very best bid no matter in what form it was
submitted;

(d) the operator may want the very best bidder to win since it entitles the operator to a higher fee, or it may wish the best bidder of the prescribed bid to win
in order to avoid a claim for damages by him.

---

[2] M Korybut, 'Online Auctions of Repossessed Collateral under Article 9' (Fall 1999) *Rutgers
Law Journal*, Vol 31, No 1, 33–129 at 41.
[3] *Andersson v Wisconsin Cent Ry* 107 Minn 296, 120 NW 39 (1909).

It is advisable that the membership terms or conditions of sale stipulate which **10.05** types of bids are acceptable. It is not really possible to make any general recommendation on this issue. It must be decided in each individual case whether it is appropriate to allow different media for submitting bids. To avoid uncertainty it ought to be expressly regulated in the conditions of sale or membership terms how a bid should be submitted. It is advisable to stipulate explicitly that no other medium than the ones listed are acceptable for submitting valid bids.

Furthermore, it is advisable to introduce a scheme for situations where there is no **10.06** obviously appropriate way to select the winner. This is particularly so in the case of simultaneous bids. The ways to deal with such a problem are to:

(a) open a re-auction;
(b) divide the goods (when possible);
(c) toss a coin (or by other means randomly select a winner); or
(d) have a pre-decided objective rule (stipulating, for instance, that the bidder located geographically closest to the auctioneer is awarded the merchandise).[4]

The price to pay

The price to pay the seller

There is no single way of determining the price in a contract concluded in an **10.07** auction or exchange. Different schemes are used. It may be uncertain what price the winning bidder is supposed to pay or get paid. The winner sometimes does not have to pay the amount corresponding to the bid he submitted but only the equivalent of the second best bid or the second best bid increased by a fixed amount. This is not infrequent in relation to sealed-bid auctions, English auctions and reverse auctions where some or all bidders have submitted bids in advance. It may also happen in audible-bid rotation systems.

A corresponding problem in determining the price may occur in Dutch and **10.08** Japanese auctions where there may be a question about how large a lot the winning bidder is obliged to take Here are three examples illustrating different methods of determining the price:

(a) In the traditional sealed-bid auction and English auction, the winner is the highest bidder and the winner pays the amount which he bid. This format is the *first-price* auction. The sale occurs at the first or highest price bid. In a first-price auction, the bid price determines both who is the winner and how much is to be paid. There is an incentive for a bidder to set a price towards his maximum limit, in order to avoid missing out on a chance to buy the item

---

[4] R J R Cassady, *Auctions and Auctioneering* (University of California Press, 1967) 89.

for less than it is worth to him. However, once the bid is within a range where the bidder will be the likely winner, he will scale his bid price downwards in order to avoid paying more than he has to.[5]

(b) William Vickrey invented another type of auction, the *second-price sealed-bid* auction, often called the Vickrey auction. In this model, the winner pays the runner-up's bid price. Bidders submit their bid prices without seeing rival bids. The winner is the bidder with the highest price. However the winner pays the price bid by the runner-up bidder, ie the price of the second best bid. In a second-price auction, the bid price does not determine how much the winner pays. Rather, it determines only who the winner is. Because the price to pay is set by another bid, the winner's bid price makes no difference to the price the winner pays. Notice the connection between the second-price auction and the English auction. In both models, the winner is the bidder who places the highest value on the object, but the winner pays a price controlled by the value of the runner-up. There is one difference in detail—in the English auction, the winner may pay the runner-up's value plus the bid increment, whereas in a second-price auction, the winner always pays the runner-up's value.[6]

(c) In double auctions and exchanges problems may arise in relation to the matching of bids. If the exchange has certain hours during which it is closed, the opening of the exchange can be problematic because of overlapping of bids. This occurs when the sellers offer to sell at lower prices than the buyers are willing to buy at. Matching bids at the level where most deals can be closed often solves this problem. All bids that overlap are matched at that level. There are two alternative methods. Under the first method, all bids over the matching level are matched at the level that they offered. Under the second method, the whole volume is placed at the lowest price. In the latter case, the strategy for the buyers is then to provide a high bid, but if everyone uses this strategy the total price is increased. After this first opening matching, ordinary continuous bidding starts based on the reference price established by the initial matching procedure. Since the bids are transparent, overlaps do not occur—no buyer is likely to submit a bid higher than the lowest seller's bid.

These examples show that it is not always obvious what price the buyer should pay. Consequently, it is necessary explicitly to regulate the method for determining the price in the conditions of sale or membership terms.

Fee to the marketplace

10.09 When the marketplace charges a fee according to the amount of the winning bid, it may be uncertain as to whether the fee to the marketplace is to be paid by the

---

[5] R E Hall, *Digital Dealing: How e-markets are transforming the Economy*, 2001, at <http://www.stanford.edu/~rehall/LinoleumReport.pdf>, 39.   [6] ibid, 40 ff.

seller, the buyer or both. This ought to be explicit in the membership terms. Furthermore, it is advisable that the fee is known to the participants while the auction procedure is pending, so as to avoid any potential misunderstandings. In this context it should also be clear whether the liability of the seller or buyer towards the marketplace is joint and severable or not.

Apart from transparently disclosing any fees to be paid by the parties to the **10.10** marketplace, the membership terms should specifically address the problem as to the operator's fee where the buyer does not pay the purchase price to the seller or when the deal is later cancelled.[7]

Has the operator of an electronic auction or exchange any right to use the sold **10.11** property as a lien for its fees? How does the operator establish a security for his fees? In traditional auctions the auctioneer had control over the goods and many legal systems allowed the auctioneer a lien over them. In electronic auctions where the goods are transferred directly from seller to buyer, the operator's fee becomes a non-secured claim. If the operator manages the payment transaction, there is good opportunity to make sure that the fee is paid out of the purchase price.

To whom should a successful buyer/bidder make the payment? To the operator or **10.12** to the seller? This ought to be made clear explicitly in the conditions of sale and be synchronized between seller and buyer, seller and operator, and buyer and operator. When the membership terms and conditions of sale are silent on this point it is difficult to make a general comment about whether the operator is entitled to collect payment and what the consequences are when payment is given to the wrong party. In many jurisdictions the buyer risks having to pay twice if he pays to a wrong party.

Taxes and fees to third parties

When an Internet marketplace is open to the whole world, the participants and the **10.13** marketplace itself may be exposed to the tax laws of all states. It is extremely difficult to regulate the tax consequences in the membership terms or conditions of sale. This study will not be examining questions of tax law. However, it is worth noting that taxation in relation to auctions is only rarely covered in multilateral or bilateral tax agreements. Since auctions have traditionally been geographically located in a certain state, it has not been important to regulate them at an international level. The emerging electronic auctions and exchanges will change the close territorial connection and we are likely to see future multilateral or bilateral tax agreements for auctions and exchanges. Until this actually

---

[7] Two English cases on real estate illustrate the problem: *Peacock v Freeman* (1888) 4 TLR 541, CA and *Shinner v Andrews and Hall* (1910) 26 TLR 340, CA. Both cases are from B W Harvey and F Meisel, *Auctions Law and Practice*, 2nd edn (OUP, 1995) 46.

happens, those involved in electronic auctions and exchanges should be aware of the risk of chaotic and unpredictable tax consequences of transactions made on such auctions and exchanges.

10.14 National law often requires that certain fees be paid to authorities or other bodies. Such fees are difficult for electronic auctions and exchanges, since it is uncertain to what extent the national law in this respect is applicable to Internet transactions. As far as possible, it is therefore advisable that the conditions of sale or membership terms address which of the participating parties and the marketplace operator is ultimately to bear the cost of such fees. Because of the uncertainty in accurately predicting the exposure to these national fees, it is difficult to make provision for distributing liability.

CONFIRMATION BY THIRD PARTIES

The problem

Sometimes the law stipulates that a deal concluded by auction must be confirmed **11.01** by a third party. Such provisions may cause huge practical problems as to what happens when a deal cannot be completed because there has been no confirmation or there has been a delay in the confirmation. The problem is exacerbated in an international setting as confirmation requirements usually vary across jurisdictions and thus may apply differently to different bidders—and this is of course against the fundamental feature of an efficient auction where all bidders should be treated equally. As said in paragraph 6.01 above, there is a general problem of a private international law nature as to which law is the applicable law when the transactions are made in one (or no) state, the participants come from many different states, and the object put up for auction is located in yet another state (or located only in cyberspace).

Examples in national law

There are examples of national legislation requiring approval or confirmation for **11.02** transactions made by auctions. To illustrate the problem, I will give two examples of legislation requiring confirmation by third parties. The examples show that national law requirements on confirmation can either be based on the situation of the participants, or on the nature of the object put up for sale. The consequences in the examples vary according to the legal situation of the parties during the time when it was not yet clear whether confirmation was given or not. The consequences also vary according to when confirmation is denied.

(a) Under US law, the court must approve sale of goods sold by a trustee of a bankrupt's estate, in accordance with the Bankruptcy Act § 70(f). The court must ascertain that the goods are not sold for less than 75 per cent of the appraised value. The bidder is bound and may not withdraw during the period up until confirmation has been granted or denied by the courts.

(b) Buyers of Norwegian farmland need permission from the state. In auctions where the highest bidder is considered to have offered too much for the property—that is to say, more than the farm is deemed to be able to finance by itself—the farm is allocated to the bidder who has provided the highest 'appropriate' bid. It may seem strange that the farm is not allocated to the highest bidder for the 'appropriate' price, but such a solution would only encourage bidders never to stop outbidding each other.[1]

Solutions in the conditions of sale or membership terms

11.03 The marketplace must take notice of national law requirements for third-party confirmation. This can be done by different means:

(a) by forbidding transactions that require confirmation by third parties to be made at the site;

(b) by informing the bidders of such regulation and of the risks involved when permission is not granted;

(c) by restricting the types of bidders to categories not needing permission, ie deny access for participants from certain states;

(d) by connecting the marketplace to a confirming third party who may quickly provide automated confirmations whenever possible.

It may be difficult to work out appropriate consequences for those invitors that neglect membership terms which stipulate that they are not allowed to participate when the object put up for auction requires third-party confirmation, or neglect an obligation to disclose the need for such third-party confirmation. Possible sanctions to impose include threatening such participants with future access denial or fees to be paid to the marketplace. The same goes for bidders who participate in auctions without disclosing that they need special permission or confirmation to finalize the deal.

11.04 The problem is that national confirmation rules are often stipulated for the protection of third parties and apply irrespective of what is said about the applicable law in the membership terms or conditions of sale. Alternatives (a) and (c) above are not feasible solutions when the marketplace is not really in a position to know about all specific regulations that may exist in different states. For such situations, it may be advisable to stipulate that those participants who suffer loss due to a permission not being granted or to a time delay in the permission procedure, shall be compensated by the party who ought to have disclosed that permission was needed.

---

[1] See Angrefristloven nr 11/1972 at lov nr 5/1998; and tvangsfullbrydelseloven nr 86/1992, 11–44 tredje ledd; S Breckhus *Omsettning og kreditt* 2, 2nd edn (Universitetsforlaget, 1994) 416, and the Norwegian case NRt 1999 s 673.

Alternative (b) above ensures transparency and is to be recommended. It makes **11.05** each participant aware of the potential risks that may follow from national law. However, the transparency will most certainly create confusion when the information is about general risks that cannot be specified and thus cannot be reduced by insurance or other means.

Alternative (d) is obviously only feasible in marketplaces that are restricted in the **11.06** geographical sense and about certain types of transaction. Furthermore, this alternative presupposes that the confirming body is able to handle confirmations electronically and automatically and is willing to collaborate with the marketplace.

In electronic auctions and exchanges that are limited to a specific type of object, **11.07** it is usually easier to make a prediction as to what extent national law imposes confirmation procedures. Consequently, alternatives (a), (b), and (c) can be used in combination or individually for such markets.

ILLEGAL TRANSACTIONS

Transactions forbidden in national law

In national law we find that certain objects may not be sold and that it is forbidden **12.01** to provide certain services. States have different rules as to what transactions are allowed. Areas often restricted are pornography, copyright material, alcohol, and pharmaceuticals. We also find restrictions in relation to export control laws and trade sanctions. Other areas forbidden in national law may be transactions deemed by a national state to threaten interests of a religious or political nature. A well-known example is the French law forbidding the sale of Nazi memorabilia. Yahoo.com's auction site enables private persons (consumer-to-consumer) to offer Nazi memorabilia to be sold by auction. This is not forbidden under US law. Of course, the combination of differences in national law and the difficulty in establishing where the transaction is made, the nationality of the involved parties and the nature of protective intention behind the national restriction makes it particularly hard to determine the applicable law. Furthermore, it is in practice difficult for the national state wishing to enforce its restrictions to give them international force.

Not only does the subject matter of restrictions vary among states, so do the **12.02** consequences for breach of the restrictions. Sometimes the transaction may be void, at other times there is the sanction of a legal penalty. Sometimes only the seller or the buyer is held responsible, at other times the marketplace operator is held liable for facilitating the illegal transaction.

The problems, seen from the perspective of the marketplace, are the following. **12.03**

(a) The marketplace wishes to attract liquidity (many participants) and is thus unwilling to restrict access solely on the ground of the participants' nationalities.
(b) Even when it is technically possible to restrict access to certain participants acting from certain states, it is still difficult to know the individual participant's true nationality.
(c) It may be costly and cumbersome for the marketplace to discover all the potential restrictions in each and every state.

(d) It is normally a question of mandatory law and, consequently, cannot be solved by regulation in the membership terms or conditions of sale.

12.04 The marketplace is advised to be cautious and ensure that the transactions do not violate restrictions in national law. In allowing access, the participants should be obliged to certify that the transactions are permitted under the law in the states (1) where he lives, (2) where he holds his citizenship, and (3) where he makes the transaction. If the participant has made inaccurate certifications about these matters, the membership terms should stipulate that he be denied further access and that he compensate the marketplace operator for any losses caused by illegal transactions carried out in the marketplace. As between the contracting parties, the conditions of sale should stipulate that when the parties are acting under different jurisdictions—one where there is a restriction and another where there is no restriction—the party making an illegal transaction should compensate the other party for any losses caused by the 'semi-illegal' transaction.

12.05 It should be noted that the content of the membership terms and conditions of sale are not always upheld by the national state the law of which imposes a restriction. The national law may provide for mandatory consequences making the contractual agreement invalid. The national law may also protect the rights of third parties, for instance within the area of intellectual property. In a German case the operator was held liable for trade-mark infringement made by a participant.[1]

Ownership—transactions in stolen goods

12.06 Several investigations show that many products sold in electronic auctions are stolen or illegal software. In traditional auctions there is also a great risk of trade in stolen goods. Traditionally, this has been prevented by national legislation which for example requires the auctioneer to supply catalogues of the objects put up for auction or which provides for mandatory licensing of the auctioneer. In order to attract trustworthiness, the operator of an Internet marketplace is well advised to implement schemes that prevent sellers from making transactions with objects that they are not entitled to sell.[2]

12.07 There are reasons other than ensuring trustworthiness for ascertaining that the objects in the marketplace are not stolen. In some jurisdictions the operator has a

---

[1] *Landgericht Köln Urteil vom 31 Oktober 2000—33 O 251/00*. See further on German law, G Spindler and A Wiebe, *Internet-Auktionen. Rechtliche Rahmenbedingungen*, (C H Beck, 2001). For US law see M R Geroe, 'Agreements between an Electronic Marketplace and Its Members' (Fall 2001) *The International Lawyer*, Vol 35, No 3, 1069 at 1074.

[2] See Software & Information Industry Association (SIIA) and its recommended policies and procedures for the auction of software on Internet auction sites with three proposals for policies to prevent auctioning of pirated software: <www.siia.net/piracy/programs/suggestedonlineauctionpolicies.htm>.

responsibility for the seller's right to transfer ownership of the object.[3] If so, the buyer may claim compensation from the auctioneer when the buyer does not acquire the title to the goods. In the area of consumer law such responsibility of the operator may be mandatory. Mandatory legislation presents a problem since the interest of equal treatment of all bidders is not met. A bidder who can rely on its own mandatory national law stipulating that he has an action against the marketplace operator where the goods are stolen is in a better position than a bidder without such national legislation to protect him. This will make it impossible to make their bids commensurable (wholly comparable). As said earlier, the fact that different national laws may apply to the same transaction is troublesome.[4]

The operator is recommended to: **12.08**

(a) introduce a procedure that prevents stolen goods from being sold in the marketplace;

(b) stipulate in the membership terms that the operator does not take any responsibility for the seller's right to transfer title to the goods;

(c) stipulate in the membership terms that if, under mandatory national law, the operator is liable to compensate a buyer due to the seller's lack of a right to transfer title in the goods, the seller must compensate the operator; and

(d) stipulate in the membership terms that sellers selling goods without proper title will be blacklisted or expelled from future participation.

---

[3] For US law see Geroe, (n 1 above) 1073, explaining that the auctioneer normally bears responsibility towards the buyer that the seller is the owner of the goods, unless the auctioneer has disclaimed such liability.

[4] See ch 4 above.

SETTLEMENT

Introduction

It is fairly straightforward to design a marketplace where bids are matched. It is **13.01** quite another matter to create a system whereby performances of obligations of the buyer and seller are settled. A minimalist marketplace may only offer an opportunity for the buyer and seller to meet and conclude the deal. After this, it is up to the parties themselves to settle the transaction. Other marketplaces may offer more extensive services including the transfer of payment and transfer of title. To a great extent the range of services provided by the marketplace depends on the types of objects put up for auction, ie, it is easier for the Internet marketplace to administer the transfer of title when the transactions deal with stocks that are electronically registered than to transfer the title of antique furniture in the seller's physical possession. This chapter will provide a brief introduction to the general problems related to settlement and illustrate some ways of limiting the problems in the Internet environment.[1]

Credit risks

In traditional physical auctions the goods and payment are exchanged simulta- **13.02** neously. This is difficult to accomplish in the electronic environment. Who is at risk—the seller or the auctioneer—when the goods are handed over to the buyer before payment and payment is subsequently not provided? Also who—the seller or the auctioneer—is at risk when the buyer cannot pay (and the goods are not handed over to the buyer) and the goods sold in a reopened auction are sold at a lower price?[2]

---

[1] For German law see G Spindler and A Wiebe, *Internet-Auktionen. Rechtliche Rahmenbedingungen* (C H Beck, 2001), chapter on '*Hilfe des Auktionshauses bei der Vertragsabwicklung*'.

[2] English cases referred to in B W Harvey and F Meisel, *Auctions Law and Practice* 2nd edn (OUP, 1995) 56, illustrate how uncertain this is.

13.03   There are several risks related to the settlement procedure. The payment must be transferred to the seller. In most electronic transactions it is not possible to exchange the goods and payment simultaneously and thus either party must take a credit risk.[3] There are several ways of transferring this risk to a third party, for example a bank or an escrow service.[4] This study will not examine the use of third parties in this respect.

13.04   When third parties are not appointed to limit the credit risk, the participants will be anxious to evaluate the creditworthiness of the other party. The marketplace may have prerequisites or conditions for participation in the marketplace including guarantees of the participant's financial status. The marketplace may even require each participant to provide security for its potential obligations before submitting an invitation or a bid. Another means of evaluating the creditworthiness of the participants is to allow them to rate each other.[5] Yet another solution may be to connect the marketplace to relevant white lists or black lists, or to enable the individual invitors to exclude certain bidders from participation.[6]

13.05   Sometimes, although this is rare, the marketplace assumes the risk of a failed settlement. This is to say, when one party commits a breach of contract the marketplace will compensate the suffering party and in turn direct a claim against the party in breach.[7] Marketplaces sometimes provide an escrow service, under which the buyers deposit money in trust with the marketplace operator who will not release the funds until certain conditions are met or verified. The more restrictive the access controls, the more likely it is that the marketplace will be willing to undertake responsibility for non-performance by the sellers and buyers.

13.06   This question of creditworthiness is also related to anonymity. When the identity of the bidders is not disclosed even after the deal is concluded, the transaction cannot be enforced and it is thus natural that the marketplace assumes liability in relation to the breached party. In some business-to-business exchanges the identity of the successful bidder is revealed automatically as soon as the transaction is concluded.[8]

13.07   When the marketplace has undertaken responsibility for breach of contract by either party, the calculation of damages should be specified in the membership

---

[3] For the risks involved in auctions directed at consumers see P Selis, A Ramasastry and C S Wright, 'Bidder Beware. Toward a Fraud-Free Marketplace—Best Practices for the Online Auction Industry', a Report for the State of Washington Attorney-General's Office (17 April 2001) at <http://www.law.washington.edu/lct/publications.html#bidder>.

[4] See <eCredit.com> and S Ellis, 'Financial Services for B2B Exchanges' in A Sculley and W Woods (eds), *Evolving E-markets: building high value B2B exchanges with staying power* (ISI Publication Ltd, 2000) 169–75. See also PayPal (<www.paypal.com>). Tradenabler provides escrow services (<www.tradenabler.com>). See also Selis, Ramasastry and Wright (n 3 above) 21.

[5] As in the consumer-to-consumer system provided by eBay.

[6] <FruitLine.com> has such a scheme. See on this issue paras 16.16–16.25 below.

[7] In consumer auctions such 'insurance' programmes are also offered. See Selis, Ramasastry and Wright (n 3 above) 19.

[8] See further on identity of counter parties paras 14.28–14.33 below.

terms. Damages for wrongful cancellation and termination are often quite straightforward to handle since there is an easy way of calculating the damages due to the ever-present marketplace. Calculating the damages and making hypothetical assumptions has always created many problems in settling disputes. When the sold object can easily be resold in the marketplace these problems are largely resolved. This in turn leads me to the conclusion that the restrictions put on the remedy of termination (rescission) need not be imposed in regard to transactions made in an electronic marketplace with high liquidity, ie where deals are concluded continually at close intervals.

It is advisable that the extent of the marketplace's responsibility for breach of contract by the seller or buyer be explicitly regulated in the conditions of sale or in the membership terms in order to avoid any uncertainty.   **13.08**

Place of delivery

With the trade of physical objects, it is usually necessary to transport them to the buyer. It is crucial that the conditions of sale point to the place of delivery, since the rules in national law may differ and thus create uncertainty and unequal treatment of bidders. It is advisable to make a reference to the well-established transportation clauses as defined by INCOTERMS where the liabilities of the seller and buyer are stipulated in a variety of ways.[9] For auctions initiated by the seller I would strongly recommend using the INCOTERM Ex Works, under which delivery takes place at the seller's premises, in order to achieve maximum equality in the evaluation of submitted bids and complete certainty as to where the liabilities of the parties shift. Conversely, in a reversed auction initiated by the buyer it is advisable to use the INCOTERM DDP, under which delivery takes place at the buyer's premises. When the marketplace uses the ICC Model Sale Contract for manufactured goods the INCOTERMS automatically form part of the terms. It is generally advisable that marketplaces use the ICC Model Sales Contract when the objects sold are manufactured goods as it provides a balanced allocation of risks between the seller and buyer.   **13.09**

As noted above, the parties may wish to negotiate on terms other than the price. One term that is frequently negotiated is the delivery term. In an auction or exchange it is difficult to allow for simultaneous bids to be submitted on price and delivery terms. In individual negotiations it is easier to provide electronic schemes where the delivery terms form part of the negotiations. There are, however, programs available for electronic auctions making it possible to submit bids covering several issues besides the price and making it possible for the invitor to evaluate and compare the bids.[10] The only feasible solution when such   **13.10**

---

[9] See <www.iccwbo.org>.   [10] See <Tradeextension.com>.

sophisticated programs are not used is that the delivery term is fixed beforehand and fixed also with respect to the geographical location of delivery.

Transfer of title and retention of title

13.11 The transfer of title often cannot, by agreement between the parties, affect third parties whose rights are infringed. This regulation varies across national laws. Is the fall of the hammer equivalent to notice? Is the transfer of the physical object necessary? Can the contract protect the buyer from the seller's creditors? National law differs widely as to the question of how retention of title is established and to what extent the mere contract between seller and buyer is sufficient to protect the seller's claim against the buyer's other creditors.

13.12 The marketplace is advised to consider carefully how the participants can meet requirements in national law for an effective transfer of title and retention of title. The marketplace may introduce links to national registration bodies or strive towards meeting national requirements for publicity. There is, as yet, no international harmonization of law with respect to property law.[11]

13.13 Furthermore the marketplace is advised to direct the participants' attention to the problems that may occur in relation to transfer of title and retention of title in the international context.

[11] Quite a few initiatives have been taken, such as the UNIDROIT ongoing work on a Mobile Equipment Convention (see <www.unidroit.org>) and the Teams on Security and Transfer of Ownership in the Study Group for a European Civil Code. See also BOLERO at <www.bolero.net>.

INFORMATION

Introduction—generally about information in marketplaces

A marketplace can be seen as a forum for conveying information. There are many **14.01**
points to note about the type of information which can be shared in the marketplace. It is essential to provide accurate information about the object put up for
auction or exchange so that it can be accurately identified and evaluated. This is
a necessary requirement, which may entail awkward problems in relation to standardization.[1] The marketplace may also have information facilitating evaluation of
the object for sale. Evaluation depends on the quality of the object and on its
present market value. The market value is determined by the current state of
supply and demand for the object—the marketplace could provide such information. There are also other surrounding circumstances that might affect the evaluation. All these various categories of information will be examined from a legal
point of view in detail below.[2]

---

[1] About the need for shared ontologies, see M Bichler, *The Future of e-Markets*, *Multidimensional
Market Mechanisms* (CUP, 2001) 2.6.3.
[2] The membership terms or the conditions of sale may regulate the question of what participants
may or may not do with information provided by the marketplace (with respect to confidentiality,
copyright and redistribution). See R Lee, *What is an Exchange? The Automation, Management and*

14.02   It is not unusual for national legislation to require a marketplace to provide certain types of information. This is particularly so for exchanges in financial markets and auctions. Regulation of mandatory information is mainly intended for the protection of weaker parties by preventing detrimental insider trading and transactions in stolen goods—in short, to maintain trust and confidence in the marketplace.

14.03   A marketplace may choose to provide and reveal only limited types of information beyond that required by mandatory regulations. How much and what type of information is dependent on what would attract the most transactions and what liability the marketplace is willing to undertake for inaccurate or incomplete information. Research suggests that the information needs of a market grow whenever the market becomes larger and more complex.[3] According to this theory, information on prices and rates is not sufficient. It is also important to provide the participants with information about underlying values and sophisticated applications for portfolio analysis as well as other information affecting their decisions.

14.04   For some marketplaces it may, however, be more attractive to the participants when only very limited information is made available.[4] The following transcript from <NYTimes.com> is an example:[5]

> A new company called SplitTheDifference (<www.splitthedifference.com>), based in New Haven, hopes to cut through these difficulties with an online negotiating tool that it plans to operate on its own and license to other companies. 'Think about the typical business deal,' said Barry Nalebuff, a management professor at Yale and a game theorist who is chairman of SplitTheDifference. 'There's all this gamesmanship: "You go first," "No, you go first." Do I tip my hand or do I bluff? Well, we've acted strategically in designing the game so the players don't have to act strategically when they play it.' SplitTheDifference operates like a combination neutral mediator and escrow service while creating an environment that safeguards buyers' and sellers' confidential information: reserve prices, identities and willingness to sell. 'This approach promises to get people to resolution very quickly,' Mr. Nalebuff said. 'It also allows people to do transactions on the Web without posting prices and to put different prices to different players.'

Information related to the quality of the object

14.05   A problem in relation to electronic transactions is that it is usually not possible to provide an opportunity for physical inspection of the object for sale. For some

---

Regulation of Financial Markets (OUP, 1988) 106 ff. Some of the problems related to protecting confidentiality by contractual arrangements are described at ibid 155–8.

[3] C Ciborra, *Teams, Markets and Systems* (CUP, 1993) 188.

[4] R E Hall, *Digital Dealing: How e-markets are transforming the Economy*, 2001, at <http://www.stanford.edu/~rehall/LinoleumReport.pdf>, 10, explains the often important interest of sellers that prices are not disclosed. See for an example of how to deal with non-disclosed information M Naor, B Pinkas and R Sumner, 'Privacy Preserving Auctions and Mechanism Design' Proceedings of 1st ACM conference on E-Commerce (EC-99), 3–5 November 1999, Denver, Colorado.   [5] 13 December 2000.

types of objects physical inspection is not important, eg financial instruments, standardized commodities and services. For other types of objects, however, we are more accustomed to touch and smell them before making an assessment of their value, eg used cars and fresh flowers. For some auctions national legislation may require that there must be an opportunity for physical inspection. This is the case under the law in some US states in relation to the sale of repossessed collateral.[6]

The dual benefits of expanding the pool of potential bidders beyond the **14.06** geographical location of the sale site and reducing the costs of attracting remote buyers should be balanced against the risks of diminished marketability and poor purchase prices when there is no reasonable opportunity to inspect the goods put up for auction. A limited solution would be to permit 'cyberspace inspections' using web technology, ie communication through text, sound pictures and videos. Another solution would be to provide grading information. It does seem likely that as electronic marketplaces continue to develop, commercial customs and practices for selling goods will change to require less reliance on physical places and physical inspection in order to sell goods.[7]

Quality assessment referring to standards

The marketplace must accurately describe the object put up for auction. This is **14.07** fairly easy to do when the product is standardized. More and more sectors are becoming standardized and, consequently, it becomes possible to trade the products efficiently in auctions and exchanges without physical inspection. In areas where there are no general standards developed, the marketplace itself can provide standard descriptions and thereby undertake an important role as a provider of standards. It is recommended that the conditions of sale or membership terms clearly identify to what standardization schemes they refer. When competing standards exist, it is very important that the participants' attention is specifically directed to what standard the marketplace applies.

Grading information

For certain types of products standardization is not sufficient. This is the case for **14.08** used goods and for objects where 'the smell and feel' are important, such as flowers, fish, tobacco and used cars. Despite the difficulties in describing the qualities of such products, it has turned out that they can be successfully sold in electronic auctions and exchanges without prior physical examination by the potential

---

[6] As to this problem see M Korybut, 'Online Auctions of Repossessed Collateral under Article 9' (Fall 1999) *Rutgers Law Journal*, Vol 31, No 1, 33–129, particularly at 119. Also German law requires the possibility for inspection but there are exemptions to this rule: see T Stögmöller, 'Auktionen im Internet', 9/1999 *K&R Heft* 391–6.   [7] Korbybut (n 6 above) 112–23.

bidders. In electronic auctions of goods requiring examination it is quite common that an independent person makes a quality evaluation at the premises of the goods. Such an evaluation is often called 'grading information' or 'certification'.

14.09   AUCNET (Internet auctions for used cars in Japan) use a successful method of establishing the quality of the used cars before putting them up for auction. The operator makes inspections and provides a standardized product representation together with a grading scale from 0 to 10.[8] A similar method is used by Autodaq (a US auction site selling used cars business-to-business). Grading information administered by the operator is also common in Dutch flower auctions where quality control and specification are of the utmost importance.[9]

Description by photograph

14.10   Another means of providing information about the object for sale in electronic auctions is to show pictures or allow for 'cyberspace inspections' in three-dimensional pictures or videos where the buyer may 'move around' by the use of a camera lens. The experience from Dutch flower auctions indicates that video shows of the flowers put up for sale did not function as well as using independent evaluators to grade the quality of the flowers.[10]

14.11   Whatever method is used it must be tailored to the object in question. When photographs are used to describe the object put up for auction, it should be remembered that they may constitute misleading descriptions.[11] A photo is a representation similar to a description in words and can serve as a basis for the seller's liability (see below).

The seller's liability for defects

14.12   When the traded object does not correspond to the description, grading information or photographs, the seller is usually liable to the buyer for compensation. National legislation often lays down detailed rules. If the transaction involves a private buyer and a commercial seller national law rules are often mandatory under protective consumer legislation. Outside mandatory consumer law, the parties are normally free to decide the liability in the conditions of sale. We often see in such conditions that the seller is liable for defects but that the remedies available to the buyer may be limited.

---

[8]   See <www.JapanCars.com/aucsat.htm>.

[9]   E van Heck and M Ribbers, 'Experiences with Electronic Auctions in Dutch Flower Industry' (1997) *Electronic Markets*, Vol 7, No 4, 29 at 33.   [10]   ibid, 33.

[11]   See the English case *Atlantic Estates v Esekiel* (1991) 2 EGLR 202 where a photo depicted a thriving wine bar but the liquor licence had been revoked. See also the English case *Marylebone Property Co Ltd v Payne* (1994) EG 156.

It is not uncommon for conditions of sale to be provided by the seller and one-   **14.13**
sidedly favourable to him. A marketplace that is anxious to attract buyer participants should be careful before introducing unbalanced conditions of sale in this
respect. The need for trustworthiness should encourage marketplaces to provide
fair and balanced conditions of sale. It is rare that buyers actually make an examination of the conditions of sale and carry out a thorough risk analysis before
accepting them. By using documents drawn up by neutral organizations, the
marketplace may indicate that the conditions of sale are acceptable to the buyer
(without him having to read and analyse them). A contract that may be used is the
ICC Model Sales Contract that has been adopted for use in the web-based environment.[12]

The operator's liability for defects

The allocation of risks in relation to wrongful description and grading may vary.   **14.14**
Thus it is essential to regulate the responsibilities explicitly in the conditions of
sale and in the membership terms. The disappointed buyer may have a claim
against the seller, or against the evaluator, or against the marketplace, or against
all or some of them. There are three main problems or questions to be answered.

(a) How should the evaluation be made (what is the appropriate standard of
care)?
(b) How can the economic detriment be established? Should the buyer be entitled to damages and price-reduction and/or termination?
(c) Should the operator have any responsibility for defects in the goods?[13]

Generally, it is not advisable to make the marketplace operator liable for misleading photographs unless the photograph was taken by an agent on behalf of the
marketplace operator.[14]

National law varies concerning to what extent the auctioneer or marketplace   **14.15**
operator has any liability for defects in the goods.[15] For instance, under Spanish
law the auctioneer is liable for hidden defects jointly with the seller when the
auctioneer fails to provide appropriate information about the object put up for

---

[12] <www.iccwbo.org>.   [13] See paras 17.07–17.11 below.
[14] I do not address problems in relation to copyright.
[15] For an investigation as to the responsibility of US art dealers, see K B Singer, ' "Sotheby's sold
me a fake!"—Holding Auction Houses Accountable for Authenticating and Attributing Works of Fine
Art' (Spring 2000) *Columbia-VLA Journal of Law and The Arts* 437. In US law a case holds that in
the absence of wilful intent to deceive and where the auctioneer provides a catalogue with a disclaimer
of any genuineness, a buyer assumes the risk as to the genuineness of the good purchased (*Weisz v
Parke-Bernet Galleries Inc* 351 NYS 2d 911 (1974)). US case law also establishes that when an
auctioneer discloses the identity of his principal (the seller) to the buyer, no liability rests on the
auctioneer for breach of warranty of quality (*Hayes v DPS Nichols Co* 64 Pa Super 273 (1916)). For
German law see G Spindler and A Wiebe, *Internet-Auktionen. Rechtliche Rahmenbedingungen* (C H
Beck, 2001) ch II.1; and B Heiderhoff, 'Internetauktionen als Umgehungsgeschäfte' *MMR* 10/2001.

auction.[16] There are also variations in national law as to what extent the market-place operator may exclude such liability. In Swedish law, for example, an auctioneer cannot exclude his liability for hidden defects in the goods when the buyer is a consumer.[17] When the marketplace operator's liability is mandatory and protects some bidders but not all, once again we are faced with the problem of not being able to receive commensurable bids.[18] For this reason, the market-place operator should be careful not to allow participation by bidders from states protected by mandatory legislation. Another way of making the bids commensur-able is for the marketplace operator generally to assume liability that corresponds to the most protective legislation.

Information related to the trade— transparency about price, quantity, and bids

Asymmetric information—transparency against opaqueness

14.16 From a theoretical point of view, the price-setting mechanism is most efficient when all participants in the marketplace have equal access to information. However, often participants wish to take advantage of superior knowledge and may be unwilling to participate in marketplaces where information is conveyed openly to all. In order to attract the highest liquidity, every marketplace should assess to what extent their particular sector is interested in having information openly provided in the marketplace.[19]

14.17 When the marketplace decides only to convey a small amount of information some participants may have more knowledge than others, depending on how much cost and effort each individual participant is willing to spend on obtaining the relevant information on their own. In some marketplaces some participants are treated unequally in the sense that only privileged participants get access to certain types of information, or get earlier access to information than others do. It is much more controversial when the marketplace provides information to only some participants than when the marketplace does not provide information to anyone. In both situations we see that the participants act with asymmetric infor-mation, but the fact that the marketplace treats its participants differently is likely to cause irritation among the participants who do not have full access to the infor-mation. Another positive consequence of transparent activities is that the risk of bribery, undue influence and corruption is lower. Thus, the trustworthiness of the marketplace may be damaged when information is not distributed equally and transparently.

---

[16] Ley 7/1996 *de Ordenación del Comercial Minorista* Arts 58 and 61.
[17] Consumer Sales Law § 1 (SFS 1990:932).   [18] See para 4.65 above.
[19] Hall, (n 4 above) ch 2, describes different bidding strategies depending on how transparent the price-setting mechanisms are.

As described in chapter 5 above, a fundamental feature of an exchange is that **14.18** prices are revealed to all participants. Whether this is a necessary feature of an auction is uncertain (sealed-bid transactions may or may not be defined as auctions).[20] When the price-setting mechanism is disclosed to all participants, they are able to assess supply and demand and thus take into account the present situation and evaluate the object for sale accordingly. There has been an intense debate as to whether it is acceptable, efficient and fair not immediately to disclose the prices in financial markets. Outside the scope of mandatory regulation a marketplace may provide more or less information to certain participants. There is a difference between information *during* the bidding and transparency *after* the deal is closed. When information about prices is provided immediately after each individual deal is concluded, there is in effect less opaqueness, since the participants may decide their bids with the reference price of the last deals.[21]

Unequal treatment of different participants is sometimes considered to be prefer- **14.19** able and to protect the efficiency in the price-setting mechanism. The main argument in favour of allowing non-disclosure of prices in an exchange has been expressed this way: 'Transparency is good in reasonable doses and fundamental to the very existence of exchanges. But excessive transparency will harm very large orders. These are likely to move prices, and when the reason becomes known, competitive activity will intensify the movement. Therefore, very large orders benefit from opaqueness, and when it is regulated away, they start avoiding the exchange, thereby downgrading its liquidity and the information it provides.'[22] According to this opinion, the strategic non-disclosure of prices and quotes is a central element in all markets' architecture.[23] When all participants are aware of the risks and opportunities in relation to the price-setting mechanism, they can adjust their behaviour and strategies accordingly.[24]

An exchange may also choose to restrict transparency in an attempt to let its **14.20** members obtain better information than other market participants, and thus enhance liquidity in the exchange. When the information in the exchange is non-transparent

---

[20] See paras 4.90–4.95 above.

[21] Hall, (n 4 above) 66, with a reference to US Treasury auctions.

[22] R Laulajainen, *Financial Geography—a Banker's view* (Göteborg, 1998) 129.

[23] In some OTC markets the very large transactions are subject to a one-hour delayed notice in the market. The reason is that the market dealer is exposed to a great risk when putting up a larger order, which he needs to allow for. This is so in the London Stock Exchange (Laulajainen, (n 22 above) 129). In traditional auctions like fish the amount of available fish is not always disclosed (R J R Cassady, *Auctions and Auctioneering* (University of California Press, 1967) 250 ff).

[24] In many auctions the bidders are uncertain about the number of participants. McAfee and McMillan showed that if bidders were risk averse and had constant or decreasing absolute risk aversion, numbers uncertainty led to more aggressive bidding in a first-price sealed-bid auction (R P McAfee and J McMillan, 'Auctions and Bidding' (1987) 25 *Journal of Economic Literature* 701. However, numbers uncertainty had no effect on bidding strategies under the three other auctions rules. Consequently, numbers uncertainty favours the first-price sealed-bid auction (M Bichler, *The Future of e-Markets, Multidimensional Market Mechanisms* (CUP, 2001) 104).

it gives traders who have access to the information an advantage over those who do not. Any cross-subsidies arising from such a market structure, such as from retail to institutional traders, will however generally be unsustainable, if it is possible for alternative trading systems to cater solely to the groups of market participants that are being exploited.[25] Opaqueness is also thought to hinder off-exchange deals and thereby create a competitive advantage for the marketplace.[26] The more information provided in the exchange, the easier it is to make off-exchange transactions.[27]

14.21 Although opaqueness has its advantages, transparency is generally and increasingly regarded as beneficial to financial markets. Many believe that it enhances the liquidity of markets. Most market participants are likely to favour environments where all participants to the greatest extent possible have the same opportunity to access correct information. Furthermore, most participants are likely not to prefer marketplaces that do not accurately reflect the presently available supply and demand. Wholly automated exchanges tend to allow full and immediate information.[28] Much experience gained in stock exchanges is also useful in Internet marketplaces where objects other than financial instruments are being transferred.

14.22 The US Division of Market Regulation has claimed that liquidity for both listed and OTC equities increased following the adoption of the quote and trade transparency rules, despite initial resistance from both the exchanges and the NSAD. The Division thus dismissed the claim that transparency increases the position risk of dealers.[29] Having a national legal regulation imposing mandatory transparency leads to difficult problems in relation to the non-national nature of Internet marketplaces.[30] Even if the nation state is unable to impose and execute mandatory information regulations, in most cases market forces will lead to transparency in marketplaces.[31]

Some practical examples of transparency policies

14.23 Hall provides the following examples of how transparency about the bidding process is dealt with in practice:

[25] Lee (n 2 above) 261.   [26] ibid, 257.   [27] ibid, 99.

[28] Laulajainen (n 22 above) 132. <FruitLine.com> immediately shows all offers that are put into the system, for how long they are available and when they are closed. In its marketing FruitLine particularly points to the transparency in the exchange as an advantage compared with the traditional non-exchange trade in fresh products.

[29] Lee (n 2 above) 257. According to the SEC, extensive information about prices and size must be communicated by the broker or ECN (electronic communication network) to the exchange.

[30] See ch 2 above.

[31] Lee (n 2 above) ch 11, explains the problems related to mandatory transparency regulation.

1. In FreeMarkets' answer to transparency the bidders know the prices bid by other bidders in time to respond during the auction. Nothing is ever disclosed about the terms of the actual deal.

2. For eBay transparency is quite different. The only information about bids disclosed during an auction is the current auction price. Because the current price may be below the maximum price of the leading bidder, bidders don't know how much they would have to bid in order to become the winner. Also, bidders cannot find out about the most important bids, those that come in at the last second. After the auction closes, eBay publishes the maximum prices of all bidders except the winner. The bidders can find the winning price of the winning bidder on eBay by displaying the closed auctions in the product category that is of interest.

3. It is often helpful for other participants in an e-market to learn the prices paid in earlier transactions. However, the participants' interest in disclosure may not coincide with the interests of the marketplace operator. Visteon, a large maker of car parts, can extract the lowest price from a supplier of plastic mouldings by keeping the price secret, but other buyers and sellers of similar mouldings would benefit from knowing that price. Such a solution may hamper the other participants' trust in the marketplace.

4. In the US stock markets, the public interest acts through the Securities and Exchange Commission (SEC), the regulator of the stock market. It is illegal for anyone but private individuals to trade stocks without reporting the trade ('printing the trade,' as they say on Wall Street) to the New York Stock Exchange, Nasdaq or another exchange. Although other players would be interested in knowing the terms of deals, the balance favours keeping the terms secret in many cases. Even in the stock markets, the require-ment for printing trades makes it easy for dealers to see what their rivals are up to. If the dealers in a stock make an agreement to keep the spreads wide, they are much more likely to spot cheaters and enforce the agreement if they all can see the terms of each trade.

5. In a procurement consortium such as the automotive industry's Covisint, secrecy about trades is virtually mandatory. First, the members of the consortium compete with each other and do not want their rivals to know about their costs. Second, anti-trust law frowns on any arrangement under which a group of companies work jointly to depress prices paid to suppliers—this violates the same laws that forbid conspiracies to charge customers high prices. To avoid falling foul of anti-trust regulations, a consortium must have convincing firewalls isolating one member from another.[32]

Another example is Priceline. The company lets buyers specify what they want to buy and name their price. Priceline then forwards the bids to participating sell-ers, who can anonymously accept the request or reject it.[33] The lack of trans-parency in the marketplace ensures that sellers do not jeopardize the prices in their conventional sales channels. **14.24**

These examples show that price development is not always disclosed to bidders. The bidding may be conducted in several stages. During each stage the bidders submit bids without knowing what bids others submit. In the next stage only active bidders are allowed to participate and once again to submit bids, now **14.25**

---

[32] Hall (n 4 above) 20–22.   [33] <www.priceline.com>.

knowing the bids in the previous bidding stage. This continues until there are only
two bidders left. The reason why it may be favourable to use such a method is to
slow down the process thus enabling the bidders to feel less stressed and instead
have ample time to make decisions that are well thought out.

14.26 Since this study focuses on law, this is not the place to elaborate further on how
best to balance transparency against opaqueness. The reason for this introduction to the topic is simply to point out the need for the marketplace operator to
consider carefully how information about prices, supply and demand should be
displayed. When a marketplace decides to distribute information unequally
among its participants, it is crucial that this policy is openly communicated to all
participants. Some participants may find this irritating, but the crucial trustworthiness may be adversely affected if the policy is kept secret and only discovered
later. The marketplace must also ensure that national legislation does not forbid
unequal distribution of information, which is often the case in financial markets.
It is also important that the membership terms regulate the liability of the
marketplace operator where the information presented is inaccurate or incomplete.[34]

14.27 It is not unusual for the marketplace operator to stipulate that the marketplace is
shut down where there are informational problems. For instance, Norex
Exchange—a Scandinavian exchange for equities—has the following provision
(4.8.1):[35]

> Where the general public does not have access to information regarding a particular
> Instrument subject to equal terms and conditions or does not have access to information
> regarding the issuer of an Instrument to a sufficient extent, or where special cause exists,
> the Primary Norex Exchange may effect a trading halt (suspension) in the Instrument.

Information on other matters

Identity

14.28 The identities of the invitors and bidders are often not revealed in the marketplace. There are many reasons for not disclosing identities. Individual participants may not wish to publicize their present need to sell or buy or to disclose their
bidding strategies. Furthermore, the identity of a bidder may influence the price-
setting mechanism in an auction or exchange.[36] It may also be that information
about participants' identities infringes rights of privacy.[37]

---

[34] See paras 16.40–16.42 below.   [35] See <www.norex.com>.

[36] J Garfinkel and M Nimalendran, 'Market Structure and Trader Anonymity: An Analysis of
Insider Trading', Working Paper, August 2000; E Theissen, 'Trader Anonymity, Price Formation and
Liquidity', Working Paper, 2000.

[37] The aspect of Internet privacy is not examined in this study.

In independent exchanges, the general custom is to keep the identities of potential **14.29** traders secret until the deal is made. An important motivation behind this is to force the parties to make their deal on the exchange and to pay its fees. On eBay, where all parties are identified before the auction closes, it is common for the seller to propose an off-eBay deal, to limit the fee that eBay earns. It is difficult to enforce eBay's rule against this scam.[38] Yet another reason for not disclosing the identities of the bidders is to prevent auctions rings and collusion. In an investigation made by Bichler a surprising number of English auctions went against traditional English auction theory by providing the bidders with each other's contact information, making it possible for rings of colluding bidders to form.[39]

Sometimes, however, it is essential that the participant's identity be commun- **14.30** icated, for instance when the bidder wishes to convince the market that he does not have any inside knowledge.[40] In the stock market, this problem is common, because of inside information. An insider in a company may be selling because he knows the secret that the company has lost an important customer. As a buyer, you would like to know whether the seller is an insider or just another outside investor. In a sell-side auction, bidders benefit from knowing the identity of the seller. First, they care about the reputation of the seller in regard to describing the product accurately and for delivering it as promised. Secondly, sellers may have special knowledge that makes buying from them dangerous. A key factor in favour of concealing the identity of bidders in a sell-side or a buy-side auction is discouraging collusion among the bidders. If one bidder in a procurement auction sees a particular rival pushing the price down, the bidder can contact the rival and propose eliminating the competition by dividing the market in advance.[41]

Each marketplace should consider to what extent the identities of participants are **14.31** to be disclosed. There are many different modes of disclosure available.

(a) In so-called 'sunshine' trading a participant is offered the choice of releasing information about the trades he wants to undertake, what type of trader he is, and, in some instances, his identity.[42]

(b) In the London Stock Exchange the order book does not disclose the identity of the order originator. The trading partners, however, will learn their mutual identities in the London Stock Exchange. Trades in the e-market through dealers are partially anonymous—the dealer knows what broker a trade comes from, but not the identity of the customer.

(c) At <FruitLine.com> the identity is not revealed until after a deal is concluded. At <FruitLine.com> all the participants are listed. When a participant making a bid is unwilling to conclude a deal with certain participants

---

[38] Hall (n 4 above) 21.   [39] Bichler (n 1 above) 133. See paras 15.08–15.15 below.
[40] Lee (n 2 above) 99.   [41] Hall (n 4 above) 21.
[42] Lee (n 2 above) 99, with a reference to POSIT.

he may individually exclude them from the list and thereby avoid his bid being matched with the excluded participants.

(d) At Arbinet-thexchange all members are treated anonymously and settlement is made via the neutral marketplace operator.[43]

(e) In FreeMarkets the buyer initiating a procurement auction knows a great deal about the bidders/sellers, because they first go through a bidder qualification process where the auction sponsor checks their credentials. A bidder does not know other bidders' identities, neither during the auction nor afterwards.

(f) A bidder-buyer can learn the eBay name and email address of the seller and all the bidder buyers at any time. Participants can check the feedback and ratings about any of them. Bidders can find the identity of the winning bidder on eBay by displaying the closed auctions in the product category that is of interest.

(g) In a captive business-to-business e-market, the identity of the company sponsoring an auction is known for sure, or is known to be a member of a consortium. As a general rule in those markets, the identities of the bidders— would-be suppliers or purchasers—are not disclosed at any time. Hall believes the primary motivation for secrecy is to discourage collusion among the bidders.[44]

14.32 When the system does not allow anonymous bidding, it should be remembered that it is in practice often possible for participants to use a proxy bidder. To discourage such behaviour, the membership terms may impose severe sanctions against it. As a provision on mandatory disclosure of identity is fairly easy to avoid, a marketplace ought to have only limited rules on mandatory disclosure of identity.

14.33 When identity is hidden and there is no possibility of excluding certain persons or companies from concluding a deal, some participants may wish to withdraw from a concluded contract when the counterparty's identity later becomes known. It is recommended that the conditions of sale and membership terms explicitly address to what extent such withdrawal is permitted. Generally, it is not advisable to allow withdrawals due to the identity of the counterparty, because the need to protect the speculative element and to prevent parties from cancelling contracts because of a bad deal are often more significant than the need to protect participants from concluding contracts with unwanted counterparties.[45]

Surrounding factors

14.34 The marketplace may provide information about surrounding factors not directly connected to the object put up for sale. Examples of the type of information that may be of interest are the weather, political conditions, scientific reports, indexes

---

[43] <www.thexchange.com>.   [44] Hall (n 4 above) 21.   [45] See ch 8 above.

and financial analyses. Often such surrounding information is welcomed by the participants and may help the marketplace to acquire liquidity. Sometimes inaccurate information about surrounding matters may be used to manipulate prices.

It is essential that the membership terms clearly stipulate to what extent the **14.35** marketplace operator is obliged to provide this type of information and to what extent the marketplace operator may be held liable if the information is inaccurate or incomplete. One site contains the following reported disclaimer:[46]

> Please be aware that the information on this site contains forward-looking statements that are based on our management's beliefs and assumptions and on information currently available to our management. Forward-looking statements include, for example, the information related to our possible or assumed future results of operations, business strategies, financial plans, competitive position, potential growth opportunities, the effects of future regulation and the effects of competition. Forward-looking statements include all statements that are not historical facts and can be identified by the use of forward-looking terminology such as the words 'believes,' 'expects,' 'anticipates,' 'intends,' 'plans,' 'estimates,' or similar expressions. Forward-looking statements involve risks, uncertainties and assumptions. You should understand that many important factors, in addition to those discussed elsewhere on our site, could cause our results to differ materially from those expressed in our forward-looking statements. Additional information concerning these risks and uncertainties and other factors you may wish to consider are provided in the 'Risk Factors' section of our Prospectus filed with the Securities and Exchanges Commission. Actual results may differ materially from those expressed in these forward-looking statements, and you should not put undue reliance on any forward-looking statement. All information contained on our site, including forward-looking statements as well as historical information, is meant to be effective as of the date the information is posted on our site. We do not have any obligation to update information after such date or to disclaim the accuracy of information should facts change after the date of posting.

It is not uncommon for third party 'watchdogs' to provide information about **14.36** prices outside the marketplace.[47] The responsibility for such 'watchdogs' is closely related to the general IT-law debate on the responsibility for URL links. When the Internet marketplace provides links to other websites with information, it is often clear that the marketplace undertakes no responsibility for the accuracy of the information to be found at these other websites.[48] However, in order to avoid any ambiguity in this respect, it is advisable to regulate the question of responsibility explicitly in the membership terms. In a market exchange for pharmaceutical products the following disclaimer is reported:[49]

---

[46] S Bain and F Lawrence Street *B2B Exchanges: Critical issues*, Practicing Law Institute, 21st Annual Institute on Computer Law.

[47] This is for example done by a company called ClearCross.

[48] I do not address the question as to what extent it is permissible to refer to other web pages or to what extent such linking needs to disclose that linking is made.

[49] Bain and Street (n 46 above).

You understand we act as a passive conduit for, and do not control, or attempt to control, any information, data, text, software, sound, photographs, graphics, video, messages or other materials, that you, or any other user of the Site, uploads, posts or transmits to or through the Site (the 'User Content'). You acknowledge and agree that you are solely responsible for any User Content that you upload, post or transmit to or through the Site, including, but not limited to, its legality, reliability, accuracy, integrity, appropriateness and originality. You represent and warrant to (operator) that you will not upload, post or otherwise transmit any User Content to or through the Site that: (1) is unlawful, harassing, libellous, defamatory, abusive, threatening, harmful, vulgar, obscene, profane, sexually oriented, racially offensive, inaccurate, or otherwise objectionable; (2) violates any law, rule or regulation; (3) infringes, misappropriates or otherwise violates any copyright, trademark or other intellectual property right, right of privacy, right of publicity or any other right of any entity or person; (4) encourages conduct that could constitute a criminal offence, give right to civil liability or otherwise violate any applicable local, state, national or international law rule or regulation; (5) contains software viruses or any other computer code, files or programs designed to interrupt, destroy or limit the functionality of any computer software or hardware or telecommunications equipment; or (6) advertises or otherwise solicits funds or is a solicitation for goods or services. We reserve the right to refuse or delete any such User Content from the Site. You further represent and warrant to (operator) that you will not: (1) impersonate any person or entity, including, but not limited to, a (operator) official, or falsely state or otherwise misrepresent your affiliation with any person or entity; (2) use the Site for chain letters, junk mail, 'spamming,' solicitations (commercial or non-commercial) or bulk communications of any kind, including but not limited to, distribution lists to any person who has not given specific permission to be included in such a list; (3) 'stalk' or otherwise harass another user of the Site; or (4) collect, store or use personal or other information about other users for any commercial purpose or obtain direct financial gain. For example, use of user information for mass marketing is strictly prohibited. You grant (operator) and its affiliates a perpetual, irrevocable, world-wide, royalty-free, non-exclusive right and license to use, reproduce, modify, adapt, publish, translate, create derivative works from, distribute, publicly perform and publicly display the User Content you upload, post or transmit to the Site (in whole or part) and/or to incorporate it in other works in any form, media, or technology now known or later developed. You also grant each user of this Site the right to access, display, view, and reproduce such User Content for personal use. You represent and warrant to (operator) that you have the right to grant the licenses stated above. You acknowledge and agree that you may not upload, post, reproduce, or distribute any User Content on or through this Site that is protected by copyright or other proprietary right of a third party, without obtaining permission of the owner of such right. Any copyrighted or other proprietary content distributed with the consent of the owner must obtain the appropriate copyright or other proprietary rights notice. The unauthorized submission or distribution of copyrighted or other proprietary content is illegal and could subject you to personal liability or criminal prosecution. If you believe that your copyrighted work or the copyrighted works of others have been infringed, please send a written notification of claimed infringements to (operator) with the following information: (a) an electronic or physical signature of the person authorized to act on behalf of the owner of the copyright; (b) a description of the copyrighted work that you claim has been infringed; (c) a description of where the allegedly infringing material is located on the Site; (d) your telephone number, address and email address; (e) a statement that you have a good-faith belief that the disputed use is not authorized by the copyright owner, its agent or the law and (f) a statement by you, made under penalty of perjury, that the information in your notice is accurate and that you are the copyright owner or authorized to act on the copyright owner's behalf. Upon receipt by (operator) of notice of a claimed copyright infringement containing the information specified above, (operator) will promptly remove the allegedly infringing material from the Site. (Operator) shall have no liability to any user of the Site for the removal of any such material.

So far we have addressed the liability of the marketplace operator for inaccurate **14.37** or incomplete information.[50] It is also advisable to make explicit provision in the conditions of sale between buyer and seller for the consequences of inaccurate information. When one of the parties has relied on inaccurate information provided in the marketplace—directly or by URL links—he may claim that the mistake is not binding on him. Most national law stipulates that such mistakes in assumptions or motives are not excusable. Also in electronic auctions and exchanges it is normally advisable to allocate the risk for mistakes in assumptions or motives to the mistaken party.[51] To eliminate any uncertainty in this respect it is recommended that the conditions of sale clarify this issue. A market exchange for metal products is reported to use the following disclaimer:[52]

Member is solely responsible for information which it posts on the Site. (Operator) does not endorse any information posted on the Site by Member or third parties. Member agrees that (operator) has no obligation to monitor the content on the Site, the Exchange or links to other Websites, and expressly disclaims any responsibility of (operator) to filter any such content. However, we may take any action with respect to such information we deem necessary or appropriate in our sole discretion if we believe such information may give rise to liability to us or other parties or interfere or impair our relationship with any Member. Information posted at the Site (a) must not be fraudulent or involve the sale of stolen items; (b) must not infringe any third party's rights of publicity or privacy; (c) must not violate any applicable law, statute, rule or regulation; (d) must not be obscene, indecent or contain pornography; (e) must not be defamatory, trade libellous, threatening or harassing; and (f) must not link directly or indirectly to or include descriptions of products or services that (i) are prohibited by this Agreement or (ii) are concurrently listed for sale on a Website other than the Exchange. In addition, you may not post on the Site or sell in the Exchange any product or service which, by paying us our Transaction Fee, could reasonably be expected to result in a violation of any applicable law, statute, rule or regulation.

---

[50] As to German law see G Spindler and A Wiebe, *Internet-Auktionen Rechtliche Rahmenbedingungen* (C H Beck, 2001) and the operator's liability to provide accurate information about the participants' identities. In US law a case indicates that a provider of a stock exchange index presented at a Chicago commodity exchange was not liable for an erroneous calculation of an index, since it had disclaimed such liability: *Rosenstein v Standard & Poor's Corp* 636 NE 2d 665, 666 (Colo Ct App 1970).   [51] See ch 9 above on mistakes.
[52] Bain and Street (n 46 above).

Checklist for types of information

14.38 Lee provides a helpful list of 18 types of information. The list is designed for financial markets but can also be used for other markets:

1. price of last trade;
2. quantity of last trade;
3. time of last trade;
4. identities of parties to last trade;
5. high, low, opening and closing, trade prices;
6. aggregate price data and price indices;
7. cumulative trade volume;
8. best bid and ask prices;
9. quantities at best bid and ask prices;
10. identities of parties who placed those orders;
11. bid and ask prices behind the best prices;
12. quantities at those prices;
13. identities of parties who placed those orders;
14. high, low, opening and closing, mid-quote prices;
15. requests for quotes;
16. identities of parties who requested quotes;
17. number of individuals logged onto the system;
18. identities of those individuals.[53]

To this list could be added information about:

19. the object put up for auction;
20. surrounding factors;
21. the participants' track record (black or white listings);
22. the identity of the participants allowed to participate.

[53] Lee (n 2 above) 98.

PRICE MANIPULATION

Introduction

It is of fundamental importance that the participants do not influence the price-setting mechanism by fake invitations and bids or by establishing auction rings or other types of collusion. Furthermore, it is important that false information that may influence price setting is not distributed to the marketplace. Manipulation of the price-setting mechanism is sometimes facilitated when the marketplace provides information about the flow and variations in the supply and demand in the marketplace. In the following paragraphs, some types of price-manipulation activities will be presented together with suggestions as how to avoid or regulate them in electronic auctions and exchanges.[1]   **15.01**

Phantom bids ('puffing' or 'shilling')

A 'puffer' is a person—normally the seller—who makes fictitious bids to drive   **15.02** up the price of an item and force unsuspecting bidders to increase their bids to acquire the item. This is also called 'bid shilling'. The concept is that when only one bidder remains in the auction the seller can try to drive up the auction price higher by bidding against the sole remaining bidder. In traditional English auctions (oral) it is not uncommon for the auctioneer to pretend that he has received a counterbid in order to push the would-be buyer to a higher level, with the effect that, when unsuccessful, the object remains in fact unsold.[2] In reverse auctions the puffing works so that the shilling buyer submits lower bids against

---

[1] See for a more in-depth analysis of strategies that may amount to price-manipulation, R E Hall, *Digital Dealing: How e-markets are transforming the Economy*, 2001, at <http://www.stanford.edu/~rehall/LinoleumReport.pdf> ch 5.

[2] R J R Cassady, *Auctions and Auctioneering* (University of California Press, 1967) 160.

the sole remaining seller. Should fictitious (or phantom) bids be allowed in electronic auctions?[3] Bichler states, 'of course, shilling is not allowed in online
auctions . . .'.[4] However, as will be explained below, it is not always necessary to
forbid such behaviour.

15.03   The problem of bid shilling is closely related to the invitor himself making a bid
or having stipulated a hidden reserve price.[5] As analysed in paragraphs 8.26–8.44
above, the disadvantages and benefits for allowing such behaviour vary across
different marketplaces. The important thing is that it is clear from the membership terms to what extent puffing is allowed. Because of the risk for the invitor
that the transaction does not lead to a final deal when no bids are provided after
the invitor's bid, there is generally enough disincentive on the invitor not to try
to influence the price-setting mechanism unduly by submitting bids himself.
Hence, it is often not necessary to forbid puffing or fictitious bids.

15.04   A particular feature of puffing is that the fictitious bid is provided by the auctioneer and not by the invitor. This suggests that the auctioneer is not a neutral party
providing a marketplace to both sellers and buyers, but mainly functions as an
agent for the invitor. In some jurisdictions auctioneers are considered to be agents
of the seller and not neutral intermediaries. An electronic marketplace is consequently well advised to clarify whether the marketplace operator has a neutral
role or is acting mainly on behalf of some participant or group of participants.
When the marketplace intends to take a neutral role it is essential to ensure the
impartiality of the operator and it is not advisable that the operator be allowed to
influence the price-setting mechanism by making fictitious bids. Another situation where it may be advisable not to allow puffing is when the auction is not held
by a neutral intermediary, but initiated by the invitor himself. From a contract
negotiation point of view it may even be considered to be an act of bad faith when
the invitor/operator submits bids and as such will not be allowed under some
national law.[6] When the invitor/operator intends to submit fictitious bids it should
be clear from the membership terms or conditions of sale that such puffing is
allowed. When the rules in this respect are transparent, the bidders are aware of

---

[3] The following US case is a significant example. Two men who defrauded eBay buyers out of
$450,000 in an attempt to sell a fake painting purportedly by artist Richard Diebenkorn have pleaded
guilty. Kenneth Walton and Scott Beach pleaded guilty in federal court in Sacramento, California to
eleven counts of fraud between them. They reportedly used illegal 'shills' (self-bids) to inflate prices
in more than half of the 1,100 auctions they hosted on eBay between late 1998 and May 2000. A third
man indicted in the scam, Kenneth Fetterman, 33, remains a fugitive. As part of their plea, Walton and
Beach agreed to pay back nearly a combined $100,000 and to refrain from engaging in any Internet
auctions for a period of up to three years. Walton was also disbarred as an attorney in California. The
two men had faced up to five years in prison for each of the criminal counts but authorities agreed
under a plea bargain to recommend a lower sentence if the pair co-operated. Further information may
be found at <http://www.ecommercetimes.com/perl/story/9045.html>.

[4] M Bichler, *The Future of e-Markets, Multidimensional Market Mechanisms* (CUP, 2001) 135.

[5] Hall (n 1 above) 51 ff, describes the strategies and dangers related to the invitor participating in
the bidding process.   [6] UPICC, Art 2:17 (<www.unidroit.org>).

the potential risk that the invitor/operator is manipulating the price-setting mechanism, and are thus able to develop their bidding strategies accordingly.

The conditions of sale or membership terms should furthermore consider whether **15.05** to allow bids by the invitor or operator to be submitted anonymously or whether it must be disclosed to the participants that it is the invitor or operator that submits the bids. When there is a risk that the participants' trust and confidence in the marketplace is harmed by puffing or fictitious bids, it is recommended that such activities be made transparent to all participants.

Actions destroying the flow

Many exchanges and auctions are dependent on an efficient flow, ie that the trans- **15.06** actions are conducted without interruption and at a continuous speed. The transactions are many and the participants are often well-trained in handling the speedy procedure and adjust their bidding strategies accordingly. When the flow is disturbed, the price-setting mechanism may be affected. An individual bidder may destroy the flow of the auction by interrupting it.[7] The interruption or disturbance may take the form of unnecessarily hitting the 'panic button' or revocation of invitations and bids. It is, however, not likely that such disturbances will have any significant impact on the price-setting mechanism. Naturally, it is important that actions distorting the flow are prevented by having an efficient technological structure for marketplaces. Apart from this, it is normally not necessary to take precautions to protect the flow of the transactions.

The expected increasing use of electronic agents may disturb the price-setting **15.07** mechanisms. It is easy to imagine a participant having several electronic agents and that the aggregated effect of these agents leads to (unintended) price distortions. It is recommended that the membership terms only allow accredited types of electronic agents so that it can be ascertained that they are compatible with the structure of the individual marketplace and do not contribute to price distortions.

Auction rings and collusion

There is a well-known phenomenon from traditional auctions that bidders in **15.08** auctions make arrangements beforehand to manipulate the price-setting mechanism. Auction rings are agreements between bidders to co-ordinate their actions to increase their surpluses above non-co-operative levels. The main concern is that the sharing of information by competitors could lead to price fixing or other

---

[7] See Cassady (n 2 above) 169, 170.

anti-competitive behaviour. There are also examples of collusion taking place in electronic auction marketplaces.[8]

15.09   When collusion and auction rings occur, the efficient price-setting mechanism is destroyed and this, in turn, negatively affects the fundamental trust in the market-place. Hence, it is crucial for the operator of the marketplace to prevent collusion. The conditions of sale or membership terms may forbid collusion and auction rings. It is advisable to stipulate severe consequences where collusion is discovered (ie high fees and/or exclusion). Furthermore, the opportunity for sharing information among the participants should be limited so as to prevent collusion.

15.10   We also often find in national law legislation against collusion. For example, the purpose of the English Auction Act 1969 is to prevent bidding agreements. When there is an unlawful bidding agreement the seller-invitor may avoid the contract and is entitled to damages covering the difference between the sale price and the true fair price.

15.11   In practice, however, it is often difficult to discover collusion. Sophisticated technological programs are available that detect unusual behaviour. Such programs are frequently used in financial markets to identify insider trading. The market-place is advised to use such technological help when transactions in the market-place are exposed to a risk of collusion.

15.12   Another practical problem is to distinguish between permitted agreements to buy the goods on joint account and unlawful bidders' rings. This problem is well known in traditional auctions. For example, in the US a promise not to bid in an auction is not enforceable on the ground of public policy and anti-trust law. However, an agreement between two or more persons to bid for their collective benefit is valid because it is ancillary to the relationship of a joint venture.[9] In the electronic marketplace the conditions of sale or membership terms may regulate to what extent participants are allowed to act on joint account and whether such joint actions must be disclosed to the marketplace.

15.13   There are also technological means for preventing collusion. Different types of price-setting mechanisms are exposed to collusion in different ways. Some types of auctions increase the risk for collusion. Robinson makes the point that a collusive

---

[8] On 7 June, eBay officials confirmed that the FBI has begun a probe into whether users have committed fraud by bidding up the prices of each other's items on eBay. Apparently eBay is actively assisting the authorities in their investigation of self-bidding, also known as 'shell bidding'. The investigation began after a May auction of a painting with an opening price of 25 cents. The description of the painting suggested that it may have been an undiscovered painting by Richard Diebenkorn, whose works sell for millions. The painting was finally sold to a Dutch collector for $135,805. However, e-Bay voided the sale saying it had detected 'shill' bids during the course of the auction. The FBI is reportedly investigating whether the seller was part of a ring of people fraudulently cross-bidding on each other's eBay sale items to drive up the price. In an attempt to detect shill bidding eBay uses proprietary 'Shill Hunter' software. Information given by eBay in Autumn 2000.

[9] A E Farnsworth, *Contracts*, 2nd edn (Little, Brown and Co, 1990) 357.

agreement may be easier to sustain in a second-bid auction than in a first-price auction. In a Dutch or first-price sealed-bid auction the designated winner will be advised to place a bid slightly higher than the seller's reservation price, whereas all other ring members are asked to abstain from bidding. However, each bidder can gain by placing a slightly higher bid, in violation of the ring agreement. Not so under the English auction. Here, the designated bidder is advised to bid up to his own valuation and everyone else is advised to abstain from bidding. No one can gain by breaking the agreement because no one will ever exceed the designated bidder's limit. That is to say, the English auction is particularly susceptible to auction rings, and it is advisable to opt for a Dutch instead of an English auction if a risk of auction rings has been identified.[10] Sealed-bid auctions, where the prices of bids are not disclosed to other bidders, make it more difficult for bidders to collude. Another type of auction that is said to prevent auction rings is the time-interval auction where a bidding deadline is stipulated giving the bidders the incentive to deviate at the last moment and not abide by the auction ring agreement. Another way of preventing collusion among the bidders is not to make their identities known until after the deal is closed.[11]

Participants that form forbidden auction rings or otherwise take part in collu- **15.14**
sion may be held responsible to the marketplace. A related question is to what extent an individual participant harmed by the auction ring or collusion has any claim for compensation. Many jurisdictions provide remedies in contract law for individuals damaged by anti-competitive behaviour.[12] It is advisable that the conditions of sale or membership terms expressly regulate to what extent a deal concluded in the marketplace is valid when it later turns out that the price-setting mechanism was distorted by an auction ring or other collusion. A problem in this respect is that the actual deal may have been concluded by two participants that did not take part in the collusion. Consequently, it is recommended that the conditions of sale or membership terms distinguish the situations when one of the parties has participated in an auction ring or other collusive actions, on the one hand, and when both parties are 'innocent', on the other hand.

A participant harmed by an auction ring or collusion may, furthermore, claim **15.15**
compensation from the marketplace operator. The membership terms should regulate to what extent the operator has any liability where there have been price manipulations by collusive participators and whether there is a duty on the operator to investigate such activities. In other words, the issue is whether the

---

[10] Bichler (n 4 above) 105 with reference to M S Robinson, 'Collusion and the choice of auction' (1985) 16 *Rand Journal of Economics* 141–5.   [11] See paras 14.28–14.33 above.
[12] Article 81.2 of the EC Treaty. See R B Bell and W F Adkinson Jr, 'Anti-trust Issues Raised by B2B Exchanges' (Autumn 2000) *Anti-trust*, 18; and Linklaters & Alliance in Goldman Sachs Global Equity Research, *B2B e-Commerce/Internet Europe—The Old World Meets the New Economy* (2000) (at <https://www.gs.com>) appendix B, 143 ff.

marketplace operator should be liable for collusion of which it was, in fact, unaware but was deemed to have known about (constructive knowledge).

Bid shielding

15.16 Bid shielding occurs when two bidders conspire to place one bid high enough to scare other bidders off and one bid lower than the fair market value, and then the higher of the two withdraws at the last minute, thereby defrauding the invitor of the value of the object as determined by open, competitive bidding. As mentioned in chapter 8 above, bid shielding can be prevented by forbidding withdrawal of bids. When this is not an available solution, the marketplace operator may introduce automated systems identifying bid shielding. It is recommended that the membership terms contain severe disincentives against bid shielding (or suspected bid shielding) by imposing high fees or denying further access whenever such behaviour is identified.

Fraudulent outsiders

15.17 It may happen in Internet marketplaces that someone takes on another's identity. If for instance S is interested in selling product P, he may falsely enter the site as merchant B and place a big buy order, thereby increasing the apparent demand for P, which will lead to a higher price. S then, in his true S capacity, sells at a high price. It is later discovered that B was not acting but that an unknown person committed a fraud. This situation ought to be avoided by making it difficult to appear with a false identity at the site. In auctions and exchanges—which are exposed to a fairly high risk of price manipulation, as large monetary gains are at stake—it is recommended that there should be strong identification measures.[13]

15.18 In regard to the liabilities of the involved parties, of course S is liable when he can be identified as having fraudulently held himself out as B. This should be described as a breach of the membership terms and should have serious consequences. If S cannot be traced and B is able to show that he did not initiate the bid, he is not bound by any contract under general default contract law. However, it is not uncommon for membership terms or conditions of sale to impose liability on B in a situation like this—that is to say make him liable for transactions made with his electronic identification device. The membership terms should regulate to what extent the marketplace operator has any liability towards B's contracting party in the situation where B has no liability. If neither B nor the

---

[13] There are many solutions available to ensure the identity of the sender of an electronic message. See also paras 16.24–16.25 with reference to using a false identity in order to escape from bad ratings or access denial.

marketplace operator is to bear any liability, the risk will fall on B's counterparty. The membership terms should then regulate the procedure for reopening the transaction.

In the previous paragraph we assumed that S had acted with an existing person's identity. The situation is different when the false identity which S takes on is non-existent. The marketplace operator could be held responsible in such a situation for not having checked the identity of the bidders beforehand. There are examples from traditional auctions where the highest bidder has been allowed to 'arrange things' before paying and thereafter not reappeared.[14] It should be clear from the conditions of sale to what extent the auctioneer must ascertain the identity of the bidders as well as the consequences where there has been a breach of any such duty.

15.19

---

[14] See the English cases: *Hibben v Bayley* (1860) 2 F & F 48; *Cyril Andrade Ltd v Sotheby & Co* (1931) 47 TLR 244; *Alchemy (International) Limited v Tattersalls Limited* (1985) 2 EGLR 17.

16

EFFECTS OF BREACH AND POTENTIAL BREACH: EXCLUSION, RATINGS, AND FEES

Introduction

As has been said many times before in this book, an Internet marketplace is **16.01** dependent on trust in order to attract liquidity. It is crucial to implement disincentives against individual participants behaving in a way that threatens the trustworthiness of the marketplace. Participants may be denied further access to the marketplace for violating the conditions of sale or membership terms. Before such a draconian sanction is used, there could be other consequences, such as warning other participants against making a deal with the misbehaving participant (rating or blacklisting) or fees to be paid by the misbehaving participant to the marketplace. Furthermore, the marketplace could require that participants be scrutinized before being accepted in the marketplace.

16.02   AUCNET—a marketplace for used cars—has two sanctions for misbehaving participants: fines and exclusion from the site. Because the opportunity to trade on AUCNET is greatly valued, withholding permission to access AUCNET is a sanction sufficiently severe to ensure compliance for most member dealers.[1]

16.03   In auctions where the person taking an initiative to the auction commits himself to accept the best bid, it is particularly important that the bidders are examined before they are admitted to submit bids. Contrary to traditional individually negotiated procurement schemes, where potential counterparties could be scrutinized after the negotiations had started, the auction does not allow for *ex post* examination. As soon as the bidding starts, all participating bidders must qualify as potential contracting parties.

16.04   In order to enhance confidence in the marketplace it is essential that participants be well informed about the risks involved. Openly disclosed risks will enable participants to protect themselves and avoid negative surprises, which may ultimately harm the trustworthiness of the marketplace.[2] It is thus recommended that participants be warned about potential risks when becoming members and that any educational schemes contain information about the risks.

16.05   It can generally be said that the more the marketplace depends on trustworthiness, the more restrictions are needed before a participant is accepted. These restrictions can relate to rapid price variations, to the need for adequate quality of the objects sold in the marketplace, or to the need for ensuring participants' creditworthiness.

16.06   Traditional marketplaces are also dependent on trust. There are many examples of how access is restricted in traditional marketplaces. In stock exchanges, for instance, the participants often need to ensure that they are familiar with the procedures and have sufficient financial strength before becoming members. Commodity trading floors may either require membership or have implemented a strong, silent, social pressure that ensures accurate behaviour.

16.07   Accessibility in Internet marketplaces is often more transparent than the hidden social disincentives established in traditional marketplaces. The operator of an Internet marketplace is recommended to design appropriate sanctions against unwanted behaviour by participants and to codify these sanctions expressly in the membership terms. This chapter will analyse some available sanctions.

16.08   When the marketplace is dominant within its area of trade, it may be required to allow access under anti-trust and competition law. The operator needs to ensure

---

[1] Ho Geun Lee, 'AUCNET: Electronic Intermediary for Used-Car Transaction' (1997) *Electronic Markets*, Vol 7, No 4, 24 at 27.

[2] P Selis, A Ramasastry and C S Wright, 'Bidder Beware. Toward a Fraud-Free Marketplace—Best Practices for the Online Auction Industry', a Report for the State of Washington Attorney-General's Office (17 April 2001) at <http://www.law.washington.edu/lct/publications.html#bidder> 41.

that participation in the marketplace is not limited to specific market competitors. Exclusion of specific entities may classify as per se anti-competitive in some jurisdictions. It is a delicate task to balance, on the one hand, the interest of high trustworthiness and, on the other hand, the interest of allowing many players in the market. These two conflicting interests can be analysed from the marketplace's point of view and from society's point of view. Both the individual marketplace and society share the conflicting interests of enhancing trustworthiness and ensuring high liquidity in the market. As long as there are sufficient other means than exclusion to ensure trustworthiness there need not be a conflict of interest. However, it is clear that the most effective way of protecting trust in the marketplace is not to admit participants that may adversely affect that trust. Here I shall deal further with access to the market as a way of preserving trust.[3]

Initial approval of participants

Is initial approval necessary?

Some marketplaces do not need to have an approval procedure before allowing participation. For instance, eBay has a scheme under which all participants are rated by other participants. Thus, the marketplace takes no overall responsibility for the credibility of the participants other than displaying how each individual participant is rated. In short, eBay has chosen open access and has no initial approval.   **16.09**

<Fruitline.com> makes it possible for each bidder to exclude their bid from being matched with unwanted participants by indicating in a list that the indicated participants should not be matched with a submitted bid. Such a scheme lessens the need for an extensive initial approval. <Fruitline.com> only makes sure that an applying participant operates within the fresh produce business before allowing participation.   **16.10**

At the Yahoo! auction site invitors may prevent specific bidders from bidding. Furthermore, Yahoo! invitors can set a minimum bidder rating and thereby only allow bidders that have received a good rating in earlier transactions an opportunity to submit bids. The invitor thus reduces the risk of bidders in bad faith and the operator need not have extensive prerequisites for initial access.   **16.11**

Other marketplaces may be more sensitive to the overall reputation of participants and, consequently, require certification in advance that certain standards are met. Covisint (for car manufacturers and their subcontractors) is an example of a marketplace which has an extensive approval procedure before allowing subcontractors to participate.   **16.12**

---

[3] See Linklaters & Alliance in Goldman Sachs Global Equity Research, *B2B e-Commerce/ Internet Europe—The Old World Meets the New Economy* (2000) (at <https://www.gs.com>) Appendix B, 143 ff.

16.13 These examples show that there is no single solution as to whether initial approval is needed or how extensive the examination should be. Access to particular sites may be particularly restricted—such as manufacturers creating auctions sites for submanufacturers. Because of the need to establish a high level of quality and performance in time, bidders are often carefully scrutinized before being given access to such marketplaces.[4] Other sites, however, feel no need to have initial approval of participants, such as auction sites offering newly manufactured goods to consumers.

Factors of relevance to initial approval

16.14 There are a number of factors that may be of interest before a person or company is admitted to participate in an electronic auction or exchange:

(a) the credibility of the participant in terms of its ability to pay and deliver the promised quality;

(b) that the participant has used an appropriate technique to identify itself;

(c) that the participant is familiar with the procedures in the marketplace;

(d) that the participant is in the relevant sector of business;

(e) that the participant uses the correct software and hardware;

(f) that the participant is a member of associated websites (for instance sites providing settlement services, such as <Bolero.net>);

(g) that the participation of the participant does not, because of the law applicable to the transaction under private international law, lead to the conditions of sale or membership terms being set aside due to mandatory national law or *ordre public*;

(h) that the participant does not participate in competing marketplaces.

This list is not exhaustive nor is every factor listed relevant for all marketplaces. The determination concerning to what extent these factors are of relevance should be made individually for each and every marketplace. It is strongly recommended that the marketplace openly communicate the prerequisites, qualifications or conditions for becoming a participant. Such transparency is likely to enhance the trustworthiness of the marketplace and also to prevent suspicions and accusations of behaviour inconsistent with this trustworthiness.

16.15 This study will not analyse each of the potentially relevant factors listed, except for factor (h), namely the restrictions on the participant's ability to make deals in other exchanges. Such a possibility is restricted in the New York Stock Exchange during on-hours. The rationale behind this is to keep the market concentrated and thereby to preserve maximum liquidity. The only exception is big deals with an

---

[4] R E Hall, *Digital Dealing: How e-markets are transforming the Economy*, 2001, at <http://www.stanford.edu/~rehall/LinoleumReport.pdf> 55.

immediate impact on the market price, which could be permitted to be negotiated outside the New York Stock Exchange. An Internet marketplace may wish to limit side activities by its participants in order to achieve a wholly transparent information structure. However, the parties involved in the big deals have a legitimate interest in negotiating the transaction outside the marketplace in order not to influence the market price while the negotiating is going on. If this is denied, the marketplace may lose important participants and thus the desired liquidity.[5]

Rating, blacklisting, and whitelisting

Positive and negative rating systems

As mentioned above, there are means other than access denial for ensuring suffi- **16.16** cient trust in a marketplace. A method that works particularly well in the electronic environment is evaluation of the individual participants' degree of trustworthiness. The rating methods may be of a positive nature, ie pointing to participants that have formerly proved to fulfil their obligations accurately, or of a negative nature, ie pointing to participants that have failed to fulfil their obligations. It is also possible to have a system combining positive and negative ratings.

The relation between rating and liquidity

The benefit of rating systems compared with access denial is that each participant **16.17** may decide what level of trust it requires from its counterparties. At least from a theoretical point of view, it would be highly satisfactory if every participant carefully considered how risky their position was and thereafter decided what level of security and trust it required from its counterparties. In practice, however, it is highly probable that most participants would feel uncomfortable taking a known and transparently displayed risk even if it is small and insignificant. Instead the participants are more likely to decide to put up excessively high security and trustworthiness requirements. This, in turn, would be detrimental to the marketplace as a whole since its liquidity would be unnecessarily lowered by excessive requirements of trustworthiness. It is thus a delicate task for the marketplace operator to balance, on the one hand, the individual participant's interest in making an individual choice as to what risks it is willing to take and, on the other hand, the general interest of the marketplace in ensuring high liquidity without risking the general trust in the market place.

---

[5] R Lee, *What is an Exchange? The Automation, Management and Regulation of Financial Markets* (OUP, 1988) 99 and ch 10; R Laulajainen, *Financial Geography—a Banker's view* (Göteborg, 1998) 131.

Rating and anti-trust effects

16.18 As mentioned earlier, access denial may cause problems in relation to rules on anti-trust and competition law. By excluding access for certain potential participators, the free price-setting mechanism may become distorted. Rating systems may at first appear less detrimental than access-denial systems to competition laws. After all, it is a legitimate interest of every participant not to be required to conclude deals with persons it does not trust. The rating systems may, however, be against anti-trust regulations since they in effect may lead to anti-competitive behaviour. This is particularly so when requirements of existing positive ratings in effect constitute a barrier to entering the market. All new participants that have not yet received any rating are thereby excluded from participation. The individual participant may be allowed access to the marketplace, but if no one would be willing to conclude a deal with a participant that cannot show a positive track record, it is in effect a barrier to entering the market. This study will not go any further into the issue of anti-trust law, but would only like to draw attention to the problem that rating systems, like rules on access denial, may constitute anti-competitive behaviour.[6]

Who handles the rating?

16.19 The *participants themselves* could handle the rating systems. Participants could be required after each deal to provide information concerning to what extent the other party performed according to the agreement. Such information would be automatically available in the marketplace. Future participants could afterwards stipulate that only bids from bidders with a certain degree of acquired trustworthiness are accepted or reject transactions with participants showing a bad track record. Another method is to make it possible for each participant to scroll down a list of potential bidders and mark which of them it accepts or, alternatively, does not accept to conclude deals with. Such a list would show to what extent the potential bidders have acquired positive or negative responses in former deals. The drawbacks of using the participants as evaluators are that:

(a) the rating is highly subjective;

(b) there is no guarantee that there in fact was good or bad behaviour by the rated participant; and

(c) there is a risk that an evaluating participant might provide incorrect information in order to harm a competing participant; and

(d) there is a risk that a participant might rate itself in order to create a more favourable track record.

---

[6] Linklaters & Alliance in Goldman Sachs Global Equity Research, *B2B e-Commerce/Internet Europe—The Old World Meets the New Economy* (2000) (at <https://www.gs.com>) Appendix B, 143 ff.

Another method is that not the participants themselves but the marketplace **16.20**
operator handles the rating system. Participants could submit complaints to the
marketplace operator who would make an individual determination as to how
serious the complaint is and whether to disclose this information to other participants. It is particularly important not to allow the participants themselves to
handle the rating system when there is a risk that competitors will discredit each
other by false complaints and false blacklisting. The drawback of having the
operator manage the rating system is that it slows down the flow of information. There is necessarily a period of time during which the operator must evaluate the participants' information. Another disadvantage is that when the
operator handles the rating system the participants may be less inclined to
provide information; either because it is more complicated to submit explana-
tions or because the participants feel offended by not being trusted and by
having to be controlled by the operator. A third disadvantage with having the
operator handling ratings is obviously that it is more costly than when the
participants do it on their own.

Yet another possibility is that a *third party*, a professional rating institute, could **16.21**
handle the rating system.[7] Such institutes are frequently used where the crucial
factors for assessing trustworthiness are other than how the parties act in the
particular marketplace. There are organizations keeping track of business behaviour generally and others specialized in particular aspects, such as for instance
creditworthiness.

Furthermore, the rating system could be synchronized or co-ordinated with *other* **16.22**
marketplaces or website activities. When a participant has lost trustworthiness or
has a negative reputation in one marketplace, such information could also be
automatically displayed in other marketplaces.[8] It is likely that we will see many
such disseminative systems in the future. Naturally, it would be devastating for a
blacklisted person if the blacklisting information was spread throughout every
marketplace and for every type of activity. However it would also be very serious
if participants were not warned about the risks involved in making transactions
with a person who has a bad track record. The marketplace operator must decide
which activities are relevant to the activities carried out in the particular marketplace. The marketplace operator should make sure not to include information
about irrelevant activities if this would lower the liquidity in the marketplace, but
at the same time include relevant information that will contribute to enhancing
trust in the marketplace.

---

[7] B Temkin, 'What's Next? E-Marketplaces Set the Stage for New Business Networks' in
A Sculley and W Woods (eds), *Evolving E-markets: building high value B2B exchanges with staying
power* (ISI Publication Ltd, 2000) 163.
[8] VISA maintains a 'bad merchant' database of sellers who have been expelled from the VISA
merchant system, and this database is available to issuers.

16.23   This overview illustrates that different bodies could be in charge of handling the rating system for marketplace participants. Naturally, it is possible to have a rating system that is a mixture of information from the participants, the operator, third party rating institutes and connected websites.

Avoiding negative rating by using a false identity

16.24   If an actor (potential participator) has obtained a bad rating, he may avoid the negative rating by acting under another name. When access requires a positive track record, such behaviour could be prevented. Furthermore, it could be prevented by making certain in the access procedure that a participant is only allowed to act under his real identity. The use of electronic signatures does not necessarily deal with the secure identification of participants. It all depends on the type of electronic signature. One of the most important matters in deciding whether the electronic signature provides enough security is how the user of the electronic signature is originally identified. Many existing types of electronic signature are not secured by appropriate original identification methods for the holders of the signatures. Other types may provide excessively high and costly security and may be difficult to use in the marketplace from an administrative point of view. Furthermore, requirements for electronic signatures may harm the liquidity in the marketplace by making access unnecessarily complicated for potential participants. The marketplace could often ensure adequate security as to the identity of the participants by using its own identification methods and simple password techniques. However, the more speculative the marketplace is, the more security is needed. For highly speculative markets it may be necessary to use electronic signatures with a high degree of security.[9]

16.25   Another way to avoid a negative rating is to act under another participant's name and use it as a decoy. This way a participant could benefit from the decoy's track record or hide its own bad ratings. Using a decoy entails collaboration with the decoy. When such collaboration is obtained it is in practice rather easy to use the decoy's identity. Obviously, the membership terms should forbid participants from allowing others to use their identity in the marketplace. However, such collaboration is difficult to detect and prevent in practice. It may be some comfort

---

[9] Council Directive (EC) 99/93 on a Community Framework for Electronic Signatures makes a distinction between 'ordinary' electronic signatures and electronic signatures issued with a qualified certificate (providing a high level of security and also imposing mandatory liability on the issuer of the electronic signature certificate). Article 5(2) stipulates that an electronic signature should not be denied legal effect solely on the ground that it is not based on a qualified certificate. In this context it should be observed that national states imposing form requirements of signature for concluding deals in an auction or exchange may have enacted legislation requiring that certain types of techniques for electronic signatures be used in order to satisfy such form requirements. The question of legislative form requirements should, however, be kept apart from the question of how the marketplace may best ascertain that the paticipants are using their correct identity. In this chapter I only deal with the latter question.

that not many serious participants would be willing to risk their own good reputation in the marketplace by letting less trustworthy participants use their identity. To take such a risk the intermediary would be likely to ask for high economic compensation to cover the extra trouble and risk, and this itself would be a deterrent to participants to avoid a negative rating by using another's identity.

Fees

As described many times earlier in this book, there is sometimes a need to create **16.26** a disincentive against certain behaviour by participants and the threat of being expelled is often an efficient disincentive. However, sometimes this sanction is too harsh. A fee may be a more balanced and appropriate sanction or consequence for breach of the rules. In order to find such a well-balanced sanction, it is important to synchronize or provide co-ordination between the fee to be paid to the operator of the marketplace on the one hand, and the compensation to be paid to other participants on the other hand.

When determining the appropriate fee to be paid to the marketplace operator, it is **16.27** essential that the breach harms or damages the marketplace as a whole. If the harm or damage is only to an individual participant, the appropriate sanction is often individual compensation to that actual participant instead of a fee to the marketplace operator. There is, however, rarely a definite borderline between individual harm and harm to the marketplace as a whole. Often many small losses by individual participants will contribute to the marketplace's general loss of trustworthiness. Consequently, breaches that mainly harm an individual participant may also justify a fee being paid to the marketplace operator.

Another situation when it is appropriate to pay a fee to the marketplace operator **16.28** is when many participants have been harmed economically but only in small amounts or amounts that are difficult to assess. Instead of compensating each participant it is often more efficient for there to be an obligation to pay a fee to the marketplace operator. In such cases it may be that it is more important to create a deterrent against a participant committing a breach than compensate individually each participant suffering slight economic harm.

The reason for introducing fees in a marketplace is not only to provide a balanced **16.29** sanction. Fees may at times be a more efficient sanction than exclusion. This is particularly so when the marketplace is not dominant in its field and a participant breaking the rules may conclude deals just as easily outside the marketplace. Thus, for newly established marketplaces, it may be particularly important to use fees instead of exclusion as the main sanction. Another situation where fees may be more efficient than exclusion is in marketplaces for one-off procurement transactions. In such marketplaces the risk of not being allowed to participate in the future may not be sufficient disincentive for participants against breaking the rules. A more appropriate sanction could be damages to the individually harmed participants instead of a fee paid to the marketplace.

16.30 An advantage in using fees as a sanction or consequence for breach is that the fee can be decided beforehand as liquidated damages. The use of liquidated damages saves time when a breach has occurred and the amount of damages to be paid would otherwise have to be assessed. In some jurisdictions the use of liquidated damages is complicated by rules on punitive damages (for instance in the US). In other jurisdictions there is no equivalent to the rules on punitive damages, but liquidated damages may be adjusted if they are excessive and unfair (as in Scandinavia). In order to avoid any problems in this respect, it is recommended that the fees or liquidated damages to be paid to the marketplace operator should not be excessive, but should correspond roughly to the economic harm caused by the breach. Therefore it is necessary that the marketplace operator estimates beforehand the potential harm caused by different types of breach in order to find the appropriate fee (or liquidated damages). In determining what the potential economic harm to the marketplace is, the cost of damaged trustworthiness should be taken into account. This in turn would allow for rather high fees as preserving trustworthiness is so important for the marketplace.

The liability of the marketplace operator for wrongful access denial, rating, fining, or exclusion

16.31 When the marketplace operator wrongfully imposes a sanction on a participant, the operator commits a breach of contract. The breach could be either that the sanction was wrongfully imposed (too harsh) or that the reason for imposing the sanction was wrong (the participant had committed no wrong and consequently should suffer no sanction). Since the relationship between the marketplace operator and the participant is contractual, the contract may stipulate what the effects should be in case of such a breach. Thus, the membership terms may regulate what the consequences are where the marketplace operator wrongfully imposes a sanction on a participant.

16.32 The effect in national law is usually that the operator should compensate the harmed participant for its economic loss. The economic loss could be substantial in a situation where the participant is excluded from participation and loses favourable deals or has to shut down its operations.[10] The economic loss is likely to vary among different participants. Furthermore, it is difficult to estimate the economic loss when it is based upon deals that were not actually concluded but are in fact hypothetical. In order to treat all participants equally and to avoid the

---

[10] See ch 17 below on the operator's liability for inaccessibility.

difficult problem of assessing the adequate amount of damages, it is recommended that the membership terms allow liquidated damages to a participant that has suffered from a wrongfully imposed sanction. Generally, it is important to compensate a participant generously in such a situation, since it is often crucial to restore the participant's trust in the marketplace.

Wrongful fee

If a fee is wrongly imposed on a participant, it is quite easy simply to state in the **16.33** membership terms that the fee should be repaid to the participant together with a fixed generous interest rate.

Wrongful rating or blacklisting

If the participant is wrongfully blacklisted or rated, appropriate compensation is to **16.34** post explicit information to all other participants about the mistake and to ensure that the participant's reputation is restored. The disadvantage is, however, that such information is perceived as boring by other participants and only rarely read. A technological solution may be that each time someone declines to conclude a deal with the wrongfully blacklisted participant information is conveyed to the participants so declining. In addition to the measures for ensuring accurate information about the participant that has been wrongfully rated, it could be appropriate to compensate the participant economically. Naturally, it is extremely difficult to determine the amount of economic harm, therefore it is advisable to compensate by the use of liquidated damages in such instances. Another complication is that the wrongful rating may not have been caused by the marketplace operator but by other participants' ratings or third parties' ratings. In marketplaces where the marketplace operator does not handle the rating system, the membership terms should stipulate whether the marketplace operator undertakes any liability for wrongful blacklisting.

When a participant has been wrongfully 'whitelisted', that is to say when a partic- **16.35** ipant has received a better rating than it should have, the harmed party is normally not the whitelisted participant itself but the party concluding a deal with this participant. That party may face a situation where the wrongfully whitelisted party does not fulfil its contractual obligation and has no economic ability to provide sufficient compensation. Other participants harmed by wrongful whitelisting may be bidders who were forced to submit higher bids in English auctions or lower bids in reversed auctions to match bids submitted by a wrongfully whitelisted participant who was not entitled to participate. As said above, the amount of liability allocated to the marketplace operator depends on who it is that handles the rating system. When the marketplace operator is in charge and responsible for the wrongful whitelisting, it may be appropriate to allow for compensation from the marketplace operator. It should be clear from the membership terms who is entitled to compensation: only participants concluding deals with a wrongfully whitelisted participant or also participants submitting bids in parallel with the wrongfully whitelisted participant. It is furthermore advisable that the membership terms stipulate liquidated damages. Finally, the membership terms should regulate to what extent the wrongfully whitelisted participant is required to reimburse the marketplace operator since it is by no means self evident that a participant who did not itself contribute to the wrongful whitelisting should be liable to reimburse the marketplace operator.

Wrongful exclusion

16.36   If the participant is wrongfully excluded from participation, it should of course be reinstalled as a participant as soon as possible. Normally, it would also be advisable to pay compensation with liquidated damages depending how long the participant was wrongfully expelled. In volatile and speculative markets it is always difficult to determine hypothetically how many transactions the wrongfully expelled participant would have made and whether these transactions would have been economically successful or not. It is extremely difficult to determine an appropriate level of liquidated damages for volatile marketplaces.

16.37   It may also be difficult to determine whether the wrongfully expelled participant ought to have conducted the equivalent transactions in other marketplaces while being expelled from the actual marketplace. The more opportunities there are for the participant to make transactions elsewhere, the lower the liquidated damages should be.

16.38   A wrongfully expelled participant may suffer severe losses when its own operations are being integrated with the operations carried out in the marketplace. In marketplaces where the participants are highly integrated technologically (such as Covisint), it is recommended that the participants be allowed generous liquidated damages for wrongful exclusion. Furthermore, where there is no direct connection between rating and exclusion information should also be provided to other participants indicating that the exclusion was a mistake, as otherwise exclusion could create rumours that in practice would have a blacklisting effect.

Wrongful denial of access

16.39   A more difficult situation is when a potential participant (an applicant) has been denied initial access. In such a case there is no contractual relationship between the operator and the applicant. According to the fundamental principle of freedom of contract, the operator is not obliged to contract with parties with which it does not wish to contract. The effect of this is that the operator has no obligation to compensate an applicant that is denied access despite the fact that it fulfils all the stipulated requirements for access. When the operator has made a wrongful decision and wrongfully denied access, it could be advisable to allow the applicant compensation ex gratia, ie without being obliged to do so in law, in order to avoid the marketplace receiving a bad reputation which may harm its trustworthiness. It should also be noted that the principle of freedom of contract is sometimes limited by national law, for instance anti-trust law or the law on non-discrimination, and may require the marketplace operator to contract with certain persons.

The liability of the marketplace operator failing to take measures against participants breaking the rules

In this section I analyse the situation when the marketplace operator has failed to **16.40** exclude or deny access to a misbehaving participant or failed to provide accurate information to other participants with respect to the rating of an individual participant. It is easy to imagine that deals are concluded between participants that would not have been concluded had one of them been denied access or been blacklisted.[11]

As between the contracting participants, the buyer and the seller, it is evident that **16.41** when one of them fails to perform, it is under an obligation according to the conditions of sale to compensate the other party. The conditions of sale may, however, not provide full economic compensation to the harmed party. Another reason why the harmed participant is not fully compensated may be that the participant in breach has insufficient funds to pay the compensation. The unsatisfied participant may then wish to direct a claim against the marketplace operator, arguing that the deal would never have been concluded had the operator enforced the sanctions of access denial, exclusion or negative rating stipulated in the membership terms. It should be clear from the membership terms to what extent the operator has such liability.

It is not generally possible to say what liability is most suitable to impose on the **16.42** marketplace operator where it has failed to exclude, deny access, or blacklist a participant. In marketplaces where it is essential to preserve the participant's trust in the marketplace, it may be appropriate to allow for generous compensation from the marketplace. An alternative is, of course, to compensate the harmed participant by providing in the conditions of sale for full compensation from the participant in breach. A disadvantage with stipulating harsh consequences for breach in the conditions of sale, out of proportion to the risk allocation for breach in the relevant trade, is that it may generally deter participation. Normally, most

---

[11] As to German law in this respect see G Spindler and A Wiebe, *Internet-Auktionen. Rechtliche Rahmenbedingungen* (C H Beck, 2001) in the chapter on '*Haftung für Rufschädigung durch Ratingseiten*'.

standard terms have limited liability. If the conditions of sale used in the market-place are different from what the participants are accustomed to, the market-place's liquidity may be hampered. Furthermore, the solution of providing full compensation in the conditions of sale does not cover the situation where the participant in breach has no funds.

17

THE OPERATOR'S LIABILITY IN CASE OF INACCESSIBILITY

The problem

An electronic marketplace may be inaccessible, which may cause losses for the **17.01** participants when they are dependent on its availability. This is the case when objects exposed to rapid price variations are being sold and bought and when alternative marketplaces are not readily available, because either the marketplace is dominant or competing marketplaces have time-consuming access procedures. Another example of dependency is when the participant is buying or selling continually and has adopted its logistic system to a continuous flow of small deals in the marketplace.

Participants in traditional marketplaces may also suffer from inaccessibility. An **17.02** example is the IRA's bombing of the Baltic Exchange for ship-broking in London in 1992. The fact that the physical marketplace was demolished severely interrupted the whole business and caused huge losses to participants.

Disruptions may occur either because the whole marketplace is inaccessible to all **17.03** participants or because a particular participant is unable technically to participate in the marketplace activities. The membership terms should address this issue and set out the liability of the marketplace operator for failure to provide participation.[1]

---

[1] See ch 12 above for the marketplace operator's liability for illegal transactions. As to German national law see G Spindler and A Wiebe, *Internet-Auktionen. Rechtliche Rahmenbedingungen* (C H Beck, 2001) in the chapter on '*Nichterrechbarkeit des System wegen Netzstörungen*'.

The cause of inaccessibility

17.04   When the cause of inaccessibility lies within the sphere of the participant's control the marketplace would generally not be willing to undertake any responsibility. However, when the marketplace operator has installed the relevant malfunctioning software or hardware, it may be appropriate to allocate the risk for inaccessibility to the operator.[2] The same should apply when the marketplace has undertaken to provide a properly functioning interface for the participant and has provided assurance that it is compatible with the participant's systems.

17.05   When the cause of inaccessibility is within the sphere of the operator, the operator is likely to face some responsibility under the default rules in national law. In most jurisdictions this responsibility is not crystal clear and it is recommended that the issue be regulated expressly in the membership terms.[3]

17.06   The membership terms should, furthermore, address the question as to who has the burden of proof for determining the cause of the inaccessibility, ie whether the technical problems were within the sphere of the participant or the operator.

The operator's liability for best effort, force majeure, and the amount of damage

Strict responsibility—responsibility for best effort

17.07   In situations where the liability falls on the marketplace operator it may wish to limit its liability to situations that are caused negligently in order to avoid strict liability. Such limited liability is often phrased as a 'performance of best efforts'—or reasonable efforts—as opposed to a strict duty to perform a specific result.[4] Responsibility for best efforts means that the operator is obliged to act with care and to do his best in order to avoid disruptions. When the operator is unable to prevent the disruption because it was out of the operator's sphere of control, the operator is not in breach. The membership terms may list what kinds of precautions are required of the marketplace in order to fulfil the requirement of best effort. Sometimes the notion 'reasonable effort' is used instead of 'best effort'. If this is the case the operator's liability is more limited.

---

[2] The question of time and place of sending and receipt is dealt with in the US Uniform Electronic Transaction Act (UETA), Art 15. It may serve as a source of inspiration in determining the liability for an Internet marketplace operator. See <www.uetaonline.com>.

[3] The marketplace operator should, of course, make an analysis of its risk exposure in relation to what liability software suppliers and like persons have towards the marketplace. Normally, their liability is limited.

[4] See UPICC, Arts 5.4 and 5.5 (<www.unidroit.org>). In some jurisdictions this distinction between best effort and specific result is well established. It has been criticized for creating confusion. However, in writing contracts it is a helpful concept to use in order to make clear the distinction between different main types of duties.

Force majeure

Another technique to achieve limited responsibility for the operator is to include **17.08** a force majeure clause in the membership terms, stipulating that disruption constitutes a breach but excluding the operator from the liability to compensate the participants for their losses. Such a limited liability is usually based on the argument that the marketplace otherwise would have to increase the price of its services in order to cover the risk exposure. It is not advisable simply to refer to force majeure, but rather to specify what types of situations constitute force majeure. ICC is presently working on a general, modern, force majeure clause.[5]

Burden of proof

In limiting the responsibility of the marketplace operator, it is crucial to address **17.09** the question of burden of proof. Who is to prove that the operator did/did not exercise best efforts? Who is to prove that there is/is not a force majeure situation? Under national law the burden in both situations is often on the operator claiming that it is not liable for breach of contract. This allocation of burden of proof should also normally be included in the membership terms, since it would be difficult in practice for the participant to find the relevant information about how the operator had acted and what caused the inaccessibility.

Limitation of damages

For situations where the marketplace operator has a duty to provide accessibility **17.10** and is in breach of that duty, liability may be limited to liquidated damages or by a stipulation that there is compensation for only certain types of losses. It is generally advisable to try to determine what economic harm a typical participant is likely to suffer through inaccessibility and then to stipulate liquidated damages at that level. The other solution, specifying what types of losses are compensated, is in practice difficult since it entails complicated assessments and evidentiary issues for determining the actual losses.

An example

Geroe provides the following example of a disclaimer:[6]   **17.11**

You understand and agree that (the provider) does not warrant the service to be uninterrupted or error-free. You further understand and agree that (the provider) has no control

---

[5] See <www.iccwbo.org>.

[6] M R Geroe, 'Agreements between an Electronic Marketplace and Its Members' (Fall 2001) *The International Lawyer*, Vol 35, No 3, 1069 at 1072, with reference to *Scott v Bell Atlantic Corp* slip opinion 600591/00 NY Sup Ct 12 October 2000.

over third party networks or Web sites that you may access in the course of your use of the service, and that delays and disruptions of other network transmissions are completely beyond the control of (the provider). (The provider) cannot and will not guarantee that the services will provide Internet access that meets your needs.

Effects on the price-setting mechanism

17.12   Apparently it is a feature of the electronic marketplace that accessibility may be denied only to one or some participants and not to all. This is also possible in traditional physical marketplaces, where an individual participant may be hindered from participation, eg due to illness, obstacles in communications or bad weather. The fact that not all participants can at all times attend the marketplace is an inevitable risk. This is to the detriment not only of the individual participant that cannot make transactions, but also has an impact on the whole marketplace as the price-setting mechanism may be affected when one or some participants are unable to attend.

17.13   There are techniques available for disclosing when important participants are not present. Marketplaces that are particularly dependent on certain participants may consider introducing such a technique. As mentioned earlier (paragraphs 14.28–14.33 above), the marketplace could choose to disclose the identity of participating bidders. By doing so, it becomes clear to all participants when an important bidder is not present. However, for many good reasons most Internet marketplaces do not disclose the bidders' identities.

Final remarks

17.14   This is not the place to consider in depth all the different modes of structuring and determining the liability of marketplace operators for inaccessibility. The bottom line is that it is advisable to stipulate explicitly the obligation of the marketplace operator in relation to disruptions and to what extent the operator is excluded from liability for compensation of losses due to inaccessibility.

17.15   Participants are advised to note carefully to what extent the marketplace operator has limited its liability and ensure that their procedures and insurance conditions are synchronized to and co-ordinated with any limited liability of the market-place.

18

DISPUTE RESOLUTION

The importance of preventing disputes

It is interesting how rarely legal disputes in courts concern auctions and exchanges, considering the long history, the many transactions, the speculative element and the large amounts involved.[1] Auctions and exchanges appear to be transactional procedures which discourage disputes. It is wise to create the same feature when the transactions are made electronically. **18.01**

The explanation for the infrequency of disputes is probably that most auction markets and exchanges require participants to be familiar with the marketplace procedures. Many exchanges and commodity marketplaces only admit bidders and invitors after extensive years of apprenticeship or examinations ensuring that the participant is familiar with the rules of the marketplace. Furthermore, the 'social pressure' in a traditional exchange or auction is strong: participants acting against the rules and traditions can immediately feel the irritation of the other participants in the room. **18.02**

The features of education and social pressure in a traditional marketplace are not always present in an electronic marketplace. There are frequently no access **18.03**

---

[1] It is also significant how little legal literature there is analysing auctions. This is probably due to the fact that there are so few disputes relating to auctions.

restrictions that ask about familiarity with the 'rules of the game' and the social pressure is not as strongly felt in the electronic environment. There is also the fact that it is difficult to ensure that participants have read and understood the procedural regulations in the membership terms and conditions of sale. From the examples of terms given at paragraphs 7.49–7.57, it is clear that most participants are unlikely to take the time to read the terms and certainly will be unable to understand the consequences fully. This leads to a possible risk that electronic auctions and exchanges will be more litigious than physical auctions and exchanges have been.

18.04 The technical design may to some extent prevent disputes. It is essential that the technology implemented by the marketplace guides the participant's behaviour in the appropriate directions by, for instance, making it technically impossible to announce a withdrawal when withdrawal is not permitted. Furthermore, the technology should be secure and show unambiguously—openly or only to the marketplace administrators—from whom a bid is coming and make it impossible to submit bids at the same moment (Japanese and sealed bid auctions excluded). Another technological feature used in order to limit misunderstandings and mistakes is that the system provides 'warning boxes' when a participant is acting strangely compared with its previous behaviour or general participants' behaviour.

Institutionalized arbitration, ad hoc arbitration, and mediation

18.05 Many disputes can be prevented by transparency, education and efficient technology. However, disputes are not wholly unavoidable. Thus, the marketplace needs an efficient mechanism for dispute resolution.

Permanent arbitration board

18.06 Many traditional auctions and exchanges have their own dispute resolution institutes. In the electronic environment it is highly recommended that specialized arbitration boards be established that are permanently connected to the marketplace. Frequently, traditional trades offline already have special dispute resolution institutes (see for instance auctions for the sale of wool in Australia and tea auctions in London) that can be connected to an Internet marketplace.[2] The benefits of a permanent dispute resolution board are that the arbitrators can be chosen from a pre-set list of experts; this is time-efficient and ensures that the arbitrators are familiar with the type of transaction in dispute. Furthermore, such a scheme normally ensures that the dispute is handled immediately and in a rather standardized manner.

---

[2] <PaperExchange.com> has profited from the lack of a dispute resolution process in the paper industry. Previously, for example, there was no agreement on how to define 'late', or 'off-spec' or 'wrong colour'. In collaboration with SGS, the Swiss certification agency, PaperExchange has made itself the only source of dispute resolution, among its participants at least.

Ad hoc arbitration

The arbitration could be of an ad hoc nature, in which the board of arbitrators is **18.07**
specifically appointed at the time a dispute occurs. The disadvantage is that the
place and procedures of the arbitration either must be specified in the membership terms and conditions of sale or refer to national legislation on arbitration.
Furthermore, it can be time-consuming and costly to appoint ad hoc arbitrators
when disputes arise rather frequently, ie there might be efficiency of scale in
establishing a permanent dispute resolution board.

Institutionalized arbitration

In marketplaces where the frequency of disputes is not large enough to justify a **18.08**
permanent resolution board, it is possible to tie the marketplace to a general institute of arbitration.

Mediation

It is not advisable for auction or exchange marketplaces to set up mediation **18.09**
schemes. This has become quite a popular way of solving disputes, but it is not
well suited for auctions or exchanges. In auctions the parties make quick transactions and there is generally volatility in the market with varying prices. It is
thus important that the decisions in relation to disputes are made quickly.
Furthermore, the need for *rigor commercialis* points to the desirability of unam-
biguous allocation of responsibility and a high degree of foreseeability.[3] The
outcome of mediation, where the parties are often involved in a vague process of
give and take, is generally hard to predict. Furthermore, the result of mediation
does not normally provide guidance for other participants as how to behave in the
future. Another reason why mediation is not appropriate for auctions and
exchanges is that parties involved in speculative transactions are not as likely to
reach an agreement under which they renounce their legal rights.

The risk of partiality

A particular problem arises when the dispute is between a participant and the **18.10**
marketplace operator as opposed to a dispute between two participants. If the arbitrators are chosen from a list provided by the marketplace operator, there is an
obvious risk of partiality. The arbitrator may—due to self interest—be inclined to
favour the marketplace operator in order to be retained on the list of arbitrators.

---

[3] See paras 7.20–7.22 above.

18.11 For such disputes it could be advisable to refer to an unbiased arbitration institute, such as the ICC International Court of Arbitration in Paris,[4] the American Arbitration Association (AAA)[5] or the Arbitration Institute of the Stockholm Chamber of Commerce.[6] Some arbitration institutes provide simplified arbitration, which could sometimes be a suitable alternative.

18.12 A greater challenge is to create a permanent dispute resolution board with safeguards against biased arbitrators. An example of such a safeguard is to allow participants to appoint persons to the list of arbitrators and for an individual dispute resolution system to use a combination of arbitrators appointed to the list by the marketplace operator and by the participants.

Costs

18.13 The cost for the dispute resolution could either be paid by the marketplace or by the loser of the dispute or shared equally by the disputing parties. It is important to stipulate in the conditions of sale and the membership terms, in the procedures set up for the permanent dispute resolution board, or in the rules of the arbitration institute how the costs for dispute resolution should be allocated.

Quick justice as compared with the right to a fair trial

18.14 There are two conflicting interests related to the question of how *formalized* the dispute resolution ought to be. On the one hand, dispute resolution should provide an opportunity to respond extensively to the other party's arguments and to hear witnesses and experts (the right to a fair trial). On the other hand, justice requires that a decision be made quickly (1) in order to avoid one of the parties dragging out the proceedings in order to harm the other party, and (2) so that the cost of dispute resolution can be limited.

18.15 Over recent years there has been a strong tendency in both court proceedings and arbitration to emphasize the need to respect all procedural elements of a fair trial. In commercial marketplaces, however, the procedure should not be excessively formalistic. Quick justice could be advanced by for instance allowing only one written statement from each party. The need to use oral witnesses is normally limited when the dispute arises from an electronic transaction and consequently there is no pressing need for oral proceedings. The emphasis on quick justice is particularly relevant in marketplaces where the transactions are speculative in nature and exposed to rapid price variations.

---

[4] <www.iccwbo.org>.   [5] <www.adr.org>.
[6] <www.chamber.se/arbitration/>.

The electronic business models are often characterized by the increased speed of **18.16**
decision-making. Naturally, decisions taken in auctions and exchange transactions described in this book are typically made quickly. The parties need predictability in order to ascertain their level of liquidity and manoeuvring room. They are often helped more by a quick decision as how to allocate the responsibility when something has gone wrong, than by obtaining a perfectly accurate award after a long period of time. Lengthy dispute resolution is not consistent with the business needs of electronic auctions and exchanges. In designing the dispute resolution scheme for electronic auctions and exchanges it is crucial to take into consideration the greater need for quick justice and to find an appropriate balance in relation to the interests of a fair trial. It is not advisable to develop dispute resolution schemes blindly on the basis of the rules for institutionalized arbitration or national legislation on arbitration. Rules for simplified arbitration may serve as a more appropriate source of inspiration.

Enforcement

The greatest advantage of arbitration is that the awards are enforceable almost **18.17**
everywhere due to the wide adoption of the 1958 New York Convention on the Recognition and Enforcement of Foreign Arbitral Awards.[7] So far, it has proved much more difficult to enforce decisions by national courts internationally.[8]

As said above, disputes arising from transactions made in electronic marketplaces **18.18**
rarely need to be settled by oral proceedings, since witnesses are normally not of importance. It is consequently efficient to conduct the arbitral proceedings online. Under most jurisdictions this is not problematic. Requirements for writing and signatures are nowadays frequently explicitly acknowledged in legislation also when they are made electronically.[9]

The remaining problem is that in enforcing an arbitral award the New York **18.19**
Convention, Article 1(1) refers to a territory of a state where the arbitral award is made. When the arbitration is made electronically it may be difficult to establish where and in which state the award was made. In non-electronic situations, however, courts have applied this requirement rather non-formalistically.[10] Furthermore, the 1958 New York Convention has a requirement of fair trial and it is uncertain how speedy arbitration can be and still satisfy this requirement.

---

[7] See the Convention and a list of states that have ratified it at <www.uncitral.org>.

[8] At the time of writing there is work proceeding to make it easier to enforce foreign court decisions internationally.

[9] See for example <www.ueta.online>; Council Directive (EC) 2000/31 on E-commerce; and the UNCITRAL Model Law on Electronic Commerce (<www.uncitral.org>).

[10] See the English case *Hiscox v Outhwaite* [1992] 1 AC 562.

18.20   As said previously, enforcement often does not need help from national authorities. There is mostly a strong incentive for participants to comply voluntarily with arbitration awards produced as a result of a dispute in an Internet marketplace, when the consequence of disobedience is exclusion from further participation. The conditions of sale and the membership terms should contain provisions on the consequences for participants who do not voluntarily adhere to arbitral awards.

Publication of arbitral awards

18.21   The marketplace can choose to make the arbitral award secret or not. It is useful for all marketplace participants to have knowledge of the decisions by the dispute resolution institution, but the disputing parties may wish not to 'wash their dirty linen in public'. In order to meet both these points, the outcome could be published without disclosing the names of the disputing parties. The published awards may be used to show how the conditions of sale and membership terms function in practice. Furthermore, the awards may be used when making revised versions of the conditions of sale and membership terms, and in the education of present and potential participants. Naturally, the published awards may also serve as precedents for future disputes.[11] Publication of arbitral awards helps to limit ambiguities, which ultimately prevents future disputes from arising.

Effects during the dispute resolution

18.22   A general problem is that the situation may become immobilized while the dispute resolution is pending. In order to reduce the losses, it could be decided that as soon as a dispute arises, the auction should be reopened. When, for instance, the bidder argues that he was entitled to the goods at 100 the auction may be immediately reopened. If the bidder then acquires the goods at the reopened auction at 120 and eventually wins the dispute, his damage is easily established to be 120 minus 100 (20). If the bidder does not acquire the goods, but somebody else does, the bidder in the dispute could quite easily prove the amount of damages as the balance between 100 and the price for which the goods were eventually sold.

18.23   As early as 1745 the conditions of sale in a book auction said: '. . . if any Dispute arises, the Book or Books to be put to Sale again.'[12] This is also a common way of resolving disputes today.[13]

---

[11] The precedents are not of the same nature and dignity as precedents in courts, but in practice they may lead to the same effects although in a much smaller setting, limited to the internal problems in the specific marketplace.

[12] B Learmount, *A History of the Auction* (Bernard & Learmount, 1985) 47.

[13] P S Atiyah, *The Sale of Goods*, 9th edn (Pitman Publishing, 1995) 33.

Summary

Internet marketplaces are likely to benefit from special dispute resolution **18.24** schemes. In designing such schemes the following should be taken into account:

(a) the type of arbitration;
(b) how to avoid partiality in disputes between the marketplace operator and participants;
(c) procedures allowing for quick dispute resolution;
(d) rules for reopening the transaction during the dispute resolution phase;
(e) how to ensure voluntary adherence to awards;
(f) how to ensure enforcement of awards;
(g) a policy for publication of awards.

19

FINAL REMARKS

This study has focused on the need for an Internet marketplace to ensure that **19.01** there is trust and confidence in it. Because of the globalization of trade and the reduced practical means for national states to influence cyberspace with regulations and enforcement of regulations, the marketplace must establish confidence itself without the traditional help of legislation and national institutions.

The main tools a marketplace can use to establish trust and confidence are the **19.02** membership terms, the conditions of sale, the technological infrastructure and the dispute resolution forum. All these should interact and be synchronized or coordinated to achieve optimum efficiency. Trust must be established in all activities undertaken by a marketplace, which can include pre- and post-trade information, order routing, order execution, matching, clearing and settlement. The different tools can in their different ways help to create trust.

As a result of the new technological means for steering and monitoring transac- **19.03** tions made in Internet marketplaces, the marketplace's rules can be designed in a different way from rules we are used to in the industrialized society. The main change lies in being able to make a clear distinction between unwanted behaviour as between the individual parties involved in a deal on the one hand, and unwanted behaviour from the point of view of the marketplace as a whole, on the other hand. In the second situation, the consequence of unwanted behaviour is either a fee to be paid to the marketplace or denial of further access. In the first situation, appropriate rights should be granted to the individual participant suffering from the detrimental behaviour. We thus see new ways to balance efficiently the interest of preventing certain behaviour by establishing proportionate disincentives and compensating economic harm caused to an individual marketplace participant. In contrast to the general tools available to national states, the operator of a particular Internet marketplace can tailor its norms or rules to the specific needs of the types of transactions made there.

The future development of Internet marketplaces—and their relationship with **19.04** participants, persons denied access to the marketplace and the national state—is likely to generate a completely new view of the law's function and design. The great changes that e-commerce is bringing for business are going to involve corresponding changes for the law.

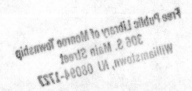

BIBLIOGRAPHY

Akdeniz, Y., Walker, C. and Wall, D., *The Internet Law and Society* (Longman, 2000)

Almén, T., *Om auktion såsom medel att åvaägabringa aftal* (Uppsala, 1897)

Ataz Lopez, J., *Régimen Juridico General del Comersio Minorista* (McGraw-Hill/ Interamericana de España, 1999)

Atiyah, P. S., *The Sale of Goods*, 9th edn (Pitman Publishing, 1995)

Bain, S. and Street, F. L., *B2B Exchanges: Critical issues* (Practicing Law Institute) 21st Annual Institute on Computer Law

Bakos, Y., 'A strategic analysis of electronic marketplaces' (1999) *MIS Quarterly*, 15(3), 295–310

Bakos, Y., 'Bundling information goods: pricing, profits and efficiency' (1991) *Management Science*, 45 (12)

Barlow, J. P., 'Thinking Logically, Acting Globally' (1996) *Cyber-Rights Electronic List*, 15 January

Barnett, R., *Contracts: Theory and Doctrine* (Little, Brown & Co, 1995)

Bell, R. B., Adkinson, W. F. Jr., 'Antitrust Issues Raised by B2B Exchanges'(2000, Fall) *Antitrust*, 18

Bernstein, L., 'Opting Out of the Legal System: Extralegal Contractual Relations in the Diamond Industry' (1992) 21 *Journal of Legal Studies* 115

Bichler, M., *The Future of e-Markets: Multidimensional Market Mechanisms* (Cambridge University Press, 2001).

Boss, A., 'The Uniform Electronic Transaction Act in a Global Environment' (2001) 37 *Idaho Law Rev* 275–342

Breckhus, S., *Omsettning og kreditt* 2, 2nd edn (Universitetsforlaget, 1994)

Brin, D., *The Transparent Society* (Reading, Mass., 1998)

Brinz, A., *Lehrbuch der Pandekten*, 2 Aufl. (Hersogt von Ph. Lotmar) IV

Cassady, R. J. R., *Auctions and Auctioneering* (University of California Press, 1967)

Ciborra, C., *Teams, Markets and Systems* (CUP, 1993)

Choudhury, V., Hartsel, K. S. and Konsynski, B. R., 'Uses and consequences of electronic markets: an empirical investigation in the aircraft parts industry' (1998) *MIS Quarterly*, 22(4), 471–507

Coase, R. H., *The Firm, the Market, and the Law* (University of Chicago Press, 1988)

Cortez, U. T., *Manual del martillero, apuntes para una reflexion* (Argentina, 1998)

Crowston, K., 'Price behavior in electronic markets', Paper presented at the 18th international conference on information systems (ICIS '97), Atlanta

Díez-Picaso, L., *Fundamentos del derecho civil patrimonial* (Madrid, 1986)

Farnsworth, A. E., *Changing your mind—the law of regretted decisions* (Yale UP, 1988)

Farnsworth, A. E., *Contracts*, 2nd edn (Little, Brown and Co, 1990)

Fletcher, R, 'An Offer You Can't Refuse', (2001) Business Law Review 162, 163

Galanter, M., 'Law Abounding: Legislation Around the North Atlantic' (1992) 55(1) *Modern Law Review* 900

Garfinkel, J. and Nimalendran, M., 'Market Structure and Trader Anonymity: An Analysis of Insider Trading', Working Paper, August 2000

Geroe, M. R., 'Agreements between an Electronic Marketplace and Its Members' (2001, Fall) *The International Lawyer*, Vol 35, No 3, 1069

Gidel, S. A., 'The Business of Exchanges', *Futures Industry*, 8 September 1997, 11–14

Goldman Sachs Global Equity Research, *B2B e-Commerce/Internet Europe—The Old World Meets the New Economy*, 2000 (at <https://www.gs.com>)

Gordley, J., *The Philosophical Origins of Modern Contract Doctrine* (OUP, 1991)

Hahn, J., 'The Dynamics of mass online marketplaces: A case study of an online auction', *CHI* 2001, 317–324

Hall, Robert E., 'Digital Dealing: How e-markets are transforming the Economy', 2001, at <http://www.stanford.edu/~rehall/LinoleumReport.pdf>

Harvey, B.W. and Meisel, F., *Auctions Law and Practice*, 2nd edn (Oxford University Press, 1995)

Heck, van E., and Ribbers, P. M., 'Experiences with Electronic Auctions in Dutch Flower Industry' (1997) *Electronic Markets*, Vol 7, No 4

Heiderhoff, B., 'Internetauktionen als Umgehungsgeschäfte' *MMR* 10/2001

Higgot R., Underhill, G. and Bieler, A. (eds) *Non-State Actors and Authority in the Global System* (Routledge, 2000)

Hirschman, A. O., *Exit, Voice and Loyalty* (Harvard UP, 1969)

Ho, G. L., 'AUCNET: Electronic Intermediary for Uused-Car Transaction' (1997) *Electronic Markets*, Vol 7, No 4, 24

Howard, P. K., *The Death of Common Sense—How law is suffocating America* (NY, 1994)

Huber, E. R., *Das Submissionswesen* (Tubingen, 1885)

Hultmark, C., 'Ny distansavtalslag' (2000–01) *Juridisk Tidskrift* 48–62

Johnson, D. R. and Post, D. G., 'The Rise of Law in the Global Network' in B. Kahin and C. Nelson (eds), *Borders in Cyberspace* (MIT, 1999)

Jönsson, C., Tägil, S. and Thörnqvist, G., *Organizing European Space* (SAGE Publications, 2000)

Jungpil, H., 'The dynamics of mass online marketplaces: A case study of an online auction'<http://misrc.umn.edu/wpaper/default.asp>

Karnow, C., *Future Codes* (Artech House, Boston, MA, 1997)

Kindervater, 'Ein Beitrag zur Lehre von der Versteigerung' in Jehring, *Jahrbucher für die Dogamtik des heutigen römischen und deutchen Privatrechts*, rsg.con Ihering VII (1865) p 2

Korybut, M., 'Online Auctions of Repossessed Collateral under Article 9' (1999, Fall) *Rutgers Law Journal*, Vol 31, No 1, 33–129

Lando, O. and Beales, H. (eds), *Principles of European Contract Law* (Kluwer Law, 2000)

Laulajainen, R., *Financial Geography—a Banker's view* (Göteborg, 1998)

Learmount, B., *A History of the Auction* (Bernard & Learmount, London, 1985)

Lee, H. G., 'Do electronic marketplaces lower the price of goods?' (1998) *Communications of the ACM*, 41(1), 73–80

Lee, R., *What is an Exchange? The Automation, Management and Regulation of Financial Markets* (Oxford University Press, 1998)

Lessig, L., *Code and other Laws of cyberspace* (Basic Books, 1999)

Lucking-Reiley, D., 'Using Field Experiments to Test Equivalence Between Auction Formats: Magic on the Internet' (Dec 1999) *The American Economic Review* Vol 89, No 5, 1063

Lucking-Reiley, D., 'Auctions on the Internet: What's Being Auctioned and How?' Available at <www.vanderbilt.edu/Econ/reiley/cv.html> (1 February, 2000)

Maggs, G. E., 'Internet Solutions to Consumer Protection Problems' (1988) *South Carolina Law Review*, Vol 49, No 4

Marsden, C. T. (ed), *Regulating the Global Information Society* (Routledge, 2000)

McAfee, R. P. and McMillan, J., 'Auctions and Biddings' (1987) 25 *Journal of Economic Literature* 701

Milgrom, P. R., and Weber, R. J., 'A Theory of Auctions and Competitive Bidding', (1982) *Econometrica* 50, 1089–1122

OECD, 'The Economic and Social Impacts of Electronic Commerce'. Available at <www.oecd.org/subject/e_commerce/summary.html> (checked May 2001)

Naor, M., Pinkas, B. and Sumner, R., 'Privacy Preserving Auctions and Mechanism Design', Proceedings of 1st ACM conference on E-Commerce (EC-99), 3–5 November 1999, Denver, Colorado

Newman, P., Milgate, M. and Eatwell, J. (eds), *The New Palgrave Dictionary of Money and Finance* (1992)

O'Hara, M, *Market Microstructure Theory* (Basil Blackwell, 1995)

Reidenberg, J. R., 'Governing Network and Cyberspace Rule-Making' (1996) 45 *Emory Law Journal* 911

Oram, A. (ed), *Peer-to-Peer Harnessing the Benefits of Disruptive Technologies* (O'Reilly, 2001)

Regelsberger, F., *Civilrechtlige Erörtertungen. I. Die Vorverhandlungen bei Verträge* (Weimar, 1868)

Ridely, M., *The Origins of Virtue* (Penguin, 1997)

Robinson, M. S., 'Collusion and the choice of auction' (1985) *Rand Journal of Economics*, 16, 141–5

Rosecrance, R., *The Rise of the Trading State* (Basic Books, 1986)

Russmann, H. and Reich, T., 'Internet als gewerbeordnungsfreier Raum?' (3/2000) *K&R Heft*

Sandel, M. J., *Democarcy's Discontent: America in Search of a Public Philosophy* (Cambridge, Mass., 1996)

Schafft, T., 'Reverse Auctions im Internet' (2001) *Medienrecht* 6, 393–401

Schlesinger, R. B., *Formation of Contracts, A Study of the Common Core of Legal Systems*, Vol 1 (NY, 1968)

Schott, *Der Obligatoriche Vertrag unter Abwesenden* (Heidelberg, 1873)

Schwartz, R. A., *Equity Markets: Structure, Trading and Performance* (Harper and Row, 1988)

Sculley, A. and Woods, W., *B2B Exchanges* (ISI Publications, USA, 1999)

Sculley, A., and Woods, W. (eds), *Evolving E-markets: building high value B2B exchanges with staying power* (ISI Publication Ltd, 2000)

Selis, P., Ramasastry, A. and Wright, C. S., 'Bidder Beware: Toward a Fraud-Free Marketplace—Best Practices for the Online Auction Industry', a Report for the State of Washington Attorney-General's Office (17 April 2001) at <http://www.law.washington.edu/lct/publications.html#bidder>

Seuffert, J. A., *De auctione*, Disseratito, Monachii 1854

Singer, K. B., 'Sotheby's sold me a fake!—Holding Auction Houses Accountable for Authenticating and Attributing Works of Fine Art' (Spring, 2000) *Art, Columbia-VLA Journal of Law and The Arts*

Spar, D. and Bussgang, J. I., 'Ruling the Net' (1996) 129 *Harvard Business Review* 125–33

Spindler, G. and Wiebe, A., *Internet-Auktionen. Rechtliche Rahmenbedingungen* (C. H. Beck, 2001)

Stögmöller, T., 'Auktionen im Internet' (9/1999) *K&R Heft* 391–6

Strange, S., *The Retreat of the State: The Diffusion of Power in the World Economy* (Cambridge University Press, 1996)

Stobbe, O., *Handbuch der deutchen Privatrechts, III* (Berlin, 1878–1885)

Theissen, E., 'Trader Anonymity, Price Formation and Liquidity', Working Paper, 2000

Thöl, H., *Das Handelsrecht. I*: 1,2, 5 Aufl, Leipzig 1875

Turban, E., 'Auctions and Bidding on the Internet: An Assessment' (1977) *Electronic Markets*, Vol 7, No 4

Wendt, O., *Lehrebuch der Pandekten* (Jena, 1888)

Wriston, W. B., *The Twilight of Sovereignty* (New York, 1992)

Wurman, P. R., Walsh, W. E. and Wellman, M. P., 'The Michigan Internet AuctionBot: A configurable auction server for human software agents', Paper presented at the second international conference on autonomous agents (Agents '98) Minneapolis

Zweigert, H. and Kötz, H., *An introduction to comparative law*, 3rd edn (Clarendon Press, 1998)

INDEX